IRELAND'S GRAMOPHONES

*MATERIAL CULTURE, MEMORY, AND TRAUMA
IN IRISH MODERNISM*

IRELAND'S GRAMOPHONES

MATERIAL CULTURE, MEMORY, AND TRAUMA IN IRISH MODERNISM

ZAN CAMMACK

CLEMSON
UNIVERSITY
PRESS

First Edition, 2021

ISBN: 978-1-949979-76-3 (print)
eISBN: 978-1-949979-77-0 (e-book)

Published by Clemson University Press
in association with Liverpool University Press

Clemson University Press is located in Clemson, SC.
For more information, please visit our website at www.clemson.edu/press.

Library of Congress Cataloging-in-Publication Data
Names: Cammack, Zan, author.
Title: Ireland's gramophones : material culture, memory, and trauma in
Irish modernism / Zan Cammack.
Description: Clemson : Clemson University Press, [2021] | Includes
bibliographical references and index. | Summary: "Ireland's Gramophones
examines the perpetual presence of the gramophone in literature of Irish
modernism: the same period in which gramophonic technology grew to
cultural prominence. The book argues that the gramophone, as object and
instrument, embodies accounts of a culture frequently traumatized
through violence and disruption"-- Provided by publisher.
Identifiers: LCCN 2021018838 (print) | LCCN 2021018839 (ebook) | ISBN
9781949979763 (hardback) | ISBN 9781949979770 (ebook)
Subjects: LCSH: Phonograph in literature. | English literature--Irish
authors--History and criticism. | Modernism (Literature)--Ireland. |
Collective memory in literature. | LCGFT: Literary criticism.
Classification: LCC PR8722.P63 C36 2021 (print) | LCC PR8722.P63 (ebook)
| DDC 820.9/9415--dc23
LC record available at https://lccn.loc.gov/2021018838
LC ebook record available at https://lccn.loc.gov/2021018839

Typeset in Minion Pro by Carnegie Book Production.
Printed and bound by CPI Group (UK) Ltd, Croydon CR0 4YY

Contents

List of Figures   vii

Acknowledgments   ix

Introduction: The Irish Gramophone   1

1   Gramophonic Trauma: Shattered Narratives and
    Undead Oralities   19

2   Gramophonic Gendering: Women, Phonographysteria, and
    the Political Machine   55

3   Gramophonic Violence: The Gramophones of the
    Irish Revolution   93

4   Gramophonic Strain: Residual Tension in
    Post-War Literature   131

Coda: Gramophonic Echoes   165

Notes   185

Index   219

Figures

0.1 Illustration of sound waves recorded on a phonograph
cylinder versus a gramophone record. On a phonograph,
the needle moves up and down in the recording trench to
reproduce sound. On a gramophone, the needle moves
horizontally from side to side.   7

0.2 A giant sculpture of a gramophone on O'Connell Street as
part of the RTÉ "Road to the Rising" recreation of April 1915
in 2015. Sculpture and photograph by Donnacha Cahill.   11

1.1 Contributions to *Dracula*'s narrative by media type.   23

1.2 Centripetal and centrifugal forces (A) in a balanced, centered
rotation on a gramophone compared to (B) those forces
working upon an object not at the center of the gramophone.   31

1.3 Order of the first 21 entries (A) as they appear in *Dracula* and
(B) in chronological order.   37

1.4 Ediphone used by the Irish Folklore Commission and housed
in the Irish Folklore Collection at University College Dublin.
Photograph: Zan Cammack.   47

2.1 A young woman transcribing from a phonograph, from
     Clarence Charles Smith, *The Expert Typist* (New York:
     Macmillan, 1922), 127, fig. 42.   56

3.1 Decca gramophone advertisement from *The Tatler*, 13
     September 1916, emphasizing the connection between war
     hospitals and gramophones. © Illustrated London News Ltd/
     Mary Evans.   96

4.1 Mainspring mechanism. Illustration by Dionysius
     Lardner, *Common Things Explained* (London: Walton and
     Maberly, 1855), 23.   133

4.2 Representations of (A) a "tired" mainspring and (B) "fatigue
     failure" in a mainspring.   133

4.3 The set for Lennox Robinson's *Portrait* and the gramophone
     used in the Abbey Theatre during the 1925 season. Abbey
     Theatre, Portrait, 31 Mar 1925 [Stage Management Files].
     Abbey Theatre Digital Archive at National University of
     Ireland, Galway, 2990_SM_0001, P1. (n.d.).   146

4.4 HMV portable gramophone, model 102, 1931. Science
     Museum Group Collection Online, 1962-154S.   157

Acknowledgments

This book grew out of a conversation with Betsy Dougherty about Elizabeth Bowen's fascination with "stuff" in *The Last September*. The gramophone in the work captured my imagination. My doctoral dissertation at Southern Illinois University Carbondale (SIU) was the result of that fascination, where Betsy, as my advisor, was and continues to be an extraordinary mentor and advocate for my research. I cannot thank her enough for always being in my corner. Many thanks also go to my dissertation committee members: to K. K. Collins for telling me, as I pitched the dissertation idea, that he could see this project as a future book; to Edward Brunner for jumping into my committee post-prelims with a whirlwind of modernist gramophone connections; and to Mary Bogumil and Anne Fletcher who helped add nuance and depth to the theatre components of this research. Each individual on the committee helped shape my research with generosity of time, expertise, and encouragement. Thank you to Jason Kirker and Marshall Johnson for reviewing my work as part of our dissertation group.

I received support for this research from the Dissertation Research Assistantship Award from the Graduate College at SIU and the Dr. Robert D. Partlow, Jr. Memorial Scholarship for Research in Victorian Literature from the Department of English. These awards helped fund research in the Abbey Theatre Digital Archives at National University of Ireland, Galway, and the National Folklore Archives at University College Dublin.

My thanks to Barry Houlihan and Simon O'Leary at each archive respectively, for helping me find materials and answering my many questions. I would also like to thank the Special Collections librarians at SIU's Morris Library for their constant help in digging out archival materials related to the Abbey Theatre and Lennox Robinson in particular.

I also received support for this project from Fulbright Canada as the 2017–18 Postdoctoral Fellow in Irish Studies, hosted by the School of Irish Studies at Concordia University. I am deeply indebted to Michael Kenneally for making my time at the School so rich by helping me connect with the larger Irish community in Montréal and Québec, as well as the vibrant academic network at Concordia. Jane McGaughey, Gavin Foster, Emer O'Toole, Gearóid Ó hAllmhuráin, and Rhona Richman Kenneally each deserve special mention for their generosity of time and for fielding so many of my questions. You are all incredible colleagues. Maureen Murphy, who was also a visiting scholar at the School during my tenure, deserves my thanks not only for donating to my Elizabeth Bowen collection but for going out of her way to share insights and advice on my project. Matina Skalkogiannis and Marion Mulvenna were also instrumental in making my time at Concordia run smoothly. I am also thankful to Anja Borck and the staff at Musée des Ondes Emile Berliner for allowing me "behind-the-scenes" access to the Berliner factory, gramophones, and records. I still can't believe that nerd-fest (for me) counted as research.

Thank you to Donnacha Cahill for his generosity of time to meet via Zoom mid-pandemic to discuss his artwork and interest in gramophones as sculptures.

A section of Chapter 2 appeared in the *Australasian Journal of Irish Studies* and a section of Chapter 3 appeared in the *Journal of Modern Literature*. My thanks to the anonymous readers for their insights and the editors for permission to reprint that material here. Additionally, a section of Chapter 4 appeared in *Science, Technology, and Irish Modernism* (Syracuse University Press, 2019). Many thanks to Kathryn Conrad, Cóilín Parsons, and Julie McCormick Weng for their excellent advice in fine-tuning my focus on the violence of the gramophone in Lennox Robinson's *Portrait* and for their brilliant work in editing such an exciting collection. Thanks also go to Syracuse University Press for permission to reprint here.

Many thanks also belong to those friends and colleagues who have supported my work along the way, despite what has been a rather nomadic academic existence for the past several years. Thank you to Trent Olsen for encouraging me to workshop a section of my project at the English Faculty Colloquium at Brigham Young University-Idaho and to all my colleagues who energetically engaged with my work in that session. Additional thanks to everyone who gave me tips on gramophones they came across in their reading as well as those who gave me gramophone novelties (bookends, mugs, Post-Its, T-shirts, coasters, cookie cutters, baby onesies) as I became "that person obsessed with gramophones." And a million thanks to Jerrica Jordan and Ellen Campbell for their unceasing encouragement and friendship. Our running/research group was essential to this project's success and you continue to support and inspire me.

My deepest thanks go to my family. Thank you to my parents, Keith and Christie Soderquist, for empowering me to jump headlong into academic pursuits: my dad for showing me what hard work looks like and what temerity can accomplish and my mum for teaching me to love literature and to ask questions. And thanks, too, Mum, for considering my book as a type of Irish modernism reading list. I'm glad you liked *At Swim-Two-Birds*. Eventually. And to Zach: you kept me (mostly) grounded through grad school, too many moves, bringing two beautiful boys—Ronan and Declan—into this world, keeping said boys alive, your work, my work, so much work, and my determination to see this book published. I am in awe of you. And thank you for doing the dishes.

Introduction
The Irish Gramophone

Few literary gramophones get as much play as the machine in James Joyce's *Ulysses*. In the Hades episode of the novel, after Leopold Bloom attends Paddy Dignam's funeral, he continues to reflect on death as he walks through the cemetery. When he observes how easily the memories of the dead fade, he considers the gramophone as a method of preserving a portion of the dead:

> Well, the voice, yes: gramophone. Have a gramophone in every grave or keep it in the house. After dinner on a Sunday. Put on poor old greatgrandfather. Kraahraark! Hellohellohello amawful-lyglad kraark awfullygladaseeagain hellohello amawf krpthsth. Remind you of the voice like the photograph reminds you of the face.[1]

In this brief description, Joyce creates an intricate network of references to the gramophone's capabilities. It is a communication device, an entertainment source, and a family memento. The machine is a method of preserving memory and is nearly supernatural in its abilities when it temporarily revives "poor old greatgrandfather" from the dead. It is a mechanical Orpheus it would seem.[2] And the gramophone's marvels in *Ulysses* don't end there.

1

In the Circe episode, the machine is granted agency in the script and stage directions. Florry's gramophone blares out the recording of "The Holy City" throughout Nighttown, intruding upon and inducing a series of hallucinations for Bloom. He envisions himself as the ruler of a new Dublin, of "Bloomusalem in the Nova Hibernia of the future."[3] The gramophone asserts its agency when it interrupts Elijah's prophecy of this new Dublin-Jerusalem:

THE GRAMOPHONE: (*Drowning [Elijah's] voice.*) Whorusa-laminyourhighhohhhh... (*The disc rasps gratingly against the needle.*)[4]

Again, Joyce's evocation of the gramophone creates a network of allusions and possibilities for the machine. It is capable of overriding and drowning out the voices of other human characters, asserting its own agency. It resides in Nighttown with the prostitutes who Bloom visits and is therefore inherently gendered as feminine and has valences of promiscuous sexuality, playing what customers want to hear ("Whorusalam..." being a key phrase here). The machine is also politicized as a particularly Irish gramophone when it enables Bloom to envision a new Dublin, free from colonial ties. These allusions unlock further potential for reading into the work's gramophones.

Gramophones proliferate throughout modernist literature (for example, T. S. Eliot's *The Waste Land*, Thomas Mann's *The Magic Mountain*, Virginia Woolf's *Between the Acts*). Yet *Ulysses* often comes up as the favorite. The trend of identifying Joyce's gramophones as particularly relevant to modernism is no doubt due in part to the high visibility of *Ulysses* in discussions of literary modernism. And yet the fact that *Ulysses* has been a perennial favorite for exploration from a range of literary and media studies scholars as a benchmark in literary gramophones led me to consider whether there might be another reason that these Joycean machines are so popular, something beyond being part and parcel of a text of high modernism. And beyond *Ulysses*, there is a remarkable queue of other high-profile modernist Irish texts that prominently feature the recording technology: Bram Stoker's *Dracula*, George Bernard Shaw's *Pygmalion*, Sean O'Casey's *Juno and the Paycock*, Elizabeth Bowen's

The Last September, and Flann O'Brien's *At Swim-Two-Birds* all high-light the gramophone as an essential apparatus in developing characters and progressing plot. In each work, the gramophone testifies, in the first place, to its own complexity as a physical object and its multiform value in the artistic development of textual material. In each work, too, the object seems virtually self-placed—less an aesthetic device than a "thing" belonging primordially to the text. Thus, the gramophone points to a deeper connection between literature and object than we perceive if we consider it as only an image, enhancement, or instrument. More specifically, there is something inherently Irish about the way these gram-ophones were culturally understood and how they functioned within Irish metonymy. That is not to say that the machines were manufactured and produced in Ireland. In fact, most gramophones sold in Ireland came from England-based companies such as Decca and His Master's Voice. But the Irishness of these gramophones comes from the physical as well as textual contexts in which we find them. Instrumentality and materiality blend to create a cultural object in these scenes. For instance, the gramophone of the Circe episode—gendered and politicized as it is—combines these two traits in the same scene to create a powerful image of a colonized Ireland.

The gendering of Ireland as female via the figure of Hibernia is embedded in Bloom's vision and compounded with negative connota-tions by the machine's voiced "Whorusalem…" When the needle rasps against the record, it draws our attention to the material object and its larger function and physical context. It is housed in the same building as the prostitutes and owned by Florry. The machine itself is rarely allowed its own voice, since, by its very nature, it is forced to play whatever record is placed upon it. The rasping needle draws attention to the violence inherent in the machine: a sharp needle drags across the scored surface of the record in order to replay its sound. When the gramophone rasps so distractingly in the Circe episode, the machine threatens no longer to stay silent or remain complacent in its voicelessness. And that threat is a reminder of the violent potential coiled in the gramophone's inner machinery and grating needle. Ireland's rebellion against its role as a gendered and subaltern state is a physical possibility embodied in the machine's autonomous behavior and cultural context. Joyce even embeds in this scene references to the Hades gramophone when Paddy Dignam's spirit appears, operating under the logic that gramophones are wont to evoke such specters. Dignam's behavior during this scene is evocative of another gramophone motif when he is described as *"listen[ing] with visible effort, thinking, his tail stiffpointed, his ears cocked"* for "My master's voice!"[5] We are meant immediately to catch the reference to the record label His Master's Voice and its accompanying logo of the terrier Nipper listening attentively to a gramophone for commands from a recording of his master. In fact, there is a strong likelihood that the gramophone in this scene originated from England, and was manufactured by His Master's Voice. Paddy's behavior, acting out the image featured on the machine, evokes the colonial motif. He is subservient to his "master," even in death. And while Joyce had a complex relationship with and attitude toward Ireland's political upheavals in the early decades of the twentieth century, he pulls no punches when he puts the tensions at play in the dream of political autonomy at the forefront of this scene. Is the gramophone a passive gendered victim or violent aggressor? Is it summoning a colonized specter or acting as a colonial oppressor? It is possible to read the gramophone as all of these things. The tangled network of allusions embedded in the instrumentality and materiality of the machine in this scene is perhaps an accurate reflection of Joyce's views on Ireland's political position. But more importantly, in the context of *Ireland's Gramophones*, this scene unlocks much of the potential to read the gramophone's actions and interactions with characters as a complex "thing" embedded in Irish culture and capable of voicing and signaling significant meaning and action in a broader Irish context.

Perhaps it is no great surprise, then, that *Ulysses'* gramophones have sparked a great deal of literary interest and interpretation, as have literary gramophones across modernism. In fact, Paul K. Saint-Amour asserts that "[l]iterary studies has a gramophone problem."[6] The problem, he concludes, is that the gramophone in literature overshadows other sound media that emerged and developed during the same time period. As evidence, he points to the gramophone in the Circe episode of *Ulysses* and how it has eclipsed the pianola scene. And he's not necessarily wrong. The range of scholarship on the gramophones of *Ulysses* alone is staggering.[7] This is due, at least partially, to the quantity of media studies scholarship available on this analog sound reproduction mechanism. The gramophone's function in literature has generally been examined in relation to Walter Benjamin's discussion of the reproduction of art through mechanical means, which emphasizes the gramophone's playback of recorded materials.[8] Other theoretical frameworks emerged in the later twentieth century—established by Jacques Derrida and Friedrich Kittler—making media analysis even more accessible. Derrida's massively influential work "*Ulysses* Gramophone: Hear Say Yes in Joyce" refers to the gramophone as an "anamnesiac machine":[9] a machine that stores and recreates memory of the written and verbal word. In Kittler's *Gramophone, Film, Typewriter* (1986), he sees the gramophone in *Ulysses* as a discourse network linking the living and the dead: the kind of information network that connects physical bodies to bodies or institutions of information and power.[10] Kittler's discourse networks and Derrida's phonocentric (dis)connections serve as the theoretical premises and groundwork for the majority of what Saint-Amour terms the "gramophone problem" in current literary studies.

There are more recent frameworks in media studies that also account for the continued discussion of gramophones in modernism. For instance, works such as *Sonic Modernity* (2013) by Sam Halliday and *Sounding Modernism* (2017) edited by Julian Murphet, Helen Groth, and Penelope Hone establish the potential to study the soundscapes created by modernism's gramophones.[11] Joyce's gramophones inevitably join this vivid soundscape, further enhancing the specific machines' profiles. And while I do not particularly engage in discussions of soundscapes in this work, *Ireland's Gramophones*, in many ways, does follow methodology established by David Trotter in *Literature in the First Media Age* (2013) in that this book seeks to situate the medium under discussion in the historical period of its acceptance, spread, and assimilation into a specific culture.[12] Unlike in Trotter's work, however, the gramophone (which is only mentioned in passing in his text) becomes the central media object under discussion. And while each of these media-oriented works supports, to some extent, Saint-Amour's point concerning how media studies methodology makes the gramophone a powerful object to grapple with, the "gramophone problem" in literary studies as I identify it in this book is not the gramophone's proliferation; instead, I suggest that the "problem" rather points to the tendency to discuss the machine's presence in literature *exclusively* as a media object.

The media studies methodology in relation to literature's gramophones, while valuable, only deals with half of the machine's potential.
Ireland's Gramophones mediates the links between media studies and the
physical presence or thingness of the object. I take my cue, in part, from
another modernist, Theodor Adorno, when he points to two distinct
aspects of the gramophone (the instrument and the object), observing
that "when gramophonic reproduction breaks down, [...] its objects
[are] transformed."[13] The breakdown of the object's traditional function
is also at the core of thing theory as conceived by Bill Brown: a study of
when passive objects transform into material and transactional "things."[14]
The gramophone, then, when it intrudes into recordings or draws attention to itself in any other way, acts as a "thing" and therefore alters the
relationships between characters and the machine. We have to treat the
gramophone as an agent and participant in the larger action of the scene
or text. I make a distinction between the gramophone as an instrument
(through which we access or hear a recording) and the gramophone as a
"thing" (an object which draws attention to itself by behaving unexpectedly, thereby forcing us to confront the object's own inherent potential).

While discussing the gramophone's thingness, it seems important
to briefly address some physical distinctions in the way I refer to the
recording technology. The terms gramophone and phonograph have often
been used interchangeably and generically: the United Kingdom and
Ireland using *gramophone* to refer to the recording technology, while in
the United States, *phonograph* was the generic term. But this undermines
the specificity of the two machines, both in terms of the physical objects
and the primary functions they perform. Both machines collect sound
waves in a horn or diaphragm that then connects to a stylus that imprints
recorded sound onto a receiving medium. And both machines are capable
of playing back that recorded sound by reversing the process and letting
the stylus retrace the path of recorded sound to amplify it through the
diaphragm and horn. But the phonograph and gramophone are still physically different machines.

The phonograph was patented by Thomas Edison in 1877. It recorded
sound on a cylindrical medium: aluminum wrapped around a cylinder in
its earliest iterations, and later cylinders coated in layers of wax. Edison
primarily envisioned the machine's use in taking down from dictation,

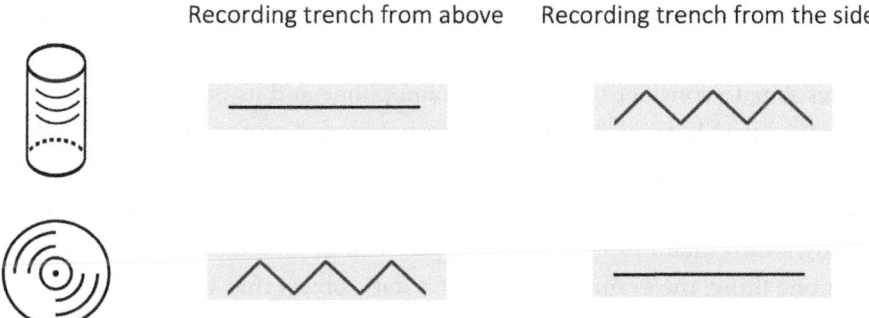

Recording trench from above   Recording trench from the side

Figure 0.1. Illustration of sound waves recorded on a phonograph cylinder versus a gramophone record. On a phonograph, the needle moves up and down in the recording trench to reproduce sound. On a gramophone, the needle moves horizontally from side to side.

which informs the nomenclature of phonograph or "sound writing." The machine was predominantly for recording the voice, with a limit to its playback abilities, since the wax recordings would rapidly wear down after several replays. Whereas the phonograph recorded sound on a cylinder in straight lines but with various depths pressed into the wax, the flat disk of the gramophone—a machine patented by Emile Berliner in 1887—wrote sound in spiraling grooves of even depth of but varying direction (see Figure 0.1). Berliner's innovation of the flat disk emphasized playback, rather than the recording of sound, since his records were made of sturdy materials like hard rubber and eventually shellac. The resilient medium also allowed for mass production, since the original could easily be used as a mold or template for new and virtually pristine copies. Berliner's machine was ultimately the more popular machine type, and is the object referred to in the majority—though not all—of the texts that *Ireland's Gramophones* discusses. In my impulse toward a pithy title (*Ireland's Phonographs and Gramophones* just does not hit the same), it might seem that I am veering into the generic use of the term *gramophone* for all recording technologies, but throughout this book I note the distinctions as they occur in each text. I try not to lose sight of the physical object.

My study of the machine as an object, rather than exclusively as an instrument, partially draws upon Elaine Freedgood's methodology established in *The Ideas in Things*, when she describes "begin[ning] with objects rather than subjects and plots and stay[ing] with them a bit longer than novelistic interpretation generally allows."[15] *Ireland's Gramophones* takes time to consider the material gramophone and its physical features, like its ornate horn or its spring motor, before returning to historical and literary contexts and realigning the object with the text's larger narrative. And while thing theory has been an invaluable jumping off point for this study, I can't claim to have stayed rigidly within its established precepts. For one thing, the gramophone is not a static object that subjects interact with. It is, instead, a quasi-human object, or "quasi-subject" as Celia Marshik describes in *At the Mercy of Their Clothes*.[16] Whereas Marshik discusses clothing as taking on human movement, the gramophone becomes quasi-human due to its voice. This voice most often comes in the form of a record that the gramophone plays back, but the voice can also come directly from the machine itself.

The transformation from medium and instrument to thing serves as a catalyst for each examination of the gramophone under consideration here, and since Saint-Amour, Derrida, Kittler, and so many others have found Joyce's *Ulysses* to be an effective starting point for their discussions of literary gramophones, it seems fitting that I have thus far followed suit. In fact, the gramophones of *Ulysses* also effectively illustrate the distinction between instrument and object. Returning to the previously mentioned episodes, the machine's physical apparatus intrudes in both scenes. We see the moment of transformation when "great grandfather" speaks from the grave, and the "Kraahrack!" and "kraark" of the machine forces us to notice the gramophone's intrinsic presence and individual voice within the recording. Similarly, in the Circe episode, the "*disc rasps gratingly against the needle*," forcing itself upon our notice, no longer content to simply play a recording. The object's "thingness" lurks behind the music and the gramophone becomes discernible as its own entity as opposed to acting as an invisible conduit. It has audibly announced its own willful autonomy, transforming from instrument to thing. It complicates our understanding of media and material cultures in the larger trend of modernism, but particularly Irish modernism.

The central argument of *Ireland's Gramophones* is that there is something culturally specific to the presence of the gramophone in its proliferation in Irish modernist literature; namely, the object most frequently crops up in tandem with aspects of national cultural trauma and upheaval. The budding recording technology grew to maturity alongside Ireland's progressively more outspoken and violent struggles for political autonomy and national stability, most particularly during the first several decades of the twentieth century. As a result, there is a forged metonymic link between the gramophone and representations of these cultural traumas. This book traces connections between the physical "thing" and its embedded or recorded cultural archives of violence, memory, and identity for Irish modernist authors and their contemporary audiences. Those cultural traumas, the result of intense social and political unrest, are archived in the gramophone. As both a voiced and mute object, the gramophone amplifies embedded accounts of a culture frequently traumatized through violence and disruption. And since trauma can also be voiced or mute, the machine is a particularly apt object to take on such intricate metonymic work.

In arguing that the gramophone takes on the symbolic weight of Irish cultural trauma, I take my definition largely from Jeffrey Alexander's work and describe it as a feeling held by a collective group that they have been subjected to a harrowing event that has left a permanent mark upon the group's consciousness that informs their memories, identities, and cultural perceptions in fundamental and irrevocable ways.[17] Cultural trauma, as an extension of trauma studies, deserves its own contextualization against Irish literature. Traumatic experiences are generally considered those that are outside normal human experience; so far outside the normal that the mind cannot process the events as it would more mainstream experiences. As a result of this very individualized mental experience, a sense of communal trauma is not a naturally occurring response to a traumatic event. Instead, communal trauma is generally cultivated by a linked narrative among a wider group. According to Alexander, the larger community or culture gains a sense of trauma from "carrier groups" who spread and frame the event, usually through a media platform. These carrier groups are generally "collective agents of the trauma process [...] with particular discursive talents for articulating their claims—for what might be called 'meaning making'— in the public sphere."[18] These carrier groups can be generational, national, religious, institutional, or marginalized classes: any group that has an outlet for articulating their particular position. The larger culture then internalizes this message of trauma.

An easily accessible example of this phenomenon can be identified in Irish history with the Easter Rising of 1916, an event that has been framed as a traumatic event on a cultural level. The violence of the week-long rebellion was largely viewed by the Irish public as disruptive and an expression of a marginal extreme faction of Irish nationalists. And yet, in the following months, the media coverage of the executions of the rebel leaders, often depicting them as martyrs to their cause, began to turn public opinion. As a result, a large demographic in Ireland became sympathetic to the Republican perspective, and the 1916 Rebellion became a catalyst for the Irish War of Independence in 1919. Even now, over one hundred years later, the Rising is considered a moment of cultural violence and trauma that is commemorated and assimilated into the national narrative of the country's independence. And while this is certainly a broad picture of a much more complex series of events, it does provide the outline for the evolution of a cultural trauma. A widely experienced trauma, carried and perpetuated by a carrier group (media), created a communal narrative.

In *Ireland's Gramophones*, I depart slightly from Alexander's ideas about the spread of communal trauma by identifying a carrier *object* rather than a carrier group;[19] I identify the gramophone as an object capable of carrying, representing, and spreading the narrative of cultural trauma in Ireland. The gramophones of this period are collective agents of the trauma process, becoming a singular media object that embodies and also disseminates the message of violent trauma (via its physical presence, primarily) to a wide community that adopts that narrative. The gramophone's proliferation throughout Ireland in the early part of the twentieth century serves as its own platform for spreading its metonymic narrative of trauma. Its presence in daily life is compounded by the narrative of gramophones in relation to trauma in cultural depictions, newspaper advertisements and articles, and in the literature of the period, as I will demonstrate. And, to briefly return to the illustrative nature of the trauma narrative constructed around the Rising, it is worth mentioning that the gramophone has recently cropped up in commemorations of the events

Figure 0.2. A giant sculpture of a gramophone on O'Connell Street as part of the RTÉ "Road to the Rising" recreation of April 1915 in 2015. Sculpture and photograph by Donnacha Cahill.

surrounding that week as an object of significance. In particular, the RTÉ's 2015 event called "Road to the Rising" strove to thematically recreate the Dublin of 1915 as a way of commemorating the events that led to the 1916 Rebellion. As part of the commemoration, a giant gramophone monument was constructed on O'Connell Street (see Figure 0.2).[20] That specific object, so visible and at the heart of such a commemoration, speaks to the role of the gramophone in the country's development during this turbulent time and its continued nuanced significance to our understanding of this period.

Ireland's cultural traumas throughout the late nineteenth and early twentieth centuries took myriad forms. In his study of Irish culture in the twentieth century, F. S. Lyons points out that between 1890 and 1939—essentially the period covered in *Ireland's Gramophones*—there was "an anarchy in the mind and the heart […] which forbade not just unity of territories, but also 'unity of being,'" that arose primarily from the "collision within a small and intimate island of seemingly irreconcilable cultures, unable to live together or live apart, caught inextricably in the web of their tragic history."[21] This description emphasizes the shattered aspects of Ireland's cultural identity: an inability to reconcile the individual perspectives into a coherent narrative. Lyons builds upon this description of fractured narrative by quoting a few lines from William Butler Yeats's poem "Remorse for Intemperate Speech" (1933): "Out of Ireland have we come; / Great hatred, little room, / Maimed us at the start."[22] Yeats's work here evokes the "maimed" psyche of the poet's country, which I read as traumatized. The final lines of the poem indicate that the damage is *inherent* in Irish culture during this period: it is something that "I carry from my mother's womb."[23] And while one wishes to avoid oversimplifying and generalizing about the psychological condition of Irish culture at large, to deny or ignore the trauma in Irish culture during this period would be "to marginalize a central dimension of the Irish historical experience and, indeed, in some cases virtually to write it out of the record," as Brendan Bradshaw points out.[24] Robert F. Garratt adds to this conclusion, explaining that trauma, as a theoretical premise, adds valence to collective memories of suffering. The framework of exploring trauma and traumatic experiences in the nineteenth and twentieth centuries allows for an exploration of characters who survived violent events during the Irish War of Independence and the Civil War, for example,

> only to be haunted by those events later. Either as witnesses or participants in the act of violence, these characters are portrayed as permanently attached to that moment, unable to let it go or to understand it with any certainty or without considerable suffering. […] They are continually haunted and shaped by previous events and moments of intense violence. The past, then, remains ongoing in the individual's consciousness, replaying previous actions and experiences.[25]

The violence, the haunting, the "replaying" of experiences are all inherently part of the theory of Ireland's cultural trauma and are also indicative of the Irish gramophone. The violence of the gramophone's initial recording process (the needle scratching into a soft surface) and the haunting revival of past speech events through those recordings become central to the gramophone's representation in the national literature.

This is not to say that all memory in Ireland is traumatic, just as not all gramophones in Irish literature function exclusively as trauma-based carrier objects. The gramophone always, inherently, evokes memory since its primary design is to replay past recording events; but the function or type of each memory can vary. There are, in fact, eight basic categories of memory, according to the Queensland Brain Institute.[26] The gramophone serves best as an analog for long-term memory (rather than short-term), which category is further divided into conscious and unconscious memory. Conscious memory includes episodic (events that happened to you) and semantic (general world knowledge) types. Unconscious memory includes procedural or motor memory as well as "priming" memory which occurs when exposure to one stimulus influences the brain's response to another. The gramophone functions on each of these levels. The replay of a recorded sound can be episodic: a specific memory of a specific event. The physical function of replay can be considered motor memory, as the machine performs a function with mechanical precision without thought. The machine's near omnipresence in the early twentieth century can be considered semantic memory. And even the skipping of a record can serve as an apt replication of priming memory; the needle skips from one section of the record to another because of scratches or dust that stimulate a correlating and unconscious change of track. *Ireland's Gramophones* is largely focused on trauma memory (a combination of these varying memory categories in a wide range of circumstances), but that does not take away from the larger nuances of memory that our minds or Irish culture are capable of embodying. And there are times when the machine operates as an agent of these wider forms of memory. That is, in part, why the gramophone is such a compelling object through which to try to understand Irish modernism; it is complex and nuanced enough to bear the scrutiny of broad mnemonic weight.

***

Ireland's Gramophones starts with an exploration of the construction of trauma narratives and the psychological parallels to the phonograph in Bram Stoker's *Dracula* (1897). Chapter 1, "Gramophonic Trauma," considers the physical and psychological trauma of the vampire attacks in *Dracula* as represented by Dr. Seward's phonograph, which sets the stage for an explication of a communal trauma narrative. Seward's phonograph is used initially as part of his practice in a mental asylum and evolves into a machine capable of revealing the trauma of the individual as well as the collective when the machine's recordings are integrated into a broader narrative. This move to the collective experience of trauma is central to the larger argument of *Ireland's Gramophones*. Seward's oral accounts also point to a larger cultural trauma in Ireland with the country's nationalistic attempts to preserve its oral culture in the wake of the Famine. While the phonograph seems an ideal piece of technology for preserving the Irish language and the country's living oral culture, it instead creates undead oralities, unnaturally preserving a culture that relies on the vitality of the storyteller to keep the tradition alive. Stoker's Irish heritage, his childhood memories of the Famine as related to him through his mother's storytelling, and his fascination with the phonographic technology used in Ireland to collect Irish folklore all reveal the author's concerns about technology's role in preserving a nation's narratives. The phonograph in *Dracula* embodies the trauma narrative of the vampire hunters, but also of a culture recovering from the widespread trauma of the Famine while trying to vocalize and preserve its history, articulating a new national identity and moving technologically into the twentieth century.

The second chapter, "Gramophonic Gendering," charts how the recording technology, from its inception, was imbued with feminine associations. This gendering took on unflattering and even traumatic overtones in relation to the rising voices and figures of female empowerment. The pseudo-psychological diagnosis of "phonographysteria" seems a common undercurrent in exploring the New Woman's (and later suffragette's) push for greater personal, sexual, and political autonomy at the same time that Ireland, a feminized space, was also pushing for greater political autonomy. The implication that women were a shrill annoyance in the face of the more masculine political agenda of Home Rule reveals aspects of political gendering in *Dracula* and *Pygmalion* (1912), as well as highlighting women's issues of education, sexuality, and independence during the period of Ireland's Second and Third Home Rule Bill debates (1880–1914).

In *Dracula*, both Lucy Westenra and Mina Murray are affiliated with the phonograph, and they are often treated as the sexual and intellectual duo of the New Woman phenomenon respectively. By explicating their interactions with the phonograph, this section argues that while Lucy is targeted as a sexual scapegoat, Mina's use of the phonograph, particularly in relation to Dr. Seward, reveals a sexual liberation that goes largely unpunished in the text. She also exposes the double standard of Ireland's pursuit of the Second Home Rule Bill without women's enfranchisement. G. B. Shaw's *Pygmalion* picks up on similar themes when, during the debates surrounding the Third Home Rule Bill, Irish suffrage was again overshadowed by the "more important" national debate. In this work, Eliza Doolittle, equated by Professor Higgins with both a phonograph and gramophone, overcomes subjugation to the machine's sexual implications by declaring her own independence from both machine and mentor. The play's finale, however—specifically its afterlives as a musical and film—is problematic in its gendering since it seeks to undo Eliza's liberation by putting her back in the machine in Higgins's study.

In the third chapter, "Gramophonic Violence," I consider the gramophone in the context of Ireland at war—World War I, the 1916 Rising, the Irish War of Independence, and the Civil War. The compounded violences of this decade draw out vivid depictions of trauma that become specific to Irish culture. During World War I, portable gramophones— colloquially known as "trench gramophones"—became a vital part of the soldiers' entertainment in the trenches and their recovery in hospitals. In hospitals, the gramophone entertained the wounded but was also controversially used as a form of distraction and even as treatment for shell-shock. Texts from the Richmond War Hospital in Dublin as well as other contemporary accounts suggest that the gramophone's functions in relation to shock quickly shifted from being representational of a larger world conflict to become a unique representation of Ireland's own cultural shock in the wake of the 1916 Easter Rising. For instance, some of the first "shock" patients admitted to the hospital were not soldiers from the war but rather civilians traumatized by the events of the Rising. As a result, "shock" or psychological trauma began to have a divergent meaning for British and Irish culture after the Rising of 1916, when the violence of war shifted from the Western Front to Irish soil. The Irish began to understand shock and trauma as the cultural inheritance of a country with divisive nationalism(s). Similarly, the gramophone—trench model or otherwise—took on divergent mnemonic and psychological meanings for British and Irish soldiers and civilians.

In Elizabeth Bowen's *The Last September* (1929), for instance, Lois Farquar's intense reaction to a gramophone's "death" suggests the object is indelibly linked to her inability to give an account of the Anglo-Irish tension festering beneath the novel's surface. This text also provides an opportunity to see the difference between the English and Irish experience of the gramophone, since Daventry, a shell-shocked English soldier, has a decidedly different reaction to its death.

In Sean O'Casey's *Juno and the Paycock* (1924), the focus shifts to a physically and psychologically scarred IRA soldier and his family as they debate the gramophone's proper function. The backdrop of the Civil War relentlessly intrudes when the Boyles' enjoyment of the gramophone—which needs "dead silence" to play, according to Captain Boyle—is interrupted by the funeral procession of the Anti-Treaty soldier Tancred:[27] a soldier betrayed to his death by the physically maimed and psychologically scarred Johnny Boyle. Johnny's experiences of the gramophone find parallels with the shell-shocked English soldiers of World War I like Daventry, but his traumas are exclusively incurred by the armed actions of Irish nationalism.

The fourth chapter, "Gramophonic Strain," examines texts written in post-war Ireland from 1924 to 1939. In these works, the gramophone's spring-powered motor demonstrates the residual cultural stress of the era that belies the post-war peace. The chapter examines a broad survey of texts, ranging from the well-known to the less popular, as an indication that gramophones from this era begin to manifest the strain of perpetual tension in both literal and metaleptic representations. The two texts of particular study in this chapter are Lennox Robinson's play *Portrait* (1925) and Flann O'Brien's novel *At Swim-Two-Birds* (1939). In *Portrait*, a play meant to be a "portrait of our time" in post-war Ireland, Peter Brandon has lived through the wars, but finds the peace just as hard.[28] In the climactic scene, a gramophone's spring stops functioning correctly, and moments later Peter erupts with disconcerting violence. Peter and the gramophone act out an extreme example of a spring wound too tightly for too long. In O'Brien's novel, a generational tension between the revolutionaries and the post-war generation is manifest when the protagonist and his uncle converse about the fear of "breakage" in the gramophone's motor.[29] The gramophone is overtly linked to war by the protagonist's uncle, but the unnamed student sees the gramophone as antiquated and its attendant potential for violence as more academic and literary than tangible. The correlation between post-war culture, gramophone spring motors, and the unforeseen violence in *Portrait*, combined with a generational history linking the gramophone to political violence in *At Swim-Two-Birds*, reveals an implied Irish anxiety about the residual cultural strain of a post-war culture.

The coda, "Gramophonic Echoes," examines the afterlife of the gramophone; how it continued to have cultural relevance in Ireland beyond its heyday. The gramophone's presence in literature from the late 1800s through the 1930s feels natural enough, given the object's popularity and relevance during these decades, but after that period the gramophone became progressively *passé*. Despite this, literature continued to evoke the machine as a signifier of trauma in Irish culture rather than merely a prop piece to establish setting. The coda surveys texts published since 1940—including works by James Plunkett, Edna O'Brien, and Patrick McCabe—that persistently depict the gramophone despite its progressively antiquated status. The gramophone's presence speaks to the largely unresolved cultural and political tensions in the wake of the Irish Revolution, since the machine still often acts in surprising outbursts in relation to violence and trauma throughout the decades.

I pay particular attention to how an anachronistic gramophone in Brian Friel's *The Gentle Island* (1971) manifests the political and cultural strain left unresolved from the early part of the twentieth century. The play is set against the backdrop of the roiling Troubles of the early 1970s and the play explodes in unexpected violence when the gramophone is repaired. The "ancient gramophone" of the play bears the metonymic weight of all the previous Irish gramophones; the disturbing ferocity of the play reveals the dangers of latent unresolved political tensions and cultural traumas.

***

Ireland's Gramophones ultimately argues that the gramophone functions as an irrepressible object that carries with it indelible archives of memory in a culture riddled with the symptoms of historically repeated violences and ruptures. This approach reconsiders the potential for "thing theory" and media studies by contextualizing them against Ireland's specific cultural traumas. The Irish gramophone is a carrier object, an active agent and portable metonymic of historical violence, that represents and collates cultural memory in its myriad strains. By considering the Irish gramophone at the intersection of media studies, "thing theory," and cultural trauma, I argue that it might speak through recorded media, but that as a cultural object of trauma it speaks even louder.

CHAPTER ONE

Gramophonic Trauma
Shattered Narratives and Undead Oralities

W hen news of phonographic technology reached Dublin in 1877 via the *Irish Times*'s correspondent in the United States, it must have sounded utterly supernatural. The machine, it was said, could preserve one's voice for an indefinite period. That voice could then be resurrected "long after [one] has turned to dust."[1] And if the recorded voice had indeed achieved "immortality," as the phonograph's inventor, Thomas Edison, suggested, then surely the immortality of entire beings was not so inconceivable.

Twenty years later, in 1897, the phonograph had evolved significantly and though far from thoroughly mainstream, it was no longer a mysterious and unknown entity. So when Bram Stoker published *Dracula* that year, filled with the scientific and technological advancements of the late nineteenth century, the phonograph's presence was nearly essential for such a cutting-edge text. Among the telegrams, traveling typewriters, and Kodak cameras of the novel, the phonograph features prominently as a newer technology and one of the primary media platforms for the narrative. And yet, despite the novel's insistence that it is thoroughly modern, with all of its technological and scientific advancements, the supernatural still creeps back in.

Dr. John Seward, a psychologist and the head of a mental asylum in London, enters Stoker's eclectic narrative via a (semi-)professional diary, "kept in phonograph."[2] His record commences with the resolve to facilitate his work at the asylum through the machine, beginning by discussing the mental state of one of his patients, Renfield. By making the phonograph an intrinsic part of his medical practice, Seward forges a connection between psychology and the machine. And as the narrative of *Dracula* unfolds, the phonograph becomes an essential tool for recording Seward's medical observations, his personal reflections about Lucy Westenra's progressing illness, his growing understanding of the nature of her demise as a victim of the undead, and ultimately his contribution to a larger group narrative of the vampire hunters and their quest to defeat Dracula.

The novel relies heavily on Seward's phonographic contribution as well as his medical perspective. As a result, it creates parallels between the psychological impact of traumatic vampire attacks and the compulsion to articulate that trauma. The phonograph becomes infinitely more complex than a mere method of preserving the human voice. In very telling ways, it physically embodies both of these concepts. First, creating a recording on a phonograph requires a needle to physically tear into the wax cylinder, leaving scars on the medium: a representation of physical and psychological trauma. Second, the phonograph represents traumatic memory with its recordings of orally delivered trauma narratives. The physical record, the wax cylinder, replicates trauma narratives as we understand them today: a memory/event that is always asynchronous and belatedly assimilated, though its assimilation into a larger narrative of the event(s) is necessary to work toward some kind of acknowledgment or recognition of the trauma. The fragmentary nature of the phonographic accounts both literally and metaphorically replicates the shattered narrative perspective of those who experience trauma. The end result is that, throughout *Dracula*, the phonograph functions as a physical and mnemonic representation of trauma and its narratives.

Stoker's use of the phonograph also takes on a larger cultural meaning when placed against the backdrop of the author's Irish heritage and his interest in oral folklore. By the time Stoker published *Dracula* in 1897, he had already used Irish folklore—passed down primarily through his mother Charlotte—as inspiration for works such as "The Invisible Giant" (1881) and *The Snake's Pass* (1890). These works use oral accounts of Irish folklore and cultural trauma, specifically in reference to the Great Famine and Charlotte's own experiences of surviving a cholera epidemic as a child, as integral to their plots and their emotional weight. The phonograph in *Dracula* therefore becomes emblematic of Stoker's interest in this Irish oral heritage, which seems to have been piqued by the use of the phonograph for collecting recordings of folklore in the nineteenth century. Stoker was aware of the phonograph's use in folklore collection; *Dracula* even predicts, in small part, many of the conundrums faced by Irish Revivalists and folklore collectors at the turn of the century. For instance, though the phonograph seems an ideal technology for preserving the country's living oral culture, it instead problematizes it. By preserving, via phonograph, a culture that relies on the vitality of the storyteller to keep the tradition alive, avid folklorists and their phonographs essentially create undead oralities: accounts that are drained of that all-important living element. And just as the vampire hunters in *Dracula* scramble to create a coherent—though always disjointed and problematic—narrative of the vampire attacks, Irish folklorists and revivalists of the late nineteenth and early twentieth centuries scrambled to collect, preserve, and assimilate oral accounts in an attempt to create a coherent—though equally disjointed and problematic—national(ist) narrative.

Of Phonographs and Psychology

The narrative of *Dracula* is constructed of myriad media types and formats, including shorthand journal entries, telegrams, letters, and newspaper clippings. The phonograph is one of the most prominent media contributors to the novel, providing over 36 percent of the overall narrative (see Figure 1.1); it is second only to personal journal entries, contributed by several different authors, including Seward, Lucy, and Mina Harker (née Murray). Except for a single (problematic "memorandum") entry by Van Helsing, the phonographic accounts are exclusively recorded by Seward.[3] Moreover, while Seward sets out to make his phonographic accounts a tool for his medical practice at the asylum, they instead become the primary account of vampire attacks and the vampire hunters' strategies to defeat Dracula. The first phonographic entry, however, illuminates how the psychologist *intended* to use the machine and its oral record as a part of his practice:

To-day I seemed to get nearer than ever before to the heart of [Renfield's] mystery. I questioned him more fully than I had ever done, with a view to making myself master of the facts of his hallucination. [...] If there be anything behind this instinct it will be valuable to trace it afterwards *accurately*, so I had better commence to do so.[4]

Seward's anxiety to "*accurately* trace" every aspect of his interactions with Renfield via his phonograph reveals the novel's near obsession with memory and its failure to provide a direct and comprehensive narrative of the encounters with the vampire. The work's fanaticism regarding memory is made particularly clear in the anonymous note before the first chapter: "There is throughout no statement of past things wherein memory may err."[5] It is also made clear in the note at the end of the work in which Jonathan Harker describes revisiting Transylvania years later with Mina: "[We] went over the old ground which was, and is, to us so full of vivid and terrible memories."[6] Since accuracy and memory are equally central to Seward's professional use of the phonograph, it becomes important to understand how Stoker came to view the phonograph as such an effective tool in psychology.

In 1880, three years after the invention of the phonograph and seventeen years before the publication of *Dracula*, Jean-Marie Guyau, a French philosopher and poet, argued that, "reasoning by analogy," the phonograph served as an appropriate equivalent for the brain's formation of memory.[7] Guyau describes the process of phonographic recording as one in which "the vibrations of one's voice are transferred to a point that engraves lines" onto the recording medium, creating "furrows" that imitate the nature of the sound. He continues that in "analogous ways, invisible lines are incessantly carved into the brain cells, which provide a channel for nerve streams." If, in this analogy, the nerve stream passes along the same channel, after a time the brain would interpret this as memory: a recalled smell, emotion, thought. In a phonograph, this is much more literal. The needle of the phonograph passes through a previously etched channel and turns that groove into voice, sound, music. Ultimately, Guyau concludes, "If the phonographic disk had self-consciousness, [...] what appears to us

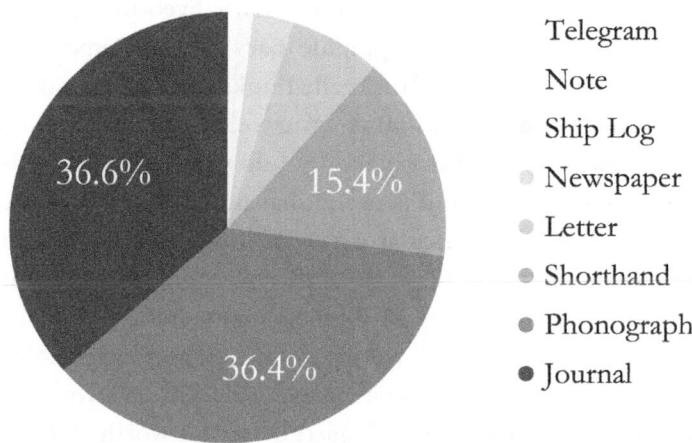

Figure 1.1. Contributions to *Dracula*'s narrative by media type.

as the effect of a rather simple mechanism would, quite probably, strike the disk as a miraculous ability: memory."[8]

Guyau's analogy relies heavily on the imagery of the carved or engraved furrows as they are formed during the recording or live event and the retracing of those furrows as the replaying or memory event. This description recalls Seward's particular emphasis on "*accurately* tracing" events after they have occurred when he creates his phonograph diary; he relies on the phonograph not only to literally retrace his recording but also to help him remember his encounters with his patients and make sense of their psychological condition.

While both Guyau and Seward see the parallels in memory and replay in the machine, they both also seem to overlook the more practical aspect of phonographic replay. The brain (which Guyau describes as an "infinitely perfected phonograph—a conscious phonograph")[9] can generally recall and replay events without effort; the phonograph, however, is a much less refined and therefore problematic system. Replaying a phonograph cylinder necessitates loading a relatively fragile wax cylinder onto the machine, then placing the needle in the groove, without the capacity to pick a specific section of sound or "memory" with any kind of accuracy. This is exactly the problem that Seward encounters when Mina asks to hear a section of his diary. Even though the doctor clearly intends to use his phonographic diary as a supplement or analog for memory, he apparently never really thinks through how the process will take place. He explains to Mina, "You see, I do not know how to pick out any particular part of the diary. [...] do you know that, although I have kept the diary for months past, it has never once struck me how I was going to find any particular part of it in the case I wanted to look it up?"[10] To contextualize the scale of this oversight, at this point in the novel Seward has provided twenty-nine phonographic diary entries and a word count beyond 35,000 words; a wax cylinder can hold approximately ten minutes of content or approximately 800–900 words.[11] Hence, Seward has accrued approximately *forty* cylinders' worth of diary before he realizes that he has no idea how to find any particular part of his account.[12] (So much for our man of science.) And yet, in taking Guyau's theories of phonographic memory formation at face value, Seward and his (sizeable) blunder ultimately signal one of the biggest flaws in the comparison; recall does not easily fit into this analogy.

While Guyau's premise may have its faults, it serves as a springboard for further explorations of connections between the brain and the phonograph. While he describes the phonographic process of a needle scratching into the surface of a phonograph cylinder, the "invisible lines" drawn upon the brain point to a different type of memory formation, and one that was only just becoming a subject of discussion in psychology in Stoker's day: that of traumatic memory. The needle's violent path, scratching those invisible lines into a pliant medium, essentially describes a physical wound or trauma. Guyau is himself aware of this parallel when he uses words like "engrave," "furrow," "carved," and "etched" in his description of the recording process. In fact, tradition holds that a physical trauma was at the heart of the inception of the phonograph.

Thomas Edison was working on an experiment related to the telephone when a stylus, attached to a diaphragm, pierced his finger when it vibrated under the influence of his voice. It was when Edison looked at his bleeding finger that he realized the potential for the phonograph. And while there is a certain amount of skepticism about this origin story, its veracity is almost superfluous: the popularity of the story became a part of the sales pitch for the machine. For instance, in May of 1878, the

Irish Times—a media outlet likely accessible to the Dublin-based Stoker—published an account of Edison's physical injury-cum-discovery:

> The little needle on the diaphragm pricked [Edison's] finger, and as he drew it away, made an interrupted line of blood upon its surface by the vibration of the point, whereupon he at once placed some Morse paper so that the diaphragm could travel over it, and speaking through the tube, found small but familiar "dots and dashes" inscribed.[13]

This particular account (published only a year after Edison's invention) might just have piqued the interest of then thirty-one-year-old Stoker. The broad strokes of the invention-born-of-blood story, at the very least, became part of the Irish cultural narrative of the invention's inception from this point forward.

And so, the phonograph needle becomes a mnemonic for physical violence, wounds, and eventual scars. These physical traumas on a phonograph cylinder would then be preserved and replayed/relived. There are definite vampiric overtones in such a description.[14] And while a vampire attack/phonographic recording would leave physical scars, the psychological scars left behind are of equal, if not greater significance. The phonograph's parallels to vampirism seem particularly relevant since the plot of *Dracula* is driven by both physical and psychological vampire attacks: the psychological aspect made all the more obvious by Seward's profession and interest in the working of the human mind. Through further explication, the physical phonograph record becomes an unexpectedly apt representation of trauma memory and narratives as we understand them today. Stoker's novel plays out these modern connections with surprising accuracy and psychological insight, considering the novelty of psychological trauma in his contemporary setting.

As a doctor of psychology, it is no wonder that Seward demonstrates a certain obsession with the human brain: an obsession that proliferates throughout the novel. "Brain" is mentioned 65 times throughout the work and often in conjunction with allusions to mental illness.[15] Each of the characters who contribute significantly to the overall narrative doubts their own sanity at one point or another. Harker's brain fever and

Renfield's madness are perhaps the most obvious examples, but there are many others as well. For instance, Harker, while at Dracula's castle and before his brain fever, describes "feeling as though my own brain were unhinged or as if the shock had come which must end in its undoing."[16] Seward, while attending to Lucy after another draining night (vampiric pun absolutely intended), reflects, "I am beginning to wonder if my long habit of life amongst the insane is beginning to tell upon my own brain."[17] Mina describes the heaviness and unreliability of her brain throughout the day after Dracula has started to victimize her.[18] Furthermore, Mina's "man's brain" and Dracula's "child-brain" come up for discussion at some length. These latter references, with their allusion to the Victorian "sex in brain" debates, reveal Stoker's interest in using contemporary science and psychological references in his work.[19]

When Van Helsing and Mina discuss the psychology of criminals in relation to Dracula, they specifically mention Max Nordau and Cesare Lombroso—two physicians and criminologists who linked physical and moral degeneracy, and a criminal type with no physical markers, respectively.[20] Stoker's characters also discuss Jean-Martin Charcot and hypnosis as a psychological access point; Charcot was a neurologist who used his theories concerning hypnotism to try to understand hysteria.[21] This allusion is perhaps intended to add a sense of realism to the vampire hunters' attempts to follow Dracula when, later in the novel, they place Mina under hypnosis. Each of these allusions lends an air of legitimacy to this story of the supernatural and definitely would have added to Stoker's image as an author well up to the mark on the psychological debates of the day.

Stoker had more than a passing interest in the study of psychology, and therefore the influence of this science on the novel goes beyond these overt references. We know, for instance, that Stoker met Charcot at the Lyceum Theatre and that Charcot had a significant influence on Sigmund Freud.[22] We also know that Stoker attended events hosted by the Society for Psychical Research, including one at which there was a report on Freud's work "Observations on the Psychical Mechanism of Hysterical Phenomenon."[23] Stephanie Moss argues that it is entirely conceivable that Stoker was also familiar with Frederic W. H. Myers's 1889 report on the distinction between the "un-" and the "sub-"conscious that ultimately served as the basis of Freudian psychoanalysis in the twentieth century.[24] Myers's report of the proceedings naturally pays particular attention to memory formation as part of this dissection of consciousness; he points out that actions that we frequently consider "automatic" or happening without our knowledge

> plainly indicate the existence of a separate train of *memory* employed upon them. And, moreover, although they take place without the agent's *knowledge*, they cannot take place without his consciousness; they cannot be truly unconscious acts. They must in some fashion belong to a *subconsciousness*, which in relation to the far more potent *upper* consciousness, may best be understood if we consider it as a *secondary* consciousness.[25]

The functioning of an upper and a secondary (or sub-)consciousness lays out the foundational understanding of modern psychology, and Moss posits that Stoker was not only aware of the report, but "knowingly inscribes the historic moment that saw the birth of psychoanalysis" in his writing of *Dracula*.[26] At the very least, Stoker foregrounded these contemporary elements of psychology in his novel.

The principles of an upper and a sub-consciousness are essential to our understanding of psychological trauma, a concept that was also picking up steam in the years before *Dracula*'s publication. Trauma, as a psychological term, was a relatively new concept in the 1890s. The first use of trauma in such a context occurs in medical journals in the years directly preceding the publication of *Dracula*. For instance, in an article from *Popular Science* in 1895, Nathan Oppenheim discusses an "obscure mental condition" that he terms "psychical trauma" and which he describes as "a morbid nervous condition caused by repeated injurious impressions" that extends beyond traditionally diagnosable (at the time) mental disorders:

> We have evidence of [injured emotional and mental activities] from such signs as [...] hysterical attacks, loss of sleep otherwise inexplicable, disturbances of the flushing and pallor, all of which may be results of psychical effects repeated again and again. [...] The continued repetition of them wears, as it were, a rut in the

brain, so that any impulse approaching it slips out of its ordinary
path in the direction of least resistance and utter distortion.[27]

Oppenheim uses phonographic imagery to describe the event of trauma
as well as its impact on the brain. The initial trauma or "injurious impression" creates a "rut in the brain" as a result of what he goes on to describe
as "mechanical repetition" of "vicious stimuli."[28] Because the trauma is
repeated so frequently, the brain reacts to any stimulus that even approxi-
mates that initial injury, slipping out of its normal trajectory to retrace/
replay the trauma impression that is so deeply ingrained in the victim's
mind. It is like a scratched record that must perpetually play the same
section of a recording due to what might initially seem like an invisible
stimulus but is actually a "rut" that causes the needle to slip out of its
normal trajectory into the scratched portion again and again. It is an unrelenting repetition of a worn path.

Jonathan Harker's experiences in the first half of *Dracula* almost
exactly replicate the process of psychical trauma as outlined by Oppenheim and thereby add force to the connection between the phonograph
and its role in representing trauma in the novel's narrative. Harker first
experiences an "injurious impression" of the supernatural events that
drive the novel when, at Dracula's castle and in a moment that pairs a
physical and psychological trauma, he cuts himself while shaving:

> Suddenly I felt a hand on my shoulder, and heard the Count's
> voice saying to me, "Good-morning." I started, for it amazed me
> that I had not seen him, since the reflection of the glass covered
> the whole room behind me. In starting I had cut myself slightly,
> but did not notice it at the moment. [...] I saw that the cut had
> bled a little, and the blood was trickling over my chin. [...] When
> the Count saw my face, his eyes blazed with a sort of demoniac
> fury, and he suddenly made a grab at my throat.[29]

It is after this first overtly violent act on the Count's part that Harker begins
to understand his precarious position and imprisonment. This encounter
occurs on May 8, and his account of his stay at the castle continues until
June 30; in this time, he is repeatedly confronted with the psychological

torment of things he cannot explain. For over a month he endures "repeated injurious impressions" that create a "rut in the brain"; so much so that he succumbs to brain fever, which, in Victorian vernacular, was essentially an intense physical illness brought on by a severe "emotional" shock. When Mina arrives in Budapest to meet a convalescing Harker, he asks her not to read his diaries, which he fears because of how his brain might react if exposed to those traumatic memories again. However, he is forced to confront these memories when he sees the Count in the London streets. Harker turns "very pale," replicating the "disturbances of flushing and pallor" Oppenheim describes, then he becomes nearly hysterical—another symptom—staring and talking to himself about the Count's appearance until he sits quietly on a park bench and falls asleep.[30] When he wakes, he resumes his ordinary demeanor: "Why Mina, have I been asleep? Oh, do forgive me for being so rude."[31] Mina sees this behavior as clearly psychological and part of Harker's past horrors when she writes, "I don't like this lapsing into forgetfulness; it may make or continue some injury to the brain."[32] She then determines to avoid asking Harker about his journey to Transylvania to prevent what Oppenheim would describe as slipping from normal thought into the deeply cut traumatic rut. This episode aligns with Stoker's contemporary understanding of trauma, and Mina's instinct to avoid the traumatic memories of Harker's past is largely successful until both she and her husband come into contact with Van Helsing, Seward, and the other vampire hunters.

Seward never turns his clinical attention to Harker specifically since, once Harker understands that his vampire encounter was not isolated to his own experience, he gains trust in his own mind again. He explains to Van Helsing, "I *was* ill, I *have* had a shock. [...] I did not know what to trust, even the evidence of my own senses," but the knowledge that others had suffered from similar experiences "cured" him of his psychological ailment.[33] Seward takes him at his word. And while Harker is largely "cured," he continues to struggle with the realities of Dracula's impact (compounded later by Mina's victimization by the vampire) for the majority of the novel. It is seemingly at odds with Seward's professional role in the novel to let Harker's condition slide. Seward instead reserves his clinical observations for his patient, Renfield, who exhibits his own set of neuroses as a result of the vampire's proximity.

Seward's first phonographic account in the novel is particularly
dedicated to an understanding of Renfield's condition. Seward describes
Renfield as a patient "who has afforded me a study of much interest,"
and Seward expresses his determination "to understand him as well as
I can."[34] Renfield's psychosis revolves around an urge to consume life (in
the form of flies, spiders, birds, and even Seward's blood)[35] in order to
have eternal life: a condition Seward describes as a "zoöphagous mania."[36]
Renfield also has an awareness and connection to Dracula which is unex-
plained in the novel, but perhaps is a result of their similar consumption
of blood/life. However, in Seward's initial phonographic record, none of
these particular elements emerge. Instead, Seward unwittingly outlines
parallels between Renfield's human mind and early phonographic and
gramophonic technology:

> I presume that the sanguine temperament itself and the disturbing
> influence end in a mentally-accomplished finish; a possibly
> dangerous man, probably dangerous if unselfish. In selfish men
> caution is as secure an armour for their foes as for themselves.
> What I think of on this point is, when self is the fixed point the
> centripetal force is balanced with the centrifugal; when duty, a
> cause, etc., is the fixed point, the latter force is paramount, and
> only accident or a series of accidents can balance it.[37]

According to Seward, then, Renfield is particularly dangerous since he
tends toward an "unselfish" if yet undetermined end: an objective bigger
than himself. A "selfish" individual will always make their own perceived
well-being the fixed point of their mania; both centripetal and centrifugal
forces equally are asserted upon the individual, creating a balance. This
is largely demonstrated in the flat disk technology of the gramophone.[38]
The center of the gramophone disk is a fixed point; the centripetal and
centrifugal forces are equally asserted upon the center, and when the disk
spins, these balanced forces keep it centered and allow the needle to progress smoothly along its trajectory. Seward posits that this equilibrium or
balance of forces in the selfish individual indicates that the person understands that harm to others has an equal risk to one's self, and therefore
violence is not a viable option. In contrast, an "unselfish" individual places

A   B

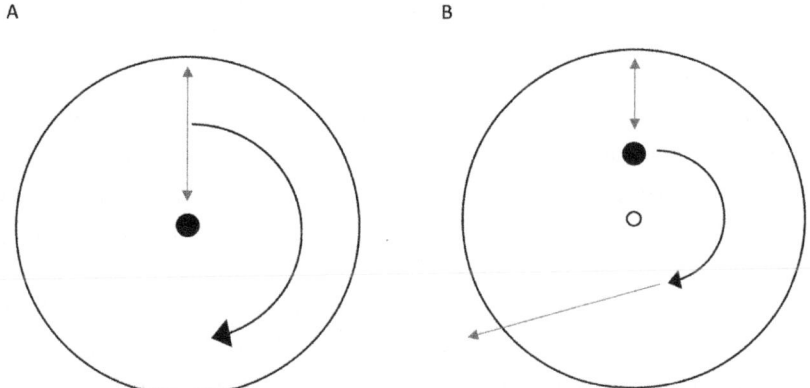

Figure 1.2. Centripetal and centrifugal forces
(A) in a balanced, centered rotation on a gramophone compared to
(B) those forces working upon an object not at the center of
the gramophone.

the duty or cause before themselves, making the "fixed point" somewhere
other than themselves. The individual's well-being and that of others is
always secondary to that duty or cause. The centripetal and centrifugal
forces are no longer balanced in favor of the course of least harm. As a
result, the individual is likely to fly off into violence or dangerous action
to themselves or others under certain circumstances. It is as if a penny
were placed on the gramophone's turntable. If the penny is placed in the
exact center of the turntable, it will not move, regardless of how fast the
turntable spins. The centripetal and centrifugal forces create this balance.
This is the "selfish" individual. If, however, the penny is off-center in the
least degree, the result is quite different. When the gramophone spins
slowly enough, the penny is stable and does not move; however, once the
turntable reaches a certain speed, the imbalance between centripetal and
centrifugal forces ruptures, and the penny will inevitably fly off the gramophone (see Figure 1.2). Seward posits that Renfield is this unselfish type
of individual, likely to put his (initially) unknown cause before himself,
and therefore Seward is wary of Renfield's moments of seeming lucidity
and his "sanguine" temperament.

Seward's hypothesis of balanced centripetal and centrifugal forces at
work in one's psyche is largely his only original foray into psychology. It

is therefore worth observing that the theory's emphasis on gramophonic principles—articulated while dictating about psychology to his phonograph—is likely not incidental. The recording industry was starting to take off in the late 1890s, and in the vernacular, the original recording was described as the "master" from which other copies were made.[39] Renfield echoes this vernacular when Dracula is near, referring to the vampire as "Master,"[40] and he repeatedly replicates the vampire's tendency to feed on living flesh. The allusion to "master" in recording parlance became poetically more complicated in the years directly after Dracula's publication. The famous image now called "His Master's Voice" became the iconic representation for the Berliner Gramophone Company, which, through the company's many iterations (Victor Talking Machines, RCA, HMV) is still in use today. In the original 1895 painting, Nipper the terrier sits in front of an Edison phonograph;[41] the story behind the iconic image is that Nipper is listening to a recording of his deceased master's voice. He remains faithful to a master who is no longer truly living but survives in a half-life through this orality.[42] In Dracula, Renfield replicates this iconic faithfulness to an un-dead "Master."

Given the importance of Renfield's account of the vampire's invasion of the asylum—not to mention Seward's particular interest in Renfield's "zoöphagia"—it is odd that Seward never thinks to have his patient talk directly into his phonograph and give an account of himself. Renfield is very clearly denied a direct narrative voice throughout this account, even in his climactic moments when his words are of the utmost importance. In the last encounter between doctor and patient, the physically shattered Renfield lies in a pool of his own blood while Seward, Van Helsing, Morris, and Holmwood all wait in an agonizingly long and tense silence for him to regain consciousness. Moreover, Seward *knows* that Renfield's account will be vital—Van Helsing explicitly states, "His words might be worth many lives"[43]—and the beginning of the phonographic account in which Seward reports Renfield's death opens with a reiterated assertion of the necessity for "exactness" in this account, since "[no] detail [...] must be forgotten."[44] And *still*, Seward does not think to bring the phonograph into the room to capture the dying man's essential narrative, even though Van Helsing, during this same period of time, has been fetched, has seen Renfield's condition, left to get dressed and fetch his operation tools, and, upon his return, sits in a sort of vigil for Renfield's last words.

Allowing a patient a direct narrative voice is common practice today, of course, but it never seems to occur to Seward, despite the novel's implication of the need to voice one's neuroses, fears, and traumas. In Seward's defense, Kittler points out that insanity during this period was considered to be "localized in the brain," and not something that could be untangled through speech. As a result, he concludes, it does not occur to Seward to "send Renfield's delirious speeches, without interface of his doctor's voice, directly into Edison's apparatus."[45] And while Kittler has a point that it was far from mainstream to think of using a patient's narrative to assist their mental recovery, it is worth pointing out that Josef Breuer and Sigmund Freud had actually published *Studies in Hysteria* in 1895—a study in which they treated traumatic memories in their patient Anna O. with the therapy that came to be known as "the talking cure." Tragically for Renfield, Seward does not place a heavy emphasis on the "talking cure" in his medical practice, even though Breuer and Freud's findings predated *Dracula*'s publication by two years. Seward does, however, seem to implement the therapy—unwitting as it may or may not be—among the rest of his fellow vampire hunters and their communal narrative of navigating vampiric trauma.

Shattered Narratives in *Dracula*

Psychological trauma, as it is understood today, is not drastically different from Oppenheim's basic premise described earlier, but it is more nuanced and provides additional insights into how the phonograph in *Dracula* serves as a representational model of trauma narratives. Trauma events are frequently described in psychological terms as "outside normal human experience," events which the mind cannot process as it would other memories. In *Dracula*, the vampire is supernatural and therefore impossibly beyond the human experience his victims are initially willing to entertain. This is Harker's reasoning when he describes his initial mental breakdown to Mina: his incapacity to process the events in Transylvania causes the breakdown. As we understand trauma now, it is because of the mind's inability to process the trauma that the event is often disconnected or separated from the rest of the mind's experiences, which explains Harker's ability to wake up from a brief nap after seeing Dracula in London and to continue as if nothing had happened. Cathy Caruth explains that the mind's disassociation of the traumatic experience from the rest of one's experiences—often because the victim fails to comprehend, much less communicate and assimilate the trauma into the conscious mind—means that the "traumatic event is not experienced as it occurs" but is instead experienced separately, belatedly.[46] Moreover, the "impact of the traumatic event lies precisely in its belatedness."[47] This complicates our understanding of memory as a chronological concept. No longer does memory easily flow from event to event in a linear progression. Rather, trauma memories become separated from the linear model and lie in an alternate stream of memory: one that the individual's mind does not consciously recognize. The mind has protected itself from this trauma by disjoining it from the larger narrative of memory. Often, the victim repeatedly relives or re-experiences the trauma *after* the initial event as part of a subconscious manifestation: something experienced in that alternate stream of memory away from the surface of consciousness. Treatment of this trauma often means confronting that asynchronous memory, and, as Freud describes it, requiring the victim to "*repeat* the repressed material as a contemporary event" (rather than remembering it as a past event) in an attempt to assimilate the trauma into the larger conscious narrative or memory.[48] By experiencing the trauma as a belated and thereby contemporary event, even when the event is assimilated, the timeline will always be a jumble of asynchronous events. In a broad generalization, instead of events occurring in a sequence (1, 2, 3, 4), trauma memory removes the event entirely from any recognizable sequence (1, 2, _, 4). An assimilation of the trauma memory will always complicate a sequential description further since the past trauma memory will now coincide or conflict with a contemporary event (1, 2, _, 4/3). When past events intrude forcibly on contemporary events as though the past is also contemporary, we can identify this as a trauma narrative. The timelines are telling.

Stoker's novel is largely constructed as a trauma narrative, with portions of the narrative contained in very literal separate streams of consciousness in the form of the individuals who contribute to the overall work. Harker, Mina, Lucy, Seward, and the rest of the vampire hunters experience the trauma of Dracula's attacks in their own (varying degrees of) consciousness. Furthermore, Jamil Khader points out that the "traumatic core" of the novel's vampire attack is not isolated to the actual physical and psychological violence, "but also in its endless repetitions."[49] And it is only after repeated traumas and experiences that the group realizes that they are all experiencing a similar trauma. They then collectively make an effort to create a larger narrative of what has happened, to assimilate their seemingly disparate, disjointed, and asynchronous accounts into a whole. As individuals, the victims are afraid to articulate their reality (we have already seen this with Harker's fear of his journal and what it contains), and therefore the attacks can only be registered in their subconscious. Once they collaborate to construct a larger representation of these traumatic events, their narratives begin to emerge from that subconscious, overlapping and creating meaning as a communal whole. But even though the narrative ultimately helps them vanquish the vampire, it remains largely fragmentary and incomplete, composed of shards of shattered individual experiences.

One of the novel's most fascinating elements is its attempt to assemble these scraps of media, narrative, and memory into a collective account. And while critics make much of the media and structural elements of the text, relatively little attention is paid to the deeply problematic anachrony of the narrative. The anachronisms reveal further parallels to a collective trauma narrative. Though the novel is constructed of disparate and even asynchronous events, the narrative still avowedly strives for chronological (linear) assimilation. For instance, after reading the note at the beginning of the work that informs us that the texts have been "placed in sequence" and are "exactly contemporary"[50]—not to mention a passage later in the novel in which Van Helsing checks that Mina and Harker "have put up in *exact order* all things that have been"[51]—we generally assume that the accounts in the novel are delivered in a strict chronological order. We take for granted that things are presented in the order that they happened. And yet, in several instances, the entries in the novel are out of sequence, often inexplicably so and to the detriment of the logic of the order of events. For instance, in the first edition text, Dr. Seward's first phonographic diary entry is dated April 25. This *pre*dates every other entry in the novel by over a week, since Harker's first entry is dated May 3. This means that, strictly chronologically speaking, Seward's entry should be the first. But this date of April 25 *cannot* be accurate, since Seward, in the diary account, refers to the "rebuff of yesterday"[52] when Lucy rejected his marriage proposal, which Lucy writes about in a letter to Mina dated May 24. The *actual* date for Seward's first entry must therefore be *May* 25 and not April.[53] And while similar small discrepancies in dates might be identified as typos—which can generally be considered oversights by the publishers of Stoker's first edition—the fact remains that, even with corrections to a few impossible dates, many of the accounts in *Dracula* are *not* in chronological order.

The first several entries of the novel are an apt representation of this anachronic timeline. Harker's journal, with which the novel starts, begins on May 3 and continues uninterrupted until June 30. However, Mina's first letter to Lucy is dated May 9, Lucy posts a letter Mina on May 24, and Seward's first phonograph entry is (presumably) May 25. Each of these entries occurs before the end of Harker's account. When we compare the first twenty-one entries of the novel to the first twenty-one entries by chronological order, we get a drastically different timeline (see Figure 1.3). And this is only a small example of the anachronic issues running throughout the majority of the novel. If we were to read the novel in this strictly chronological order, we would experience it quite differently.

What can we make of such problematic timelines, considering the multiple assurances from the text that the work is "placed in sequence" and "exact order"? The narrative structure of *Dracula* is essentially replicating traumatic memory integration. The memories of the traumatized vampire victims lie in literal alternate and separate bodies of the novel's consciousness until finally combined into a single text, but those memories are perpetually disjointed and non-sequential. Moreover, the group of victims who have collected and collated this narrative seem largely unaware that they have created such problematic timelines. The trauma is extant in the structure; the victims do not even register the existence of the problem.

These fractures in the timeline emphasize the difficulty of truly assimilating a trauma into a coherent narrative. The memories of the vampire victims can never fully assimilate and articulate the reality of Dracula's physical and psychological toll. It is these cracks of narrative that allow

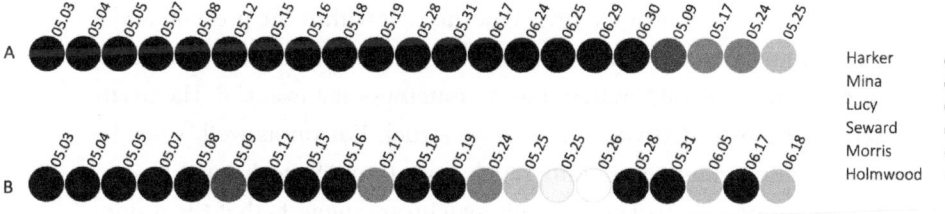

Figure 1.3. Order of the first 21 entries (A) as they appear in *Dracula* and (B) in chronological order.

inexplicable and troublesome events to occur, even after the hunters begin to work together. How else might we explain the fact that these individuals cannot seem to register that Mina begins to exhibit the same symptoms that Lucy suffered only weeks earlier? Seward, Harker, and Mina see *and* comment on her symptoms of pallor and lethargy but fail to connect them to the diagnosis of vampire attack until they are all communally confronted with a horrifying assault that leaves them in no doubt that Mina is Dracula's victim. The Count invades the asylum and attacks Mina; in Seward's later account of the attack, Dracula even taunts them that this is a repeated trauma, sneering "[I]t is not the first time, or the second, that [Mina's] veins have appeased my thirst!"[54] This attack occurs after the hunters have tried to isolate Mina from their planning and serves as a brutal reminder that isolating and silencing a strain of the trauma narrative is likely to perpetuate or compound the trauma rather than treat it. It is a hard-learned lesson, but one that seems to work; after this event, the narrative becomes much more coherent and linear. Anachronic events drop out of the narrative, and the novel becomes a direct account of the hunters' final pursuit of and confrontation with the Count.

While the anachrony of the larger narrative seems to resolve by the end of the novel, the phonograph persists as a physical reminder of the trauma narratives and a physical embodiment of the "alternate stream" of trauma memory. Seward's phonograph and its cylinders replicate the anachronic and belated nature of a trauma narrative by further problematizing our conception of chronological or linear time. When a voice recording like Seward's diary is made, a living aural event is inscribed on the wax cylinder. Any replay or replication of that recording will always be a reliving of a past event, a revival of the past within the present, and a very literal iteration of Freud's concern that trauma obliges the individual to "*repeat* the repressed material as a contemporary event."[55] The asynchrony of the recorded voice must have struck Edison as well, since he famously stated, after the phonograph's invention, "Speech has become, as it were, immortal." In *Dracula*, this anachrony suggests that the immediacy of the accounts, so valued by the assemblers of the novel's narrative, is compromised by the very technology they assume will assist them. The phonograph then gains compounded meaning. The "immortality" of the phonograph evokes the vampire's supernatural lifespan. It is not only a physical and psychological signifier of trauma memories and a literal account of the verbalized trauma of vampire attacks, but it now also creates "undead" oral and aural events in the replay of the initial "master" copy. Essentially, the phonograph's narrative in *Dracula* is also the narrative of a vampire coded into the machine.

Undead Oralities and Irish Folklore

In a novel that has sparked many a pun on "oral fixation"—the vampire's biting and "child brain," for instance, make the Freudian expression apt enough—*Dracula* takes the idea of an oral obsession in a new direction when Seward's orality, and that of anyone else using the machine, is consumed by the phonograph. Several readings of the media in *Dracula* suggest that the technology of the late nineteenth century is essential to defeating the vampire; a different reading, however, is that the phonograph is very like a vampire.[56] And considering that the phonograph is responsible for over one-third of the novel's accounts, the machine problematizes orality in the novel and the wider Irish cultural context.

When Edison's phonograph burst onto the media scene in 1877, the inventor's first "immortalized" words were a roared rendition of "Mary Had a Little Lamb," a nursery rhyme that relies largely on the oral tradition for its perpetuation. By capturing the rhyme on his machine, Edison essentially created a mechanical cognate for the tradition of passing stories, songs, and histories along to new generations; a tradition valued by largely oral-based cultures such as that of nineteenth-century Ireland. In a certain light, the phonograph may have seemed like a machine custom-made for Ireland, a country for which print culture could be perceived as "the medium of [...] colonial administration," with oral culture as the obvious antithesis.[57] Oral culture was a core principle of "Irishness" well into the 1890s, and the phonograph seemed posed as the medium to champion this tradition while also bringing the tradition and Ireland further into modernity. And yet the machine becomes a double-edged sword when we realize that the phonograph inherently transfers the tradition into a mechanism, rather than transmitting it to another living individual.

In oral cultures, or perceived oral cultures like Ireland's of the late 1800s, the essence of orality is its *living* vitality. Oral tales and songs were considered enduring media: memory and record passed on to each successive generation. This relies on the transfer of the story from person to person through an oral performance to living memory, which can then preserve the story for future iterations. And so, despite the initial inclination to consider phonographic technology as an ideal platform to preserve such orality, the phono*graph*, with its etymological emphasis on *writing* sound, tries to inscribe the words of folklore onto a wax surface. This makes these oralities artifacts, objects, things that are only revived when replayed verbatim on the same machine: only an imitation of the original speech event. And so, if words in an oral culture are living things, then any attempt to preserve them in a format other than a living body fundamentally kills what it intends to preserve. The phonograph essentially creates an undead orality. In Stoker's novel, the undeadness of the phonograph, like Dracula, haunts the narrative of the vampire hunters.

It is likely that the phonograph's oral "undeadness" was not lost on Stoker when he chose to highlight the technology so prominently in his work. His fascination with the phonograph predated *Dracula* and, hence, informed his use of the machine in the novel. He first learned of Edison's invention almost certainly while he was living in Dublin, lending a specifically Irish nuance to his perceptions of it. Reports of the phonograph's invention and its popularity were nearly simultaneous and universal; Dublin reporters and shops were as eager as any to gain access to "[o]ne of the most wonderful and interesting of many and marvelous inventions" of the era.[58] In August of 1878, only six months after Edison patented the phonograph, Mr. Robinson's store on Grafton Street advertised in many of the major Dublin newspapers—including the *Dublin Evening Mail*, the newspaper for which Stoker wrote at the time[59]—that it was displaying and demonstrating the marvelous invention for the Irish public. In an article in the *Weekly Irish Times*, the machine was reported to do "much more than write down sound—it speaks intelligible words and phrases with the most minute accuracy as to intensity of tone, pitch, or quality"; the article goes on to describe the origin story of the inventor pricking his finger, and then claims that "the voice can be *embalmed* by the phonograph, and made to last indefinitely."[60] The description of the voice as "embalmed" directly addresses the underlying cultural perception of orality in Ireland as something that is originally a living thing. To "embalm" it, then, is to acknowledge that a singular speech event, once spoken, no longer has its vitality unless transmitted to another living source, and any attempt to preserve it is artificial, and merely an attempt to prevent a speedy decay. (And while embalming might initially suggest mummification rather than vampiric preservation, I'll take my undead references however I find them.) Though we cannot with certainty claim that Stoker read this particularly apt description of the phonograph's embalming of the human voice, we can be relatively sure that he read one of the myriad accounts of the invention, complete with descriptions of Edison's inspiration drawn from blood, in the reports and advertisements for the machine that flooded the *Dublin Evening Mail*, the *Irish Times*, and other popular periodicals of the day. Similarly, Stoker almost certainly passed by the window of Robinson's store on Grafton Street, with its displays and advertised demonstrations, since this is one of Dublin's major thoroughfares. These are particular Irish cultural encounters with the machine.

Stoker had other documented encounters with the phonograph that also informed his depiction of orality in *Dracula*. In 1888 he helped arrange for the actor Henry Irving, who employed Stoker as his manager in 1878, to visit Little Menlo to record an excerpt from Monk Lewis's *The Captive*. Edison's primary agent in Great Britain, George Edward Gouraud, was based at Little Menlo—so named in recognition of Edison's location in Menlo Park, New Jersey—and was largely responsible for introducing the phonograph to British society. Irving's was one of many high-profile recordings of actors and authors of the day; the recording was also considered a great publicity platform for Irving.

Later, in 1890, Stoker accompanied Irving on a visit to Alfred Tennyson. While there, the poet's son Hallam took out his phonograph and played a cylinder of Tennyson reading "The Charge of the Light Brigade." In Stoker's own words, "It was strange to hear the mechanical repetition whilst the sound of the real voice, which we had so lately heard, was still ringing in our ears."[61] The juxtaposition of the mechanical and the real voice are markedly "strange"—he also points out that it is "hard to believe" that this was not actually Tennyson in the room again—and yet Stoker also finds the experience rather visceral. He goes on to write,

> The poem [...] is one of special excellence for both phonographic recital and was an illustration of Tennyson's remarkable sense of time. One seems to hear the thunder of the horses' hooves as they ride to the attack. The ground seems to shake, and the virile voice of the reader conveys in added volume the desperate valour of the charge.[62]

Stoker hears Tennyson's voice through the machine, of course, but is more significantly struck by the impact that the machine has on the recitation, specifically pointing out the phonograph's role in this near-bodily experience of Lord Cardigan's ill-fated charge.

Stoker's description of hearing Tennyson's recitation as "strange" and "hard to believe" was not uncommon during the early years of the phonograph. When people were still first experiencing recorded sound, auditors often struggled to come to grips with the "unnatural" or uncanny preservation of voice. For example, when the London Browning Society gathered to commemorate the poet after his death, part of the evening's entertainment included the phonograph recording of the dead poet reciting a portion of his poetry; Browning's sister Sarianna was horrified by the recording, describing it as an "indecent séance."[63] In other instances, people reportedly succumbed to faintness or "hysteria" when they heard the phonograph play for the first time.[64] Given these reactions, it perhaps comes as no surprise that Mina's first experience of the phonograph is marked by a certain amount of shock and her near-swoon. And even though Mina's shock might be a combined reaction to the narrative of vampirism she is hearing unfold as well as the machine, she clearly finds the phonograph disconcerting. She informs Seward that the machine is "cruelly true. [...] It was like a soul crying out to Almighty God" and she "hear[d] [his] heart beat."[65] Her reaction mirrors Stoker's in that it is "hard to believe" that this is not a truly living iteration of the oral event, and both Mina and Stoker respond to the recording as a very dramatic and visceral experience. The machine, for Mina, creates an uncanny half-living heart-beat with something "like a soul"; the experience of Seward's original oral recordings and her reaction is so strong that she immediately tries to minimize its impact for future audiences.

These striking moments of orality—both in Stoker's personal experi-ence and its iteration in Mina's experience—strongly suggest the author's understanding of the power of orality in both its living and undead (phonographic) forms. The nuance of his depictions of orality's power in *Dracula*, particularly in the context of trauma narratives, finds paral-lels in his own life and cultural background. We see the shadow of oral trauma narratives of the Great Famine emerge in Stoker's childhood as well as in the haunting orality of *Dracula*. In fact, there are several *specific* parallels between the representations of orality, communal trauma narra-tive, and transcription in *Dracula* and Irish folkloric accounts collected by phonographic technology in the late nineteenth and early twentieth centuries. First, the oral narratives of trauma in both instances start as individual accounts, but quickly become important to the objectives of those interested in constructing a communal narrative. Seward's accounts become vital to the vampire hunters' efforts to understand the vampire, and in Ireland, individual experiences of Famine and family lore become valued for their articulation of a national tragedy. The accounts, however, resist seamless integration into a larger narrative, replicating the trauma narrative structures that they try to recount. Next, the oral narratives are transcribed into written media, largely undercutting the value of the preserved orality: Mina chooses to eliminate Seward's emotions and idio-syncrasies from the record and folklore collectors preserved the written accounts as part of a data-collection, even though transcription presents its own set of concerns and cannot always preserve the authenticity of the original. And ultimately, many of the original oral records are destroyed, eliminating the remaining vitality of the phonograph record. Each of these parallels emphasizes the problematic but powerful symbolic *and* tangible nature of the phonograph in replicating the trauma narratives of a collective.

Oral folklore was an inherent part of Stoker's childhood. When he was young, he suffered a near seven-year convalescence following an unidentified paralytic illness. During this time, his mother Charlotte would recite stories from Irish folklore and her own experiences to entertain her son.[66] According to Joseph Valente, Stoker's "'so Irish' mother nurtured [his] nativist adherences on all manner of Irish myth, on Celtic Folklore, and, most conspicuously, on macabre accounts of the Great Famine just passed, her experience of the 1832 cholera epidemic, [...] and the horrors of the Banshee, whose wail supposedly accompanied [...] the death of her Celtic mother."[67] (With such sinister childhood stories, perhaps it is no wonder Stoker had a gift for the gothic.) Amid this flurry of storytelling techniques—Irish folklore, the supernatural, and all-too-horrific histories—what emerges as a common theme in *Dracula* and Stoker's other writings is his tendency to value and preserve his mother's oral narratives of personal and cultural traumas.

Stoker came to view this early developmental period of his life as particularly marked by a *physical* trauma resulting from the larger *cultural* trauma of the Famine. Valente points out that Stoker considered his childhood illness to be a result of the contagion left behind in the wake of the Famine.[68] Stoker was, in fact, considered a "Famine child," in that he was born in 1847, "Black 47," the worst year of the Famine. His prolonged convalescence, Robert A. Smart and Michael Hutcheson speculate, "in the midst of so much disease and death must surely have provided him with vivid images of the dead and dying victims of the invisible blight and fevers from the Famine."[69] When we combine Stoker's interest in his mother's narratives of folklore and personal and cultural traumas, as well as his own physical and psychological development which was directly impacted by a sweeping cultural trauma, we begin to understand the author's compulsion to tell a trauma narrative not only in *Dracula*, but in his earlier works as well.

In his short story "The Invisible Giant" (1881), Stoker conducts his own form of folklore collection, incorporating his mother's oral narratives into his writing. He remembered her stories of the cholera epidemic when she was a young girl in Sligo, and later, as an adult, he asked her to write down the account for him. He adapted her account into "The Invisible Giant" in ways that articulate that particular personal trauma as part of a larger cultural narrative. The story presents itself as a fairy tale—evoking the oral tradition format in which he first experienced the story—and it quickly becomes allegorical, drawing parallels between the cholera epidemic and the larger and later trauma of the Irish Famine. Charlotte described the "plague" of cholera as invading Ireland, stealing into houses and ultimately striking five-eighths of Sligo's population dead.[70] In Stoker's story, the Invisible Giant is synonymous with the Plague—always capitalized and even called the "Giant Plague" at one point[71]—sweeping over the fictional city and killing its inhabitants. This fictional version has parallels with the language used in Charlotte's account as well as broader accounts of the "plague" of the Famine. The Giant Plague is initially depicted as a looming murky figure that Zaya, the young protagonist, can see as a dark shadow, but once it enters the town it becomes an invisible killer. Zaya is also constantly near starvation and fears catching the death that the Giant Plague brings. During the Famine, potato blight brought the poor to the brink of starvation, and if they did not succumb, diseases such as typhus often claimed their lives. While Charlotte reported five-eighths of the population of Sligo dying, Stoker describes a city in which "so many people had died that one began to wonder that so many were left; for it was only when the town began to get thinned that people thought of the vast numbers that had lived in it."[72] This fictional account again evokes parallels to Charlotte's cholera experiences and the later nearly one-third reduction in population in Ireland due to the Famine—something that Charlotte lived through (though in comparative ease in Dublin) and shared accounts of with her son.

While the connections to Irish cultural trauma are fairly obvious in "The Invisible Giant," they are less overt in *Dracula*, even though many have argued for decoding the novel as an Irish narrative.[73] And while I do not venture to describe *Dracula* as an *explicitly* Irish text, there are distinct Irish characteristics present in Stoker's use of folklore throughout the narrative,[74] the overt references to "famine and disease" in a text obsessed with the consumption of food and drink,[75] the coffin ship that herald's Dracula's arrival in London—"a resonant image from Famine times"[76]—and, most importantly in the context of this chapter, the text's urgent reliance on orality throughout. This latter motif indicates Stoker's compulsion to use oral accounts of trauma as a way of working through his own personal, familial, and cultural inheritances of the Famine. In *Dracula* Stoker uses both his mother's experiences of a localized communal horror and her macabre accounts of the Famine to explore Ireland's cultural traumas and their iterations in oral folklore.

Stoker's experience of the Famine as a simultaneously personal and vicarious national oral narrative is somewhat representative of collected Famine folklore. In the final decades of the nineteenth century, oral Famine narratives were starting to take on elements of politics and nationalism. Irish Revivalism was in the air; support for bolstering the Irish language and its rich oral culture was at the heart of nearly every form of Irish nationalism. Irish orality, particularly in terms of folklore collection, became a highly valued cultural commodity. Oral accounts of the Great Famine and other Irish hardships were politicized by those with nationalist interests; the traumas experienced by the communal Irish formed a condemning narrative of colonialism. And while this nationalist outlook is a reductive way to view the instinct to collect and preserve oral folklore, and was in no way the only instinct at play, it *was* a factor. Regardless of the impetus, the coming decades saw an incredible, large-scale effort to collect Famine narratives (particularly after the formation of the Irish Folklore Commission in 1935), which created a larger communal narrative of those traumas via recorded accounts.

There is a large body of scholarship based on the work of the Folklore Commission and the collection of Irish Famine narratives, and these works take a range of directions and interpretations. However, a common thread in most work on Famine narratives is an attempt to collate the myriad experiences into a larger narrative of understanding of this traumatic event. At the same time, most works also acknowledge that the individual experiences of the Famine were deeply and personally traumatic, and that a communal representation of those traumas will always be insufficient, though still valuable. Cathal Póirtéir explains, "The picture which folklore gives us is broken and fragmentary, but that is in itself no reason to undervalue it. These thousands upon thousands of shattered pieces of memory can still form part of the mosaic of our understanding."[77] The vivid metaphor of a "shattered" communal memory finds particular resonance in the context of trauma narratives; the idea of memory creating a "mosaic" of the events that transpired produces a meaningful parallel between the communal narrative structures of the Famine and *Dracula*. The problematic timeline of Stoker's novel gains added meaning when read through this perspective of Irish communal trauma. In fact, when Póirtéir writes, "The neat chronological demarcations afforded to scholars by hindsight and the written record are not the prime concern of the folk record,"[78] he posits a rebuttal to the introductory note to *Dracula* that insists that the records of the novel must be "exactly contemporary" and "placed in sequence."[79] Tales of trauma, of orality, of communal narrative, are not meant to articulate a "neat chronological demarcation," but rather the "shattered pieces of memory [that] can still form part of the mosaic of our understanding." Shattered narratives of trauma are no less valuable for their inability to articulate precise memory; the trauma is relevant regardless.

The parallels between fictional and factual communal trauma narratives continue when we examine their continued debt to phonographic technology. The abundance of extant Famine narratives owes a great deal to the phonograph, despite the problematic "undeadness" inherent in the technology. In *Dracula*, the vampire hunters use the phonograph and other media in an attempt to collect and assimilate disparate aspects of a traumatized community into a coherent narrative. Irish folklorists of the *fin de siècle* often used the phonograph to collect, document, and assimilate aspects of their heritage and traumatized cultural memory to form a coherent national(ist) narrative. In both instances, the phonograph initially seems to be part of the solution. It is Seward's primary tool for recording the vampire attacks, and the Ediphone (a phonographic machine specifically intended for recording dictation) was considered the most important piece of equipment in an Irish folklorist's kit (see Figure 1.4).[80] But the machine quickly problematizes the process and potentially damages the "accuracy" or "authenticity" that both narratives so desperately crave.

The upswing in national(ist) interest in the Irish language and oral tradition in the late 1800s coincided with the rise of phonographic technology. Beyond the amateur and individual folklore collectors who had already begun to use the machine to archive their work in Ireland, a semi-official collection of folklore via phonograph began the same year that *Dracula* was published. In 1897 the Gaelic League hosted the

Figure 1.4. Ediphone used by the Irish Folklore Commission and housed
in the Irish Folklore Collection at University College Dublin.
Photograph: Zan Cammack.

inaugural *Oireachtas* cultural festival; in the same year there was the inaugural *Feis Ceoil*, a music festival. Both events prominently featured the
phonograph as part of the festivities. At the *Feis Ceoil*, for instance, the
phonograph recorded contestants explicitly "to admit it [the music] to
being transcribed."[81] The first *Oireachtas* also collected stories, poems, and
songs; some of these records are the earliest recordings housed in the Irish
Folklore Collection at University College Dublin. But what to do with all
of these oral recordings? Mina has the answer, which seems obvious to her
only moments after encountering her first phonograph.

When Mina first sees and hears Seward's phonograph, she is fascinated with its ability to quickly and accurately take down his account,

exclaiming, "Why, this beats even shorthand!"[82] Her enthusiasm and desire to hear the phonograph, to engage in the recording process, is similar to the reaction of many of the Irish who encountered folklorists armed with Ediphones. In fact, Briody and other folklore collectors considered the Ediphone "an enticement in itself to get narrators to divulge their lore."[83] But Mina quickly shifts from fascination to practicality. She is interested in collecting all of the narratives of those involved in Lucy's death, and she has also just exposed Seward's problem with recalling specific sections of the recording; one of Mina's first instincts is to transcribe the oral account.

In a supreme act of bureaucracy,[84] Mina sets out to create a typed version of Seward's accounts and to collate them into the other masses of written media that make up the novel. She strives to collect the disparate narratives of the vampire attacks and preserve the story as a "most accurate" and "authentic" account. But part of the process requires that the media be homogenized, standardized, and unified under a *written* language. And even though transcription of oral accounts was a logical impulse for Mina and the Irish folklorists (one of Edison's primary marketing strategies was to advertise the phonograph as a dictation device for stenographers), transcription comes at a price.

Mina understands the power of the oral language as a medium of expressing emotion through voice and inflection, something that cannot always be conveyed through the written word. The removal of that emotion and expression, however, partially motivates Mina's decision to transcribe. She points out that the phonograph is "cruelly true" and "told me in its very tones, the anguish of your heart."[85] And even though the phonograph's orality enables an immediacy and primacy, Mina overtly wants to remove this in her transcription. She concludes that "[n]o one must hear them spoken ever again," and a transcription will ensure that "none other need now hear your heart beat, as I did."[86] In this instance, Mina is subliminally acknowledging the half-life or undead nature of the phonographic recording—her repeated mention of the heart points to her perception of the recording's preserved life—and it is exactly this element that she wishes to eliminate in transcription. Beyond this motivation, however, Mina also hopes to document Seward's encounters with Renfield and Lucy to help further the hunt for the vampire. To do this, she needs to access the diary in a format that can fit in with her filing system and documentation. So, she removes Seward's oral recitations from the problematic phonograph to the bureaucratic transcript.

Transcription of phonographic accounts also became standard practice for Irish folklore collectors. After the *Feis Ceoil*, for instance, the phonograph preserved the folk songs primarily for the purpose of transcribing the music for the archive. At the *Oireachtas*, the recordings were similarly meant to serve an archival purpose. The Gaelic League went so far as to announce that "the only adequate means of preserving the vast mass of oral literature still extant is to get it into *print* as soon as possible."[87] Transcription was the standard practice and took priority over recordings in the organizations that eventually became the Irish Folklore Commission.

Transcription presents another problem for orality in its idiosyncrasies and difficulties in mediating the translation from oral to written language. Seward's accounts again provide insight into this difficulty. Leanne Page points out that the phonograph creates a change in Seward's language that we can only fully notice and appreciate after he is forced to leave it behind in London while in pursuit of the vampire, and draws attention to how much he misses the fluidity of the phonograph over the "irksome pen."[88] Seward's *written* accounts, Page argues, still have "traces of the oral style of communication demanded by the phonograph."[89] He has grown accustomed to "performing" language differently for the phonograph, and it alters his language patterns. Page specifically recognizes the use of ellipses and sentence fragments as part of Seward's language adaptation for the phonograph,[90] identifying these phenomena in his first entry when he discusses Renfield's condition: "Sanguine temperament; great physical strength; morbidly excitable; periods of gloom ending in some fixed idea which I cannot make out."[91] And while Page's identification of elements of adapted language performance is spot on, this first phonographic entry proves trickier to grapple with than mere performance.

Seward uses several phrases in this entry that make no sense in verbal communication. Can one ever orally abbreviate, with any ease of performance, Latin terminology like *verb. sap.* or *ætat* (*verbum sapienti satis est*, "a word is sufficient to a wise man," and *aetatis*, "aged")?[92] In the same entry, Seward makes a *mem.* or memorandum to himself; not only is a memorandum a distinctly written platform, but we later realize that

Seward has no idea how to retrieve any kind of memorandum from his mass of recordings, meaning the entire side note is a breakdown of the "performance" for this technology. These problematic abbreviations point to a few possible conclusions: 1) Seward's "performance" for the phonograph is still on a learning curve; 2) Stoker didn't particularly recognize these problems; or 3) this is likely some sort of transcription adaptation on Mina's part. It's likely a combination of all three, but with a heavy emphasis on transcription adaptation.

It is, after all, only halfway through the novel that we learn that Mina has transcribed the phonographic diary entries. We have, of course, already registered on some level that the account is *not* in fact "kept in phonograph" but is written. We might have initially thought that we were meant to suspend disbelief and imagine these accounts still in their phonographic form, but by mid-novel Mina and her transcriptions make more sense. Mina's role in facilitating the shift from oral to written diary partially accounts for these troublesome abbreviations and aberrations. Each of these instances of alteration, however, exposes how deeply difficult it is to represent an oral communication in a written form, underscoring the impossibility of the "accuracy" that Seward specifically desires from the initial account and on which the vampire hunters implicitly rely.

The trouble with transcription exposed by Seward's accounts highlights the same potential problem with transcriptions of Irish oral folklore: the integrity of the transcription is inherently under suspicion. Harker even points this out at the end of the novel when he writes: "In all the mass of material of which the record is composed, there is hardly one authentic document. [...] We could hardly ask anyone, even did we wish to, to accept these as proofs of so wild a story."[93] As if the undead orality of phonography were not problematic enough, the urge to document, file, and collate any communal account, whether the trauma narrative of various vampire victims or the folklore representation of a battered colonial country, alters and even homogenizes what it sets out to preserve. When we witness orality standardized and absorbed by the phonograph and into the media "mass" of *Dracula*'s fictional narrative, we witness a process that was occurring in reality in the collection of Irish music and folklore. Transcribing from the Ediphone—though it was an invaluable tool for the Irish Folklore Commission and was used by the Commission well into mid-century, long after the technology's heyday—was considered a deeply arduous task and one that heavily relied on the abilities of both collector and speaker. For Tadhg Ó Murchadha, one of the Commission folklorists, "transcription was the most difficult part of the work, especially when the speaker spoke unclearly."[94] He considered it a "heroic feat" to transcribe three cylinders of content in a day if there were difficulties with the recording; he even reported losing sleep over the stress of the activity. And if he and other folklorists couldn't understand a word or phrase, they had either to re-consult their source or leave a blank space.[95] While the dedication of these folklorists left relatively few blank spaces unfilled, the unfilled spaces that do exist further emphasize the connection to trauma narratives as well as the troubles of transcription, and mirror the blank spaces and missed time in *Dracula*.

In an ironic twist, the phonograph was also responsible for the *loss* of many folkloric accounts. While collectors, armed with Ediphones, collected works from all over Ireland, financial constraints made it impossible for them to keep and store all of the records they made. So, to economize, after an original recording was transcribed and filed, the wax cylinders were pared down, the recording removed, and the cylinder sent back out into the field to be used again (up to six times). Preservation of the original was always the ideal scenario, but shortage of funds made this paring down a necessity.[96] It was a logistical issue. Recordings that were considered particularly representative *were* preserved until they could be transferred to the more permanent (and easier to store) medium of the gramophone record. And yet, according to Seosamh Ó Dálaigh, "many informants in the early days, at least, did not realize that their recordings were not being preserved in *acoustic* format for posterity."[97] Since the contributors were not always aware of the fleeting nature of these recordings, it is highly likely that many oral accounts dropped out of living orality, under the assumption they were preserved elsewhere.

The tragic destruction of so many thousands of oral accounts is mirrored in *Dracula* when, after Mina transcribes the cylinders and Seward stores the documents in a safe, Dracula invades the asylum and sets fire to the phonograph cylinders. Holmwood tells the others that the wax of the cylinders (generally made of paraffin) not only melts, but "help[s] the flames."[98] This narrative detail draws particular attention to the (self-)destruction of the only remaining trace of Seward's oral/aural account. In this, the phonograph's climactic moment, the machine is depicted as a self-defeating means of preserving orality. The cylinders are not passive victims in the fire, but actively assist in the destruction of an oral account, fueling the flames that consume Seward's orality.

In Ireland, the early attempts to collect folklore via phonograph were efforts to combine and propagate a collective Irish narrative. That narrative would be made up of accounts in the Irish language, orally delivered, as a testament to the country's resilience against English rule and cultural traumas like the Famine. Though a laudable agenda, and one that preserved thousands of accounts that are culturally and historically invaluable, the phonographic methodology problematized as much as it assisted the agenda. The preservation of an oral national narrative via phonograph, the attempt to artificially preserve a wilting oral culture that was being sucked dry by a written culture, was essentially self-defeating: an effort to preserve a living culture through a vampiric device.

Stoker's working title for *Dracula*—"The Un-Dead"—signals the author's concern for persons or things that have been supernaturally or (in the case of the phonograph) scientifically preserved. What initially seems novel, fascinating, and exactly calculated to fit into Stoker's modern setting ultimately takes a sinister turn. The novel's antagonist, under the working title, can be interpreted as either the vampire Dracula or the vampiric phonograph and its replications of trauma and iterations of undead orality.

Conclusion

The narrative of *Dracula* crawls to a finish without an oral apparatus, and the manuscripts are all unoriginal and problematic duplicates. The final version of the story, compiled and described as "exactly contemporary," is an amalgam of different narratives that are out of sync, gaping with problematic holes and traumatic oversights, and (in Seward's case) a flattened and undead transcription of orality.[99] There are virtually no "authentic documents" left to this narrative.[100] Though we have a compilation of these miscellaneous accounts, it is still deeply flawed. The traumas endured by its authors, replicated in the phonograph's ability to preserve accounts outside of traditional timelines, contribute to the shattered narrative perspectives and undead oralities that haunt Seward's vampiric phonograph. Stoker's novel prefigures the phonograph's potential for collecting Irish oral histories, but it also problematizes the technology and points to its potential failings, especially if the original record does not survive. In *Dracula*, the loss of the records is tempered by the survival of the typed pages, but the novel ends on a note of heavy concern about the authenticity and accuracy of its account.

When Stoker put the phonograph into the novel as the particular apparatus of a doctor of psychology, he created a connection between the emerging science and the machine. The phonograph then becomes an incredibly powerful tool for unlocking our understanding of trauma narratives within the work and beyond. Contextualizing Stoker's work as a product of an Irish author transforms the oral component of the novel into a revealing exploration of Irish folklore and the emerging national(ist) narrative of a traumatized colonial culture in the wake of the Famine. The phonograph becomes the symbolic and literal apparatus capable of articulating that national and communal trauma. And while gramophonic technology continued to evolve in the twentieth century, so did Irish narratives of trauma.

CHAPTER TWO

Gramophonic Gendering

Women, Phonographysteria,
and the Political Machine

In the April 15, 1899 edition of the *Weekly Irish Times*, one article drew attention to a growing ailment that was plaguing women stenographers. The condition, the article informs us, is "phonographysteria," and sadly, "so far no cure has been discovered."[1] The condition stems from the "numerous business houses [that] have availed themselves of the phonograph for correspondence purposes, dictating letters to this familiar spirit, and then handing it over to a typewriter."[2] The typewriter, or female secretary (notice the problematic ambiguity between object and woman in the article's use of the term), then transcribes the correspondence by listening intently to the phonograph messages (see Figure 2.1). The *Weekly Irish Times* article continues:

> [U]p to the present this sort of typewriting work has been found so trying to the nerves that many girls have resigned their situations, driven away by the "uncanniness" of the mysterious voice. At first they find it rather amusing, then it becomes irritating, and invites summary destruction with the fire-irons. Finally it is positively maddening and worries the typist so much that her health suffers.[3]

While there may be a certain element of tongue-in-cheek to such an article—we shouldn't overlook the sidelong reference to the machine

Figure 2.1. A young woman transcribing from a phonograph,
from Clarence Charles Smith, *The Expert Typist*
(New York: Macmillan, 1922), 127, fig. 42.

as a "familiar spirit," an aid to those dealing in magic and witchcraft—
there are documented cases of stenographers being genuinely overcome
by the "uncanniness" of the recordings. There are numerous accounts
of "hysterics" among women who worked as switchboard operators,

for instance, suggesting that the "mysterious" and "uncanny" nature of the disembodied voice was unsettling to women primarily. It became protocol, for a time, to have additional women on call waiting to step in and take over when a hysterical fit would come over the working switchboard operators. It was an expected aspect of the job. Barbara Engh's work on this topic documents at least one instance of male hysterics in the early days of the disembodied voice, suggesting that the phenomenon was not exclusive to women.[4] Nevertheless, the nature of the fits and the more predominantly documented (and anticipated) instances of female hysterics over the disembodied voice implied that "phonographysteria" was primarily a female ailment. What's more, the *name* of the diagnosis is not one that I have been able to find anywhere but in this Irish newspaper. It would seem that phonographysteria is diagnostically isolated not only to women, but at least to some extent to women in Ireland.

By conflating the phonograph and hysteria into a single, pseudo-scientific diagnosis affecting women, the *Weekly Irish Times* article identified themes of Irish gendering and trauma that haunt the machine throughout much of the early twentieth century. Almost from its inception, the phonograph was embedded with gendered implications. A man's voice was the first to be recorded on Thomas Edison's machine, and from that moment women were primarily relegated to the role of listeners, as indicated by the cultural phenomenon of the female secretary or "typewriter," with her ear to the machine and writing out male dictation. The phonograph's early function as a part of professional and public life meant that women's use of the machine was often conducted under male supervision. And yet its physical appearance was almost overtly feminine: the horn, one of its most distinctive visual features, seems an almost embarrassingly obvious vaginal reference that grew more ornate and aestheticized in the early decades of the machine's production. In later years, when the gramophone became a more privatized and domestic machine, the horn became something of a discomfort to many female consumers, who were anxious to conceal it, even at the expense of sound quality. Kyle Barnett points out that as the machine's technology progressed, "the male of the home might accept an internal horn phonograph" (which was considered technologically inferior to the larger exterior horn), because the exposed horn "risked offending 'polite society' (undoubtedly the province of women)."[5] In this context, the male-dominant supervision of an arguably feminine and sexualized physical object/body in relation to the phonograph-turned-gramophone seems self-evident.

The *fin de siècle* also saw the rise of the New Woman and later the suffragette: women who were determined to gain autonomy from male supervision. In Ireland, this pursuit of gender equality occurred in tandem with the wider push for national autonomy in the form of Home Rule. And because Home Rule was the primary and seemingly all-consuming agenda in Irish politics for decades, women's voices were considered a shrill and "hysterical" annoyance and distraction from the "real" issue of the day. But, in an ironic twist, the Home Rule argument, stretching from the 1870s to the end of World War I, was often characterized as a gendered debate.[6] Ireland was persistently gendered as a subordinate female in the figures of Erin or Hibernia, while England was gendered as a conquering male via the figure of John Bull.[7] This gendering became highly visible during the Home Rule debates. For instance, during a 1911 debate, Austen Chamberlain of the Liberal Unionist party pointedly characterized the union between England and Ireland as a heteronormative marriage when he argued that "I see no reason for a divorce in this ancient household," adding that if Ireland chose a separation, "then at least we should not pay the separation allowance."[8] Home Rule, then, was allegorized as a debate about women's rights and autonomy under any marriage contract or dissolution of the same. Though there were dissenting views in Ireland about the Home Rule bills (Unionists, particularly in Northern Ireland, intensely resisted the dissolution of the Act of Union), the defeats in 1886 and 1893 seemed to the bills' supporters to stifle Ireland's political voice in the British government and to imply an analogous gendered hierarchy of rights.

In the following decades (1890s through 1910s), the phonograph and then the gramophone became more commercially successful, and the technology continued to be conflated with gendered stereotypes and incorporated into political references. The valences became common enough that parallels between the female body and the gendered machine were used in political debates specifically about Home Rule and the "Irish Question" after the failed Second Home Rule Bill. And while George Moore, in his 1893 work *Modern Painting*, explicitly tried to remove the phonograph from Irish political contexts, arguing that "science is not national" and that a phonograph has no identifiable country but is rather a machine of science,[9] I would suggest that the roiling undercurrent to this gendered object and Home Rule's specific political tensions subliminally captured the Irish literary imagination—perhaps even more specifically, the Irish male imagination.

Very few women writers during this era engaged with the gramophone in hyper-gendered terms. And this makes sense. The Irish New Woman authors, for instance, were less concerned with symbols, and especially not those that seemed to objectify or sexualize women, and were more interested in addressing women's issues head on. Writers like Bram Stoker and George Bernard Shaw, however, often had complicated views of and relationships with women, though both ultimately fell on the side of progressive women's rights. They both also ultimately fell on the side of Irish Home Rule despite living in England and writing largely England-based narratives. As a result, the gendered machines in their works create a complex network of metaphorized national politics and individualized women's rights.

This chapter charts the gramophone's sexual and political overtones in Ireland during the Home Rule period. More particularly, it charts the progression of the sexualized machine and its implications in relation to the rising voices seeking female empowerment. In Stoker's *Dracula*, for instance, Lucy Westenra and Mina Murray-Harker are both sexualized in their relationships with the phonograph in ways that parallel Stoker's views of Ireland's Home Rule politics. In George Bernard Shaw's *Pygmalion* (1912), Eliza Doolittle is similarly sexualized, and her identity conflated with the gramophones in Henry Higgins's study during the prolonged debates regarding the Third Home Rule Bill, which was called by some the "gramophone campaign." Eliza's declaration of independence from Higgins and his machines indicates a belief in Home Rule's success in Ireland. And yet the afterlives of Shaw's play—particularly the added scenes that show Eliza back in Higgins's study and reciting words from the gramophone—illustrate the potential for violence if the political gendering of a movement is taken too far. And while these texts function on a level of symbolic political gendering, there are roiling undercurrents of very real gender politics that demand genuine autonomy from male-driven objectifying and sexualizing of the female body via the gramophone.

The Gramophone as a Sexualized Political Body

The phonograph, and later the gramophone, seemed "charged with sexualized femininity," nearly as soon as its invention, John Picker writes,[10]
pointing out that as early as 1878 (only one year after Edison invented
the machine), George Du Maurier published an illustration in *Punch* of a
"fair female phonographer" playing poetry "in [the authors'] own original
voices" on the machine as a substitute for organ grinders in the streets.[11]
The illustration depicts a woman holding a phonograph slung across her
body, the horn of which is larger than her entire upper body and the base
of which rests on her lower abdomen. Picker points out that the "massive
machine at once presents a (male) poet's vocal organs as well as represents
the (female) phonographer's sex organs, both of which are to be 'played'
by her on the streets."[12] The fact that Du Maurier's illustration is titled
"Suggestion" only adds to the subtlety of the titillating visual. The kind
of public performance highlighted in this image demonstrates the sexually charged gender implications of the phonograph. It implies that female
interaction with the machine carries undercurrents of sexuality and, in a
Victorian context, is suggestive of loose female morals unless that interaction is carefully supervised by a male figure. And if a woman were to
record her voice, the sound reproduction (again, the vocabulary is loaded
with gendered implications) often took on more overtly sexual overtones
bordering on public performance.[13] As a result, the recorded female voice
might become a commodity or object that men could keep for their own
use and pleasure, possibly to the detriment of a woman's character. The
phonograph, then, becomes something of a threat to women if not "properly supervised."

The women in *Dracula* have just these sorts of intricate connections
to the phonograph and its gender implications. Neither woman actually
records her voice on the machine, but both are sexualized by their interactions with it. Lucy is often characterized by her sexual desirability but
is predominantly voiceless and essentially victimized through the phonograph. Mina is an intelligent New Woman whose interactions with the
machine primarily involve transcribing male dictation, its traditionally
acceptable use. Her interactions, however, have subversive underlying
sexual implications. And it is primarily through her transcriptions that

readers receive the novel's narrative, which provides her with a significant amount of power (particularly compared to Lucy). However, while Mina's interactions with the phonograph are more explicitly documented in the novel, Lucy's less overt and yet revealing connections with the machine serve as an effective starting point for examining the gendered and sexual connotations of the phonograph in *Dracula*.

The majority of Lucy's story is documented through Seward's phonograph diary. He recounts her rejection of his marriage proposal as well as her illness and eventual death. Her own diary entries are nearly swallowed up in the sheer volume of his phonographic records. And the first recording enters the semi-epistolary novel with the good doctor struggling to come to grips with the "rebuff of yesterday."[14] By turning to the phonograph post-rejection, Seward echoes an 1888 illustration that appeared in the *Pall Mall Budget* that overtly links female rejection with the phonograph.[15] Among this illustration's amusing speculations about the possible future functions of the phonograph, the top right section depicts a young woman handing a wrapped parcel to a young man, saying, "I cannot be your wife, Mr. Jones. But I have given my answer in detail to the phonograph. Set it going in say a months [*sic*] time when I am far away."[16] While the Victorian idea of breakup-by-phonograph certainly has comic payoff (and parallels to the modern breakup-by-voice message), the illustration depicts an inversion of the scene in *Dracula* when Seward licks his wounds by talking to the feminized object in his own office after Lucy has rejected his proposal. He cannot marry her, so he turns to a sexually charged, feminized object for solace instead.

This phonographic stand-in takes on more overt sexual overtones after Lucy falls ill. When Seward forges a connection between Lucy and the phonograph in his inaugural account, it signals the gendering implication of the machine, and sets up a reading of Lucy's interactions with the phonograph that deserves further explication. Lucy, we learn, has her own phonograph. And yet there is no account of her ever using it. But Seward does; in his September 18 diary entry he states "I can complete my entry on Lucy's phonograph" and then proceeds to do so: "I am entering this on Lucy's phonograph."[17] From these exchanges we get three simple facts that represent, almost entirely, Lucy's story as depicted in the pages of *Dracula*. 1) She owns a phonograph, a gendered machine traditionally used by men. Lucy could be considered sexually transgressive through her ownership of the object. 2) A man uses her machine. The needle and wax of the machine substitute for fang/transfusion needle/stake and flesh, meaning that the male use of the machine replicates Dracula's vampiric penetration of Lucy, the several blood transfusions she receives from the men around her, and ultimately the staking of her body by the male vampire hunters.[18] As a result, Lucy is perceived as even more overtly sexually transgressive and/or promiscuous since, in the case of the phonograph, it is not her fiancé but the doctor who uses her machine. 3) Lucy never uses her phonograph. Her personal narrative is largely overwhelmed by the male voices in *Dracula* and rendered almost forgettable after the first half of the novel.[19] Essentially, Lucy's phonograph metonymically embodies her story: a silent testimony to the gendered implications of the text. Lucy's overwhelmed voice and (dis)use of the phonograph suggests that her transgressive behaviors are a threat to the Victorian perception of a woman's role in marriage. As a result, she becomes a locus for gendered/sexualized anxieties in the novel. These anxieties are mirrored in the gendered political debates around Home Rule.

In *Dracula*, both Lucy and Mina have connections to Ireland: Lucy's surname Westenra ties her to the Westenra family of County Monaghan who were Barons of Rossmore,[20] and Mina's surname Murray is even more overtly Irish (etymologically derived from the Irish name Ó Muireadhaigh). While Lucy and Mina are never explicitly characterized as Irish, they may well be Anglo-Irish citizens living in England, much like Stoker himself. It is too much to assume that the Irish-born author would carelessly select names with such national implications, given his own mother's surname's roots in the Irish name Ó Blathnhaic. Furthermore, both women become betrothed to English men, modeling two different potential embodiments of Home Rule as a metropolitan marriage.

The phonograph in Lucy's possession shows a transgression of the gendered standards for the machine's use at this period. It transforms her from a tractable female to a woman whose sexuality is a threat to the marriage state. The Home Rule debates in the early 1890s witnessed a violent split in the movement between Charles Stewart Parnell and William Ewart Gladstone, largely due to a sexualized and gendered transgression.

When the House of Lords defeated the second bill for Home Rule in 1893, denying Ireland its own parliament, many viewed the bill's failure as a consequence of the very public scandal attached to Parnell; he was named as a co-respondent in a divorce case because of his relationship with the married Katharine O'Shea. The trajectory of Lucy's gendered use of the phonograph mirrors the trajectory of the gendered/sexualized implications of the failed Second Home Rule Bill.

Anxiety about gendered roles and nationality are highly visible throughout *Dracula*. The men in the work constantly discuss what is manly (iterations of "man," "gentleman," and "manly" occur over 150 times in the novel). Much of that discussion is carried on in terms of English nationality. (It is worth noting that Quincey Morris and Van Helsing are often described as displaying attributes of manliness that the English characters can appreciate, *despite* their perceived disadvantages in coming from America and the Netherlands.) This gendered perspective of nationality in the novel is no coincidence, since Stoker grew up in a household that seemed to embody the English and Irish national gendering motifs and Anglo-Irish marriage. Joseph Valente points out that Stoker's father, a civil servant at Dublin Castle, had a "strictly Anglo-Saxon" heritage, whereas his mother grew up in the west of Ireland and was a descendant of the Ó Blathnhaic Galway family.[21] Stoker grew up hearing his father's stories of the "martial valor of [his] English forebears, their enactment of an aggressive, disciplined, and dominating ideal of masculinity" as well as his mother's stories of "domestic suffering and passive endurance of her Irish peasant compeers, their conformity with a patient and subservient ideal associated with femininity."[22] Perhaps as a result of his gendered national perspective represented in his parents' marriage, Stoker viewed Irish politics from a similarly gendered stance.

Some critics have pointed to Stoker's life in England as an indication of a lack of interest in Irish politics on the author's part; others point to an anecdote from Stoker's *Personal Reminiscences of Henry Irving*, in which he self-identifies as a "Philosophical Home Ruler," as an indication of an ambivalent engagement with the Irish debate.[23] However, Stoker seemed to engage with the Irish question on a regular basis throughout his career, developing his own sense of Ireland's role within the British Empire and how Home Rule would benefit his country.[24] Valente points out that Stoker

was in favor of British imperialism *and* Home Rule. Perhaps his divided
allegiances to his parental heritage contributed to this complex stance,
and yet it was not an *uncommon* stance in Ireland at the time. Stoker saw
the need for an autonomous Irish parliament, which Home Rule would
offer, while he also saw that autonomy as making Ireland an equal partner
in the United Kingdom's imperialism: a "metrocolonial exceptionalism,
involving a liberated Ireland in the administration and the rewards of Britain's global conquests."[25] Stoker's position on Home Rule was largely based
in his desire for Ireland to maintain the metropolitan marriage contract
with England, but with greater autonomy and voice available to Ireland as
the female counterpart, and equal rights to the benefits of that contract.
This stance was definitely progressive in terms of gender equality, but not,
perhaps, as progressive in terms of the "Irish Question." Regardless, Stoker
did seem to support Home Rule in principle.

Parnell, as the leading voice of the Irish Parliamentary Party, seemed
to offer the best hope for Home Rule in terms of an altered gendering
of the Union contract altogether, essentially making it a male–male
or "real" contract.[26] In *The Myth of Manliness in Irish National Culture*,
Valente argues that Parnell—in both his "personal style of address" and
his "political agenda"—projected "an air of manliness that had a special
currency under the regime of domestic colonialism."[27] So much so that his
"air of manliness became the locus of collective transference and identification, allowing Parnell to defy colonial emasculation in the name of the
Irish people."[28] And yet, just when Parnell seemed most likely to carry the
bill through (achieving a male–male political contract), a sexual scandal
attached to his public image and led to his political fall.

In 1889 it became public knowledge that Parnell was having an affair
with Katharine O'Shea when her husband sued for divorce, naming Parnell
as co-respondent; the scandal turned Parnell's public rapidly and viciously
against him. In 1890 Gladstone threatened to withdraw his support for the
Second Home Rule Bill if Parnell did not resign. Tim Healy, the man who
once described Parnell as the "uncrowned king of Ireland," called for his
resignation.[29] His masculine public profile was now "roundly feminized
by the O'Shea divorce case" and was seen to "have permitted unrestrained
amorous sentiment to lead him into the 'feminine' realm of personal
intrigue that had long been viewed as an insidious threat to the masculine

political order."[30] Parnell resigned and died only one year later. In 1893 the bill he had championed failed to pass the House of Lords.

Stoker was clearly familiar with the Parnell–O'Shea scandal, as is evident from his recorded interactions with the Prime Minister in the weeks after the news broke. Stoker describes a conversation with Gladstone on December 2, 1890, only three weeks after the Parnell scandal broke publicly. In retrospect, Stoker considered that this conversation between himself and Gladstone took place during

> one of the greatest troubles and trials of his whole political life. The hopes which he had built through the slow progress of years for the happy settlement of centuries-old Irish troubles had been suddenly almost shattered by a bolt from the blue, and his great intellect and enormous powers of work and concentration had been for many days strained to the utmost to keep the road of the future clear from the possibility of permanent destruction following on temporary embarrassment.[31]

Stoker's allusion to a "temporary embarrassment" is definitely a reference to Parnell, whether to the marriage scandal or to Parnell's impassioned and divisive manifesto "To the People of Ireland," which served as the straw that broke the movement's back, creating the Parnellite and Gladstonian Home Rule schism.[32] Gladstone believed the bill could push beyond the scandal by creating distance from Parnell, and yet the second bill still failed to pass.

Irish nationalists, hurt and seething with anger, turned the finger of blame for these events particularly on O'Shea as a scandalously sexual woman. And perhaps Lucy's fate in *Dracula* as the sexual scapegoat in part echoes a national frustration at the bill's failure in the wake of the scandal. Lucy's sexual appetites belie her docility and conformity to Victorian ideals of femininity, and lead the men of the novel to condemn her undead body as a focal point for sexual liberation that they cannot allow. Lucy's progressively transgressive sexuality is violently treated by the men, culminating in her second, vampiric death in which she is penetrated by a wooden stake in a ritual tantamount to rape by the English lord who asserts his masculine authority over her body.

Male penetration of Lucy's body is a theme throughout the first half of the novel. Dracula has vampirically penetrated Lucy with his fangs; Van Helsing points out that all of the men trying to save her have shared blood with Lucy via transfusions performed via needle penetration; finally, Lord Godalming penetrates Lucy's body with a stake. Each of these scenes has been meticulously explicated by other critics to expose the bristling sexual implications that lie barely below the surface of Stoker's text.[33] There is, however, an additional and largely unexplored instance of penetration to be explicated in Seward's use of Lucy's phonograph.

It is during Lucy's illness that we learn about her phonograph. Seward has already taken pains, in his first phonographic account, to explain *his* reasons for owning such a machine—it is a part of his profession—but we never learn why Lucy has one. It seems, then, that Lucy's possession of a phonograph is suggestive of a certain transgression of gendered expectations. Jennifer Forrest points out that the concept of the disembodied female voice "tested the boundaries of the male listener's comfort zone, challenging the social consensus regarding gender and voice when women were connected to communication technologies; [...] women facilitated the exchange of information, but were themselves considered unfit as emitters."[34] If Lucy owned a machine, she could potentially make recordings of her voice. For all we know, she may have. ("The Suppressed Phonographic Recordings of Lucy Westenra": a fanfiction opportunity delivered on a platter.) And Lucy's phonograph and her theoretical phonographic recordings simultaneously test male listeners' comfort zones and carry implicit connections to transgressive sexuality. If her voice is recorded and played back by male auditors, it becomes something of a public performance. Female public performance during this period was generally considered a demonstration of sexuality, and in theatre, at least, there was an "implicit link between the female performer and the prostitute."[35] And this is not just a hypothetical reading of Lucy's sexuality, since she becomes progressively more public in her performances of sexuality as her story develops: she confesses to Mina that she wishes a girl could "marry three men, or as many as want her,"[36] she leaves the house in a nightgown at night, and her most overtly public performance is her undead appearance as the "Bloofer Lady" in the newspaper.[37]

Lucy's progressive public sexuality finds parallels in the media coverage of Katharine O'Shea, depicted as an English paramour. O'Shea became one of the most vilified women in Irish history, it would seem. Lambasted in Irish newspaper coverage of the scandal, she became known as "Kitty" O'Shea, a name she never personally used, which not only functions as an informal abbreviation of Katharine (and is therefore presumptuous of false intimacy), but also had connotations as a sobriquet for a woman with loose (Lucy?) morals.[38] Another parallel between Lucy and O'Shea is Lucy's seeming infidelity to her affianced husband. Even though Lucy is engaged to Lord Godalming, she continues her acquaintance with her other suitors, and it is Seward, *not* Godalming, who makes use of her phonograph, suggesting that the marriage contract between Lucy and her English lord might not guarantee her constancy and submissive obedience.

While trying to diagnose Lucy's ailment, Seward is called upon to keep watch over her during the evening, and determines to use her phonograph to maintain his diary. The language used to describe his decision, as pointed out by Picker, also carries potential sexual implications:[39] Seward "take[s his] cylinder with [him]" so that he may "complete [his] entry on Lucy's phonograph."[40] His use of Lucy's phonograph seems to support the common reading of Lucy as a focus for feminine sexuality in the novel, and suggests that Seward may view the use of Lucy's phonograph as an analogous form of sexual gratification with the woman he cannot marry. Seward also specifically identifies which of the phonograph records was created on Lucy's machine (a rare moment of filing logic on his part), meaning that the cylinder is uniquely significant and can be kept as a symbol and object of his sexual desires (almost a masturbatory prosthetic). Lucy can continue to be a fetishized object in his narrative.

Since the phonograph cylinder is an object of recorded sound, and yet Lucy's voice is (as far as we know) never recorded on her own machine, it seems that Seward's use of her machine also has connotations for the larger narrative. As mentioned earlier, Seward's phonographic account quantitively overpowers Lucy's own contributions to the vampire narrative. This discrepancy in quantity might suggest that Seward has exerted his own control over Lucy's narrative. She is literally a silent patient, denied a voice on her own machine.

Lucy's second death is also graphic and prolonged in description, in contrast with that of Dracula's (which critics generally agree is anticlimactic in comparison). Lucy seems to fall victim to Stoker's ideas about an ideal Irish Home Rule. While he desired an Irish parliamentary voice, he had hoped for a more equal (masculine) contract that Parnell's policy might have initially offered. After the Irish Parliamentary Party's split due to an embarrassing sexual scandal, Ireland seems to be again depicted as the feminine disenfranchised partner in the metropolitan marriage. And yet Stoker still desires an Irish parliamentary voice (gendered again as the feminized phonograph), and so he cannot approve of an entire break from the marriage contract motif. Lucy's sexuality suggests that a marriage is no longer a truly viable option: all the men have become her husbands through her transfusions, and Seward's phonograph use has created a new layer of sexual promiscuity between herself and a man to whom she is not betrothed. That same sexuality becomes her downfall and her punishment. Because Lucy's sexuality becomes something of a public conversation (like O'Shea's) and because of her intractability in defying the traditional gender roles in marriage, she is viewed as a threat to the period's restrictive gender norms, and the men of the novel impose silence on her through her second death.

Whereas Lucy's ownership of a phonograph suggests an overt defiance of gendered expectations of the machine's use and function, Mina's interactions with the machine are, on the surface, much less threatening. Mina enters the narrative of *Dracula* as an independent woman, working for her own support as an assistant schoolmistress and in possession of a keen mind for detail and observation. She has memorized the train listings, learned how to write shorthand, and keeps a journal with the intention of doing "what I see lady journalists do: interviewing and writing descriptions and trying to remember conversations."[41] She has invested in the current technologies of the day like the typewriter and constantly reads the newspapers. And despite her potentially ambiguous comments about the New Woman, her reference to the phenomenon shows her to be a well-informed woman engaging with current debates surrounding "New Woman authors" and the question of women's rights.[42] Mina is also engaged to Harker and intends to be an ideal helpmeet and wife to him, aiding his work through her acquired knowledge, suggesting that she is also an idealized (and therefore non-sexualized) Victorian woman; Harker, for instance, sees her as categorically different from the three overtly sexual vampire women he encounters in Transylvania.[43] However, Mina's interactions with the phonograph suggest a more subversive character than initially meets the eye.

Mina spends less than half of the novel as Mina Murray—she becomes Mrs. Mina Harker by the beginning of the ninth chapter—but, as mentioned before, her given surname Murray serves as a hint to an Irish national heritage. And it is perhaps no surprise that Stoker then creates a marriage between her and an Englishman. The political metropolitan marriage is embodied in this union in *Dracula*. She becomes Mina Murray Harker. "Harker" is a decidedly English name, with Yorkshire roots and derived from the Early Middle English *herkien*, meaning to harken or listen. And that is Mina's principal role in relation to the phonograph: to harken.

Mina is primarily associated with the machine as a stenographer. She, like Lucy, is not allowed a voice. Unlike her friend, however, Mina conforms to an accepted and gendered interaction with the machine. When Mina listens to Seward's phonographic account of Lucy's illness, her first reaction is to transcribe the oral account on her typewriter. Picker points out that Mina's role in the novel is a tangle of sexual identity,[44] since she is a bold New Woman, but also has (as Van Helsing puts it) a "man's brain."[45] And yet, in the historical context of the novel, Mina's role as scribe for the male vampire hunters is entirely period-appropriate for her gender. During the decade of 1891–1901 (the same decade in which *Dracula* was written and published), there was a 151.6 percent increase in female clerical participation in Great Britain.[46] A large number of these clerks were typists who took down from recorded dictation.[47] This brings us back to the problematic "phonographhysteria" diagnosis for those women who found recorded voices uncanny and upsetting.

When Mina first encounters the phonograph, her reaction is one of wonder and excitement. She then listens to a portion of Seward's recordings and momentarily seems likely to suffer from "phonographhysteria" when she hears his account of Lucy's death. Directly after listening to the phonograph, Mina "lay back powerless" and in a near swoon— "Fortunately I am not of a fainting disposition"—and explains:

My brain was all in a whirl [...]. It is all so wild, and *mysterious*, and strange that if I had not known Jonathan's experience in Transylvania I could not have believed. As it was, I didn't know what to believe, and so got out of my difficulty by attending to something else. I took the cover off my typewriter, and said to Dr. Seward: —

"Let me write this all out now."[48]

Both the *Weekly Irish Times* article and Mina's account of listening to the phonograph emphasize that it is the "mysterious" nature of the encounter with the machine that nearly brings on hysterics. However, in the *Irish Times* account, the phonograph drives women to abandon their typewriters, while Seward's phonograph compels Mina to "[take] the cover off [her] typewriter" in order to write down the account as a way of controlling those feelings (implying that writing serves as a form of therapy for or preventative of phonographysteria).[49] Rather than succumb to hysterics when she encounters the phonograph, Mina maintains her level-headedness and sees the potential ramifications of the recording where other characters cannot. She then asserts her authority over the situation and the machine. (The men of *Dracula*, however, remain wary of Mina's potential for hysteria, which partially accounts for their ill-informed and nearly fatal sequestration of her for fear of her inability to handle the strain of the events surrounding the vampire.) Her adept administration over the phonograph mirrors Stoker's faith in Ireland's level-headedness in its approach to Gladstonian Home Rule, its capacity for self-government and restraint, and its hope to contribute to the Empire's success, playing off the common motif of characterizing Ireland and its personification Erin/Hibernia as hysterical whenever there were violent reactions against British rule.[50] In the eyes of the British government, a country incapable of managing cultural hysteria clearly could not be left to manage itself.

In *Dracula*, however, the tenuous link between hysteria, phonograph, and female is cut even further, since five of the eight specific references to hysteria in the novel are directly attributed to men rather than women. First, a catalogue of female-related hysteria: one of the Transylvanian women is hysterical while talking to Harker; then Lucy's housemaids "cried and sobbed in a hysterical manner"; and finally, Mina supposes "I was hysterical" when she asks Van Helsing to help her husband.[51] Now a catalogue of male-related hysteria: first, Van Helsing "[gives] way to a regular fit of hysterics" and then promptly denies being hysterical; next, Renfield's hysterical antics are mentioned twice; finally, Van Helsing is again in danger of "break[ing] down and hav[ing] hysterics."[52] And while hysterics are never *directly* ascribed to Harker, his frequent breakdowns tend toward all the symptoms of such "fits." The fit of hysterics most notably missing from the novel is a demonstration of "phonographysteria" from Mina as she engages with the machine.

Mina's interactions with the phonograph also have a sexual undertone, allowing for a different reading of her seemingly conventional Victorian female sexuality. While Mina always maintains her status as an ideal of womanhood, femininity, and even (by the novel's end) maternity, she gains a level of sexual self-rule through her interactions with Seward's phonograph. And though she remains voiceless in terms of recorded audio, she uses the machine to claim her own distinct voice, essentially providing us the majority of the text through her transcriptions. Mina— invested in the marriage state, but with her own form of resistance to complete submission and exclusive male ownership within that state, as indicated in her interactions with the phonograph—serves as an analogue for Stoker's views on Irish Home Rule.

As mentioned in the previous section, Stoker's interest in Home Rule did not wane when he moved to England. Even once he left Ireland to work as Henry Irving's theatrical manager, he maintained his support for Home Rule, which sometimes exasperated his employer. Stoker writes of an instance when Irving suggested that rural England could supply the "true inwardness of British opinion" on the Irish debates.[53] To prove his point Irving suggested that a nearby police officer would supply the "Voice of England" on the matter; he asked the man "[W]hat is your opinion as to this trouble in Ireland?":

> The answer came at once, stern and full of pent-up feeling, and in an accent there was no possibility of mistaking: 'Ah, begob, it's all the fault iv the dirty Gover'mint!' His brogue might have been cut with a hatchet. [...] I came to the conclusion that Home Rule was of little moment to that guardian of the law: he was an out

and out Fenian. For many a day afterwards I managed to bring
in the 'Voice of England' whenever Irving began to chaff about
Home Rule.[54]

Stoker's delight at the "Voice of England" episode suggests a certain
approval of the subversive Irish presence and resistance to English rule.
Valente observes that the scene reveals two major facets of Stoker's
perception of Home Rule. First, "it stands as an exemplum of the mutual
ethnic incorporation that Stoker increasingly took as the bedrock reality
of the United Kingdom," meaning that the English state absorbed the
Irish officer not only as a citizen, but as an agent of its law; vice versa,
the English law becomes saturated with Irish intonations, idiom, and
attitudes.[55] Secondly, lawless violence is a logical byproduct of refusing
to acknowledge this symbiosis: the Irish constable embodies an urge to
violently react against the British aggressor that he represents.[56] I would
add to Valente's observations that Stoker depicts in this episode an Irish
voice (or political presence), not just an Irish dialect within the British
state. This voice has perhaps been underestimated, but the "Voice of
England" is a subversive representation of how the Irish voice can be
heard in unexpected ways and convey dissatisfaction within the accepted
parameters of the Union. The "Voice of England" anecdote essentially
embodies Stoker's views about Home Rule: Ireland should have a voice
and autonomy in the Union while still working within its parameters.
Mina's use of the phonograph is another example of the embodied and
ironic "Voice of England."

Mina uses the machine both to sexually rebel and, through her
transcriptions, ultimately to provide the unspoken voice for all of those
involved in the narrative of *Dracula*; after all, the novel is comprised almost
exclusively of a "mass of typewriting" of Mina's making.[57] To explicate the
sexual implications of Mina's use of the phonograph, we must return to
the scene of her first encounter with the machine. She overhears Seward
talking to the phonograph and assumes he must be talking to someone
else in the room. Upon entering the room and seeing the device, Mina
is immediately fascinated. Seward at first "replie[s] with alacrity" before
pausing and awkwardly confessing that there is a great deal of information
about Lucy in his account.[58]

Before Mina listens to Seward's accounts, the phonograph is physically moved into a feminine space—Dr. Seward "carried the phonograph himself into my sitting-room"—and Mina anticipates "something pleasant" from hearing Seward's account and getting to "know [him] better."[59] After hearing the first few cylinders, Mina returns to Dr. Seward's study, proclaiming, "It is a wonderful machine [...]. It told me, in its very tones, the anguish of your heart."[60] The phonograph has forged a new intimacy between Seward and Mina, and, according to Picker, "this new intimacy lends to their restrained professional interactions a sensual charge."[61] Picker goes on to read the subsequent passage as a scene potentially wrought with "autoerotic implications [for Mina] who satisfies standard Victorian masculine *and* feminine gender expectations":[62]

> After dinner I came with Dr. Seward to his study. He brought back the phonograph from my room, and I took my typewriter. He placed me in a comfortable chair, and arranged the phonograph so that I could touch it without getting up, and showed me how to stop it in case I should want to pause. Then he very thoughtfully took a chair, with his back to me, so that I might be as free as possible, and began to read. I put the forked metal to my ears and listened. When [...] done, I lay back in my chair powerless.[63]

Picker describes this scene as "autoerotic" and yet seems to dismiss Seward's presence throughout the scene. Moments such as when Mina puts the "forked metal" of the earphones of Seward's machine in her ears seem highly intimate in this context. Though Mina is a married woman, and therefore allowed a modicum of latitude when it comes to private interviews and social intimacy with other men, this entire evening isolates Mina and Seward in close quarters and heightens the possibility for sexual exchange.

Picker also overlooks the previous scene with the phonograph in Mina's personal sitting room (a feminine space), which is a more privatized and potentially sexualized encounter with the machine. Mina's *first* private use of the phonograph is autoerotic, and the *second* use in Seward's study is charged with a kind of sexual liberty with proximity to a man who is not her husband. In the second scene, the phonograph has been moved back to Seward's study (a masculine space), and he "placed" Mina in a comfortable chair where she could touch his phonograph "without getting up," and she is then rendered "powerless" after the encounter.

Mina's first use of the phonograph draws her closer to Seward not only through his voiced history, but also in the privatization of the experience which allows for a form of autoeroticism. After all, Mina listens to the cylinders onto which Seward has poured out his love for Lucy.[64] Her second use of the machine creates an intense intimacy between Mina and Seward in their isolated proximity to each other. Ultimately, the machine has "told me, in its very tones, the anguish of your heart. It was like a soul crying out to Almighty God. No one must hear them spoken ever again! [...] I have copied out the words on my typewriter, and none other need now hear your heartbeat, as I did."[65] The interaction between Mina, Seward, and the phonograph is described in terms of physical proximity ("hear your heart beat") and spiritual intimacy ("a soul crying out"); furthermore, Mina has isolated the intimacy of this experience between herself and Seward, since no one else ever listens to the recording.

Given the phonograph's role in facilitating a sexually charged exchange between Mina and Seward, it is perhaps less easy to identify Mina with the sexual "purity" of the idealized Victorian woman, and in fact the focus on the object allows for a certain expression of sexual liberty on Mina's part. Carol Senf argues that Lucy and Mina serve as the sexual and intellectual aspects of the 1890s woman respectively, suggesting that Mina is generally considered in intellectual, rather than sexual, terms throughout the novel.[66] The phonograph, however, reveals Mina to embody *both* aspects, drawing out a latent liberated sexuality in her character. And while Fleissner argues that the baby Mina dandles on her knee at the end of the novel replaces the erstwhile typewriter and indicates her conformation to societal expectations of maternal duties rather than intellectual pursuits, the phonograph indicates that Mina's sexual liberation makes the same baby, described as a "bundle of names [that] links all our little band of men together,"[67] a subversive locus for paternal uncertainty, undercutting the male-dominant society's feminine idealizations. And through it all, her role as a dutiful wife and mother is never questioned by the men of the novel. Her subversive sexuality via the phonograph, even with a man who is not her husband, does not seem to fully transgress the marriage contract she has entered into with her English husband. In fact, when she is victimized by Dracula and forced to drink his blood, the men do not blame her, but set out to slay the monster and defend her honor. It is in these moments that Mina's connections to Stoker's vision of Home Rule seem to emerge most clearly. In analogous ways, Mina enjoys the sexual autonomy that the phonograph offers (standing in for access to an individual political voice in an Irish parliament), but she also enjoys the protection and support of the men of the novel when she is victimized (the perks of Empire).

Mina embodies the British ideals of womanhood: she willingly commits to the marriage state, functions as a helpmeet to her English husband, adheres to gender expectations as a transcriptionist for the male voice, and ultimately resigns her work to become a mother. And yet her interactions with the phonograph belie that serene submissive surface. Mina is a sexually liberated, levelheaded intellectual. Though she is not allowed a performance of personal voice, she is the near-solitary voice of *Dracula*, since every word of the novel has been filtered through her. Her Irish heritage and English marriage, as well as her sexual autonomy within the bonds of marriage, suggest a potential reading of Stoker's vision of Home Rule.

While Stoker's vision of Home Rule was rather conservative, G. B. Shaw was more outspoken on the subject. In his 1904 play, *John Bull's Other Island*, Shaw directly addresses Home Rule and the British parliament's role in Ireland when the English character Broadbent insinuates his way into being elected the MP for the Irish community of Roscullen. Broadbent manages to win over an Irish constituency, engage himself to an Irish woman, and essentially purchase large parcels of land with the aim of developing them into a hotel and golf course. Doyle's ambiguous complicity in Broadbent's plans and his attitude toward Home Rule were particular points of concern with the producers at the Abbey Theatre, even though W. B. Yeats had commissioned the play. Shaw directly addressed this mild political controversy in his 1907 "Preface for Politicians":

> Mr. Yeats got rather more than he bargained for. The play was at that time beyond the resources of the New Abbey Theatre. [...]

There was another reason for changing the destination of *John Bull's Other Island*. It was uncongenial to the whole spirit of the neo-Gaelic movement, which is bent on creating a new Ireland after its own ideal, whereas my play is a very uncompromising presentment of the real old Ireland.[68]

As a result of these conflicting views of "a new Ireland," the play was first performed in 1904 in England rather than Ireland, and in fact was not produced in Ireland until 1907, and not at the Abbey until 1916. Though Shaw's views on Home Rule were viewed with a skeptical eye both by English and Irish audiences of *John Bull's Other Island*, in his 1912 play, *Pygmalion*, he found a way of addressing those same topics in a less overt manner, and with the phonograph (turned gramophone by play's end—more on that to come) serving as a lodestone for these debates.

The Gramophone Campaign

In 1912 a third Home Rule Bill was up for debate in parliament. When Prime Minister H. H. Asquith introduced the bill, he was presenting a measure for a devolved government that would allow greater political autonomy to Ireland within the United Kingdom. It would provide a bicameral parliament in Dublin to deal primarily with Irish national affairs; involve the abolition of the Dublin Castle administration, although retaining the Lord Lieutenant as the crown's representative in Ireland; and reduce the number of Irish MPs still sitting in the parliament of the United Kingdom. With the Third Home Rule Bill, the gendered implications of the Union, or Anglo-Irish political marriage, along with the accusations of repetitive "gramophonic" pleas for an Irish parliament, reached a crescendo.

The Irish nationalist party and supporters of the bill were frequently characterized as gramophonic in their voicing of the desire for autonomy during the debates. The *Irish Times* reported several of these instances. The Right Hon. J. H. Campbell concluded that Home Rule was a "political gramophone" which would repeat its position *ad nauseam*, and any candidate who took up the Home Rule cause had as much originality as the gramophone that played back the composition or recitation of another artist.[69] Ian Malcolm stated before the House of Commons that the representatives of the House were "reduced to a state of impotence—a sort of Parliamentary gramophone for recording the decrees of Ministers" because of "conflicting declarations of Your Majesty's Ministers on the subject of Home Rule."[70] In the same article where Austen Chamberlain evoked the aforementioned marriage motif between England and Ireland, he also characterized the bill as a "gramophone campaign," establishing a link between national and gramophonic gendering of Ireland and its political concerns.[71] And Colonel F. O'Callaghan-Westropp of County Clare described Home Rule as a "gramophone campaign" with commercial undercurrents, "not unconnected with the coin in the slot principle." He continued, "If the audience was an English one it was a 'benevolence, love, and toleration' record that was put on; if an Irish audience, it was 'Ireland, a nation': if it was an American audience then there was a strong suspicion of dynamite about the record."[72]

This latter "gramophone campaign" reference is particularly problematic in its use of the "pay-for-service" motif that not only genders Ireland as female, but as a woman who will prostitute herself to different audiences with what they want to hear in return for money. It recalls the Circe episode of *Ulysses* and the "Whorusalam" that blares from the gramophone in Nighttown while Bloom fantasizes about a Dublin reborn.[73] Joyce's work is set before the Third Home Rule Bill, in 1904, but since it was published in 1922, its backward perspective on Ireland's road to revolution makes the sexualized and prostituted gramophone reference fit squarely among the political debates of the era.

Edith Somerville and Martin Ross's novel *Mount Music* (1919) similarly takes a backward glance at Ireland's land wars, and Home Rule debates are central to questions of the eponymous Big House's survival. When one of the characters finally decides to throw himself into the political fray, engaging with Home Rule as he campaigns for office, he finds the debates exhausting. He revealingly internalizes the debates, observing "he had become a gramophone, and a tired gramophone, badly in want of winding up, at that."[74] The machines in *Ulysses* and *Mount Music* both reinforce the historical fact that Home Rule was characterized as, on the benign end of the spectrum, annoyingly repetitive like the tired gramophone in want of a wind up and, on the more virulent end of the spectrum, a form of gramophonic prostitution, playing rhetorical lip service to anyone who might listen to the constant demands for autonomy. Either way, the persistent characterization of Irish Home Rule and its proponents as mere gramophonic recordings demonstrates an inflammatory dismissal of Ireland's political voice.

So when Shaw, in *Pygmalion*, couples Eliza Doolittle with a phonograph almost immediately (and later a gramophone), it is a revealing pairing with contemporary political undercurrents. Shaw's retelling of the mythological story—in which the eponymous sculptor falls in love with his work, bringing Galatea to life—depicts a woman who struggles for sexual, intellectual, and financial freedom under the bemused tutelage of an unfeeling instructor. Eliza's story mirrors Ireland's during the Home Rule debates. Her fight for autonomy seems to begin and end with her entrance into Higgins's home, where she becomes equated with the phonograph in his study. The conflated identities are often casually sexualized by Higgins and others until Eliza liberates herself from the machine and her teaching master.

After we meet Eliza Doolittle and Professor Henry Higgins in the first act of *Pygmalion*, the second act opens in the professor's study, which includes a phonograph. It sits on a table in the corner, along with a spread of objects relevant to Higgins's profession: "In this corner stands a flat writing-table, on which are a phonograph, a laryngoscope, a row of tiny organ pipes with a bellows, [...] and a box containing a supply of wax cylinders for the phonograph."[75] As the description continues, other aspects of the room are described in relation to the phonograph's position. The stand for newspapers is between the fireplace and the phonograph; the seating arrangements in the room are sparse, except near the phonograph.[76] There is a clear and demonstrative emphasis on the phonograph's physicality. (In the 1938 film version the phonograph horn is taken to even greater extremes and is nearly inescapable as it physically looms over both Higgins and Eliza in their interactions.)

When Eliza comes to the phonetician for help with her speech in order to elevate herself from selling flowers on Tottenham Court Road to working in a flower shop, the transformation is initially centered on the idea that her speech must be modulated. One of the primary tools in phonetics at this time was the phonograph. By 1895 linguists and phoneticians had started to use the phonograph in correspondence courses. In an 1896 *Weekly Irish Times* article titled "Teaching by Phonograph," the author describes a process by which an instructor sends "twenty loaded cylinders and twenty blank ones" so that students can listen to the correct pronunciation of the language on the loaded cylinders, then recite the lesson onto the blank cylinders, sending them back to the instructor for feedback and correction.[77] In 1910 Shaw also wrote briefly about "correspondence classes with gramophone" as a method for educating young boys in *A Treatise on Parents and Young Children*.[78] And in *Pygmalion*, we learn about this educational process at closer proximity throughout Eliza's transformation.

When Eliza is announced by Mrs. Pearce to Higgins and Colonel Pickering as a woman with a "dreadful" accent, Higgins's first reaction is to consider the unknown woman in relation to the phonograph: "This is rather a bit of luck. I'll shew you how I make records. We'll set her talking; [...] then we'll get her on the phonograph so that you can turn her on as often as you like."[79] His language—"we'll set her talking"—makes it clear that he views the unknown woman as little more than an automaton. Furthermore, he makes no real distinction between the corporeal woman and her phonographic counterpart, since "we'll get her on the phonograph" implies that the woman and the machine are largely interchangeable. Higgins's phraseology further reflects the treatment of the phonograph as a gendered feminine object with the sexual connotations of the "kept woman"; the phrase "turn her on" not only connotes the operation of a mechanical object but also slang for sexual arousal.

Moments after Eliza has committed herself to Higgins and Pickering's agreement to transform her into a duchess, the sexual implications and undertones of the deal abound. Pickering asks Higgins, "Are you a man of good character where women are concerned?" (to which the professor replies, "What! That thing! Sacred, I assure you").[80] Though the "old bachelors" may have no designs on Eliza's sexuality, the underlying "kept woman" tension rears its head in nearly every act of the play and almost always in relation to "turning on" the machine.[81]

Only moments later, Eliza's father turns up (having heard of her presence at the house) and explains to Higgins, "She said she didn't want no clothes. What was I to think from that, Governor? I ask you as a parent what was I to think?" to which Higgins then asks, "So you came to rescue her from worse than death, eh?"[82] But Doolittle's interest is exclusively monetary under his paternal pretext, and the sexual implications are clear. After explaining his desire to capitalize on Eliza's new situation at Wimpole Street (with no real concern about her safety, sexual or otherwise), Doolittle candidly states, "Well, what's a five pound note to you? And what's Eliza to me?"[83] When Pickering objects, attempting to redeem this transaction from its human trafficking undertones by stating that Higgins's intentions are "entirely honorable," Doolittle calmly replies, "Course they are, Governor. If I thought they wasn't, I'd ask fifty."[84] Higgins eventually capitulates to the monetary request, saying, "There can be no question that as a matter of morals, it's a positive crime to give this chap a farthing. And yet I feel a sort of justice in his claim."[85] Higgins pays Doolittle five pounds (after offering ten) for Eliza.[86]

The prices these men toss about when speaking of Eliza are not coincidental. Doolittle's price range for his daughter—£5 to £50—exactly imitates the price range for a gramophone at the time Shaw finished writing the play in 1912,[87] turning the conversation into the buying and selling of essentially inanimate but sexualized goods. The exchange between Doolittle and Higgins solidifies the male perception of the female as object and the parallels between the sexualized phonograph and the female body. And what's more, in the post #MeToo era, these exchanges read less as laddish humor with a witty edge and more like the overt selling of a woman's sexuality that is actually occurring.[88] The phonographic objectification of Eliza draws specific attention to the menacing undercurrent of the exchange.

In fusing Eliza's identity with the phonograph as a sexualized object, Shaw was likely drawing upon literary and political influences that had been present from the time he had the first germ of the idea for *Pygmalion* in 1897, the year of *Dracula's* publication. Shaw wrote a letter to Ellen Terry on September 8 of that year in which he references a "rapscallionly flower girl."[89] It is possible that Stoker's gendered phonograph had some influence on Shaw's depiction. An even more likely influence was E. E. Kellett's 1901 short story "The Lady Automaton," as explained by Phillip Klass.[90] Kellett's work, published in *Pearson's Magazine*, tells the story of an inventor, Arthur Moore, who, after perfecting the phonograph, decides to make an "anti-phonograph," or a phonograph that can react and respond to conversation.[91] The "anti-phonograph" is created with a "sweet and beautifully modulated feminine voice" and later becomes a completed lady automaton.[92] Moore explains,

> I wanted her to be a lady that would deceive anyone. Not a thing that can only act when lifted into a chair or stuck upon a platform; but a creature that will guide herself, answer questions, talk and eat like a rational being—in fact, perform the part of a society lady as well as the best bred of them all.[93]

The automaton, Amelia, is a huge social success, particularly with men. She is capable of appropriately responding to any social stimulus, but lacks the ability to discern the problem with accepting the proposals of two young men. This recalls Lucy Westenra's desire to marry three men (and own a phonograph). Whereas Lucy knows that this is not socially allowed, the lady automaton continues with both her engagements, with the full knowledge of her creator, who bemusedly watches the social tangle play out. That is, until one of the suitors discovers her duplicity (not her status as an automaton), and stabs her at the altar during her wedding to another, resulting in a pile of spilled sawdust and broken machinery.

Kellett's "anti-phonograph" Amelia and Shaw's Eliza have much in common, though it is clear that Shaw remained skeptical of the idea that a phonograph could be perfected so easily, even in fiction. Shaw viewed recorded sound with suspicion, as is evident from his own gramophone recording, in which he warns listeners that "unless you know how to use your gramophone properly, what you are hearing may be something grotesquely unlike any sound that has ever come from my lips."[94] He cautions those who would listen to him that they cannot be sure that they are really hearing his voice unless the gramophone is playing at exactly the right speed, which is nearly impossible to discern. But he provides this tip:

> If what you hear is very disappointing and you feel instinctively, "That must be a horrid man," you may be quite sure the speed

is wrong. Slow [the gramophone] down until you feel you are
listening to an amiable gentleman of seventy-one with a rather
pleasant Irish voice. Then that is me. All the other people whom
you hear at the other speeds are imposters. Sham Shaws. Phan-
toms who never existed.[95]

His warning against the sham Shaws—embedded in his highly subjective method for finding the *real* Shaw—effectively demonstrates the
limitations of the machine, especially its replicating (or impersonating)
a human being. He also points out that while recording technology is
"steadily improving in its manner," its mechanical "wheezing and snarling
and braying" largely undercuts the verisimilitude of the recording.[96] To
create a Galatea from such raw mechanical material would be supernatural. And that is exactly how Kellett handles the transformation of the
lady automaton and her inventor.

Higgins is, by contrast, provided with an actual human. His problem
stems from his inability to acknowledge that humanity, trying largely
to reverse Moore's success, deconstructing Eliza into a pliant, perfected
phonograph. Moore succeeds in his venture, creating a woman who
completely fools society until she is publicly revealed to have committed
a social taboo. Similarly, when Higgins and Pickering bring Eliza to Mrs.
Higgins's home for a public tea, Eliza perfectly enunciates her words, but
shocks her audience with her conversational topics; she discusses "ladling
gin down [her aunt's] throat" as evidence that "them as pinched [her aunt's
hat] done her in."[97] Eliza's farewell—"Walk! Not bloody likely!"—creates a
sensation that Higgins and Pickering find amusing, but ultimately must
smooth over with the Eynsford-Hills.[98]

Though Higgins and Pickering are invested in making Eliza a social
success, they never really see her as a human being. When they consult
with Mrs. Higgins to gauge the success of their venture to date, she is
unimpressed, stating, "[O]f course she's not presentable. She's a triumph
of your art and her dressmaker's."[99] She is merely the phonographic object
that they have dressed up for the occasion. And even as Higgins and
Pickering protest against this characterization of Eliza's first outing, they
unwittingly emphasize their perception of Eliza as a living phonograph,

rather than an actual woman, when they describe their proceedings. They deliver the following speeches simultaneously:

HIGGINS. You know, she has the most extraordinary quickness of ear: just like a parrot. Ive [sic] tried her with every possible sort of sound that a human being can make—Continental dialects, African dialects, Hottentot clicks, things it took me years to get hold of; and she picks them up like a shot, right away, as if she had been at it all her life.

PICKERING. I assure you, my dear Mrs. Higgins, that girl is a genius. She can play the piano quite beautifully. We have taken her to classical concerts and to music halls; and it's all the same to her: she plays everything she hears right off when she comes home, whether it's Beethoven and Brahms or Lehar and Lionel Morickton; though six months ago, she'd never as much as touched a piano.[100]

Higgins emphasizes Eliza's uncanny ability with dialects while Pickering describes a musical virtuoso playing exclusively by ear. But rather than marvel at Eliza who, by these descriptions, is staggeringly brilliant, they leave Mrs. Higgins, dismissing her concerns about Eliza's future—"that poor woman"—while planning their next outing with their portable phonograph:

HIGGINS   [to Pickering as they go out together] Let's take her to the Shakespear [sic] exhibition at Earls Court.
PICKERING Yes: lets [sic]. Her remarks will be delicious.
HIGGINS   She'll mimic all the people for us when we get home.
PICKERING Ripping.[101]

Higgins and Pickering lose sight of Eliza the woman entirely. Instead, they brag about the "dozens of gramophone disks" they have amassed of her work and progress during the experiment, and simply equate her with the novelty of the machine and its capabilities:[102] let's have Eliza learn a new dialect, let's have Eliza play a new song, let's have Eliza mimic new people. Never mind the absolute genius they live with.

In Eliza's uncannily talented phonographic repetitions we again see shades of Stoker's *Dracula* where Mina also becomes a living phonograph. In one of her many flashes of brilliance, Mina realizes that she can be hypnotized and give an account of the vampire's surroundings. Van Helsing and the rest of the men then tend to treat her as an oral GPS report of the vampire's location. She becomes very repetitive, even mechanical in her "hypnotic reports," which continue *ad nauseam*, morning and evening for an entire month (from October 3 to November 4).[103] Her responses are described as "unvaried" and "the same as usual" for the majority of this time.[104] Her abilities make the men fear her and treat her like an object, much like Higgins and Pickering. In *Dracula*, Mina's mimicry or gramophony is distinctly unsettling to the men of the novel, and yet they must learn to value her as a tool in their pursuit of the vampire rather than leaving her outside the group as they tried to do earlier. In *Pygmalion*, Eliza's gramophony earns her a larger role in the entertainment and experiments of the two bachelors. In both instances, the women are still largely objectified as gramophonic. Their innocent mimicry has larger ramifications, since, as Homi Bhabha points out, the successful colonial mimic "depends on a proliferation of inappropriate *objects* that ensure its strategic failure, so that mimicry is at once resemblance and menace."[105] In Eliza's case, her mimicry might make her seem an "inappropriate object" that occasionally provides Higgins with a laugh, but her inevitable failure to remain an object will provide the "resemblance and menace" that Bhabha predicts.

Higgins's refusal to see the flaw in his project also parallels Kellett's short story. The inventor believes his automaton is perfect, and he gives no serious thought to the consequences of what he has created. Higgins will not understand the warnings from Mrs. Higgins and his housekeeper Mrs. Pearce about Eliza's future. Higgins and Moore believe that their creations are complete representations of the society lady, and both are forcibly confronted with their errors. Kellett's work, as Klass points out, is about "a fine prank with a piece of machinery that succeeds up to a point and then ends in so much sawdust [and a 'mad-scientist finale']," whereas Shaw's play is about "a girl imprisoned in gutters and back alleys because of a lack of education" and how "just one shred of education—in speech—could [...] make her an acceptable lady; and it ends with her giving up that fake ladyhood for genuine womanhood."[106] Shaw's work is clearly more socially conscious, but both highlight the deeply embedded, but ultimately and obviously flawed social connections between the lady automaton via the phonograph and "genuine womanhood." Eliza's final moments in *Pygmalion* depict her last struggle to free herself from the trappings of the mechanical apparatus.

Eliza asserts her independence from her Pygmalion, clearly distinguishing herself from the gramophone that he so frequently blurs with her identity. When Higgins tells her "I have grown accustomed to your voice and appearance,"[107] she identifies the surface-level capabilities of her mentor and refuses to be automatized any further in their relationship: "Well, you have both of them on your gramophone and in your book of photographs. When you feel lonely without me, you can turn the machine on. It's got no feelings to hurt."[108] Eliza and Higgins both refer to voice *and* appearance, but Eliza most heavily emphasizes her relation (or rather lack thereof) to the gramophone. The machine can be "turned on" at Higgins's whim, but it has "no feelings to hurt."

It seems, for a moment at least, that Higgins finally understands the distinction between machine and woman when he concedes, "I can't turn your soul on."[109] Forrest discusses this exact distinction between the "voice" and "soul-as-expressed-through-the-voice" as a nuance that the male creator/teacher/mentor in fiction rarely understands, since he is generally responsible for scripting his creation's words.[110] The difference between Eliza's coached gramophone voice and her physically embodied voice and personhood are utterly bewildering for Higgins to articulate in this scene. His bewilderment is echoed, over a decade later, by Theodor Adorno when he tries to dissect the recorded female voice. He claims that male voices are more effective on the gramophone (reinforcing the male speaker/female auditor dynamic); but if one *does* record the female voice, as Higgins has done, that voice becomes problematic:

> The female voice easily sounds shrill but not because the gramophone is incapable of conveying high tones, as is demonstrated by its adequate reproduction of the flute. Rather, [...] the female voice requires the physical appearance of the body that carries it.

> But it is just this body that the gramophone eliminates, thereby
> giving every female voice a sound that is needy and incomplete.[111]

The statement is, of course, utterly subjective. And it is also objectifying. Adorno's catch-22 of eliminating the female body, but still requiring the female body for effective gramophone recordings, encapsulates Higgins's conundrum. Eliza's voice on the machine, recorded under Higgins's tutelage, is a coached and prompted response. These recordings demonstrate the "needy" quality in Eliza's voice recordings (the need for the male supervisor). And Higgins seems comfortable enough with these interactions when Eliza is present. But he also acknowledges that they are "incomplete"; her physical presence seems necessary to him, though he does not necessarily want her to have independent thoughts and ideas. He nowhere acknowledges her right of individuality and autonomy but rather hopes to keep her soul—which he equates with voice and physical body—to turn off and on like a gramophone. Eliza as an obedient automaton resolves the quandary that Adorno poses. Eliza as the independent woman does not. And Eliza understands this flaw in Higgins's logic, which informs her refusal to return to Wimpole Street. Higgins doesn't really understand this actualized Eliza or her statements of independence, since, at the conclusion of the play, he clearly believes that Eliza will run his errands and return to live with him.

And yet Eliza *has* declared her autonomy from Higgins and his gramophone, and in a fashion that finds parallels in the progress and success of the Third Home Rule Bill. *Pygmalion* was written in 1912 and performed in 1914; this two-year span was also the duration of the Third Home Rule Bill's contemplation in parliament. Asquith introduced the bill in April 1912; Shaw wrote *Pygmalion* in the spring of that same year. The bill would have introduced a greater allowance of autonomy than the previous two bills and would have provided for an Irish parliament, the continued representation of Irish MPs in the parliament of the United Kingdom, and the dissolution of Dublin Castle's rule in Ireland, although the government would retain the Lord Lieutenancy of Ireland. In Shaw's play, Higgins tries to dissuade Eliza from her avowal of independence, telling her she is now fit for marriage, specifically with the "Lord-Lieutenant of Ireland"[112]—recalling (though revising) the political metropolitan marriage motif—and revealing his feeble attempts to contain Eliza's increasing self-sufficiency.

Higgins's attempt to marry her off in these last desperate moments of control also find parallels in Kellett's work. Moore has no qualms about this automaton being treated as a sexualized prize to be won by her two suitors, who largely want to possess her rather than appreciate any originality in her. And the petty, jealous young man who discovers her seemingly promiscuous duplicity attempts murder rather than confronting her, implying the melodramatic but sinister motif of "If I can't have her, no one can." Higgins clearly still views Eliza as a parcel of goods when he suggests she marry the Lord Lieutenant of Ireland. And this isn't the first time he has thought of passing her off in marriage. In the previous act, he suggests that his mother could "find some chap or other" for her, and Eliza immediately calls him out for the sexual implications of the transaction, stating "We were above that at the corner of Tottenham Court Road. [...] I sold flowers. I didnt [sic] sell myself."[113] And in her final confrontation with Higgins, Eliza scoffs at his belief that a political marriage—especially one that is framed as a transactional passing on of sexualized goods—holds any merit for a woman who seeks independence.

Pygmalion premiered on March 24, 1914, and only two months later, on May 25, 1914, the Third Home Rule Bill was passed in the House of Commons, and Royal Assent was granted on September 18, 1914. It seemed that Eliza and Ireland had finally emancipated themselves from the English resistance to Home Rule that had been described in the *Irish Times* as a "parliamentary gramophone," "gramophone campaign," and "political gramophone" over the years. And yet, despite the bill's success, the official Government of Ireland Act 1914 was never implemented; with the outbreak of war with Germany in August, the Suspensory Act of September 1914 postponed Home Rule for the duration of the war. While the suspension of the Act is viewed by most historians as a rational decision—largely due to the fact that to have enforced it while Ulster Unionists were so violently opposed would likely have resulted in armed conflict in Ireland while Britain was already at war with Germany and its allies—its delay caused intense disappointment among Irish nationalists and fostered the republican cause, leading ultimately to the 1916 Rising. Although it might oversimplify a complex political situation, some Irish nationalists felt that Britain was just not willing to let go of Ireland. Similarly, it would seem, Higgins could not fully let go of the idea that Eliza would return to him.

Higgins was not the only one who struggled to believe in Eliza's independence from both himself and the gramophone. Shaw's theatre audiences and producers seemed to prefer a "happy ending," and several productions took liberties with the final scene, including Sir Herbert Beerbohm Tree's 1914 London production in which Tree, as Higgins, threw Eliza a bouquet of flowers after she left and blew her a kiss as a kind of truce. According to Shaw's letters, Tree protested "My ending makes money; you ought to be grateful," to which Shaw retorted, "Your ending is damnable; you ought to be shot."[114] And yet Tree's perception of the play was perpetuated long after its initial run.

In the 1938 film adaptation, Eliza's triumph falters and fails with a final additional scene, filmed prior to Shaw's approval. The scene depicts Higgins furious and defeated by Eliza's decision to leave. He stomps into his study with the gramophone and starts smashing the "dozens of gramophone disks" that presumably contain Eliza's voice. He inadvertently turns the machine on, and we hear Eliza's cockneyed, "I washed my face and hands afore I come, I did" from the second act.[115] The echo of his Galatea seems to undo the professor and he drops his head into his hands. Then Eliza, the flesh and blood Eliza, is heard to repeat the phrase in her perfected English. Higgins, with unguarded delight, turns around to see her standing in his study. Then he slumps in his chair, asking, "Where the devil are my slippers?"—a repeated phrase from the fourth act.[116]

The film's ending, particularly with its overt use of the gramophone, undoes Eliza's transformation and exemplifies the male desire to continue to associate women with the machine. By echoing phrases from acts two and four, the final scene uses gramophonic repetition (literally in the first instance) to recapture Eliza before her liberation. Higgins has essentially taken her advice from their confrontation and has turned on the machine as a way of remembering his creation. Then, as if by magic, she is there in the flesh, perfectly elocuting the phonetics he has taught her. Through the power of the gramophone, Eliza again becomes the perfect lady automaton in her recitation.

This disturbing "undoing" of Eliza with the gramophone in the final scene is the version most often associated with Shaw's *Pygmalion*. Despite Shaw's protestations against Eliza and Higgins's potentially romantic reconciliation, his script for the film *Pygmalion* earned him an Oscar. The film version was, after Shaw's death, then turned into the 1956 musical *My Fair Lady*, keeping the gramophonic ending (and winning six Tony Awards). And the musical was filmed in 1964 (winning eight Oscars and three Golden Globes). These iterations of Eliza and the gramophone solidify the "lady automaton" phenomenon that Shaw fought so hard to explode with his independent Eliza.[117]

Shaw's use of the phonograph-turned-gramophone in the play illuminates yet another embedded resistance to Eliza's malleability: his insistence on her independence as a permanent state rather than one that can be rewritten. Shaw once explained to Mrs. Patrick Campbell, who played Eliza in the 1914 London production of the play, "When Eliza emancipates herself—when Galatea comes to life—she must not relapse. She must retain her pride and triumph to the end."[118] If Eliza's independence serves as an analog for Ireland's Home Rule, then it perhaps compounds why Shaw would become so defensive about her retention of "pride and triumph to the end." Shaw described himself as an "inveterate Republican and Home Ruler."[119] And as an inveterate Republican, Shaw would have seen a break between Eliza and Higgins as a similar parallel to a political break. As a result, somewhere between the second and third acts of *Pygmalion*, a very specific and significant shift occurs in relation to the machine that Eliza has declared independence from: a movement from a phonograph with cylinders to a gramophone with disks.

While many of the studies and productions of Shaw's play take for granted the interchangeability of phonograph and gramophone, it is essential to realize that these are two very distinct technologies with differently focused abilities. And in a play so concerned with language and its effects on perception, Shaw's change from phonograph to gramophone cannot be dismissed out of hand as easily as it seems to have been thus far. The *phonograph* emphasized the recording process, with wax cylinders that were malleable and receptive to dictation but limited in terms of repeated playback. It is a temporary or volatile platform for recording. As a teaching tool, the phonograph makes perfect sense. Eliza's phonographic recordings with Higgins are meant to create a transition in her speech. Each recording is only a step in her progression and is therefore temporary. It is also meant to be the place where she imitates her instructor, mimicking his speech and enunciation. The *gramophone*, on the other hand, used the durable flat-disk record, and the machine emphasized playback by largely removing the recording function. The gramophone represents a step toward permanence that the phonograph lacks. By the third act of the play, Eliza is no longer phonographically imitating Higgins. She has started to move off script with her obvious deviation of "not bloody likely." She is still imitating sounds, languages, and music, but it is being filtered through her individuality, as is made clear when Pickering points out that "her remarks will be delicious" after an evening of observing London society.[120] Pickering and Higgins are storing "dozens of gramophone disks" specifically for their novelty and replay capabilities.[121] Higgins *knows* that there has been a permanent shift in Eliza. These are his machines, after all. He just fails to understand what that permanent shift entails. An Eliza who he can no longer control. An Eliza who need only take one more step to be free, altogether, of him and objectifying machines.

By the fourth act, Eliza is permanently actualized and denounces her identity as the "perfected phonograph" and automaton. She is capable of full autonomy from her instructor. She plans to independently support herself by setting up a flower shop; she refuses to accept a sexualized double standard by scoffing at Higgins's suggestion that she "sell herself" as a marriageable market item to the Lord Lieutenant of Ireland; and she clearly and adamantly proclaims "I'll have independence."[122] Eliza entirely resists Higgins's implied reiteration of the Act of Union marriage motif in which a woman, capable of independence and personal autonomy, joins in a contract where she will again be denied her own voice and disenfranchised by England's official representative in Ireland.

When Eliza rejects the marriage as well as the stagnation of a repetitive gramophonic existence with her previous master, Higgins then betrays a potential for violence that is at the same time startling and yet completely in keeping with the roiling cruelty that characterizes his attitude toward Eliza if one reads the play without the jaunty slant that most performances embrace. He rises "*with fury*" and says, "You take one step in [that] direction and I'll wring your neck!" as he places his hands on her.[123] Eliza's reaction solidifies her independence, since she is unintimidated and even sees violence as an eventuality in this relationship: "Wring away! What do I care? I knew you'd strike me one day."[124] And upon consideration, her reaction makes perfect sense. Eliza's linguistic education has been "violent and violating" throughout the play,[125] as demonstrated by depictions of the phonograph and gramophone as part of her transformation. The needle of the machine tore into the wax cylinders of the phonograph when Eliza was Higgins's student. When Eliza declares her independence from Higgins, the metonymic violence of the recording is set and made permanent by the reference to the gramophone. The violence of recording imagery moves out of abstraction into overtly physical gestures. In this moment, Eliza emphasizes the permanence of her break from Higgins as well as its inevitability.

This climactic display of violence perhaps highlights Shaw's own foresight about the inevitable violence that might come if Ireland were not allowed autonomy through Home Rule. For some, the postponement of Home Rule in light of World War I might have had sound political logic behind it, but only two years later the Easter Rising of 1916 was an outburst of violence between the two nations that eventually led to a bloody guerrilla war for Irish independence. The permanence of the rift between England and Ireland has further parallels to *Pygmalion*, given that Shaw published a "sequel" to the play in 1916: a sequel prompted by the liberties taken with *Pygmalion*'s ending. Shaw clearly outlines Eliza's inability to return to Higgins, and instead depicts Eliza having only a cordial relationship with the two men at Wimpole Street (she is on friendly terms with Pickering and has a tempestuous truce with Higgins). Shaw clearly defines why Eliza's independence and Higgins's stubbornness make a romantic reconciliation between the two impossible. The "marriage" is off for good.

Conclusion

Throughout the Home Rule period, the gendered connotations of recording technology evolved from a concern about phonographysteria to wariness about the female voice no longer under male control. When Adorno writes about the disembodied female voice, he represents a gendered historical anxiety concerning women and the machine that emerges in some of the earliest connotations and associations of the phonograph and gramophone. The "needy and incomplete" voice of the gramophone and the physicality of the machine seem to dissect women into intellectual or sexual halves that are both negated through the object. In Irish literature at the turn of the century, the gendered object is further complicated by depictions of women in relation to the political context of Home Rule. Lucy's interactions with the phonograph show the male fear of a sexually liberated woman in terms of a threat to the metropolitan marriage contract of Home Rule. Mina's work with the phonograph indicates approval of the female intellect but the need for coded and subversive sexuality for the successful navigation of political and sexual debates. And Eliza's transition from a phonographic object, to a gramophonic record, and finally to a liberated and actualized woman finds parallels in Shaw's views of the successful passing (then stalling) of Irish Home Rule in 1914. The transition from phonograph to gramophone as a politically coded and gendered "thing" in these works also suggests the move toward a permanent and violent break in English and Irish relations in 1914. Shaw's *Pygmalion* foretells violence in this gramophonic shift, and by the time he published his 1916 "sequel," that violence had been fulfilled with the Easter Rising. The gramophone continued to serve as an object indicative of embedded trauma and violence in works that documented the wars after *Pygmalion*'s publication.

CHAPTER THREE

Gramophonic Violence
The Gramophones of the Irish Revolution

D uring the 1916 Easter Rising, Thomas MacDonagh led the 2nd
Battalion to commandeer Jacob's biscuit factory on Bishop
Street, nearly a mile away from headquarters at the General Post
Office. During the week, the factory, as a base for the rebellion, was largely
ignored by the British forces, making tedium and tension warring factors
for the volunteers. At some point during the week, according to Volunteer
Lieutenant John MacDonagh (brother to Thomas), "volunteers discovered
an old-fashioned gramophone, in a corner downstairs in Jacob's."[1] The
machine provided entertainment for the volunteers, even though the only
record they had was, ironically enough, "God Save the King."[2] They made
good use of the machine, however, since, as John MacDonagh continues:
"[O]ne day when Tom [MacDonagh] and [John] MacBride were making
their tour of inspection, it was put on to take the rise out of them."[3] By
Friday of that week, Seosamh de Brún, another volunteer, wrote in his
diary that "[i]f it was not for occassional [sic] sniping the Factory would
remind one of a huge entertainment, everybody merry & cheerful. […]
Smoking & playing cards to music of gramophone & piano."[4] Details of the
gramophone were even shared with Muriel MacDonagh, Thomas's wife,
when a family friend reported having met with MacDonagh during the
week. Muriel was told that the volunteers "were in great form—that the
only complaint they had to make was that they need not have needles for
their gramophone, and that the soldiers did [not] come out to fight."[5]

Earlier that Easter week, Sean O'Casey witnessed the march of the Irish Citizen Army and Volunteers following Patrick Pearse, James Connolly, and Tom Clarke to the GPO, and the subsequent reactions from Dubliners. He recalled a "company o' throttin' lancers" making their way to the GPO while people speculated that "the Irish Republic [was] endin' quicker'n it began."[6] Directly after this observation, O'Casey's narrative version of the events shifts to someone observing, "Looka this fella comin' along with a gramophone. Eh, sonny boy, where'd you get that?"[7] The gramophone, pilfered from a store window, signals the beginning of the looting of Sackville Street in O'Casey's version of events.

Gramophones were at the height of their popularity and accessibility during the Irish revolutionary period (1913–23), which makes their presence during crucial events of the period relatively unsurprising. And yet, *because* of their cultural near omnipresence, they crop up in unexpected places and descriptions, taking up space as more than mere background information during events surrounding Ireland's near decade of armed conflict. From Jacob's biscuit factory to Sackville Street, from the Western Front to Irish war hospitals, from country estates to tenement buildings, the gramophone unapologetically asserts its physical presence and psychological parallels throughout these conflicts.

This chapter considers the gramophone in the context of Ireland at war, arguing that the gramophones of this period, particularly in Ireland, take on valences of shell-shock or post-traumatic stress disorder by embodying memories, scars, and ghosts of the violence in Ireland during the tumultuous period of Irish revolution. Elizabeth Bowen's *The Last September* (1929) and Sean O'Casey's *Juno and the Paycock* (1924) deal directly with the armed conflict of the Irish revolution in their works, depicting the Irish War of Independence and the subsequent Civil War respectively. Inevitably, the other armed conflicts of the period are contextually embedded in these works: Bowen's novel depicts English soldiers who are veterans of World War I and who are based in Ireland during the Anglo-Irish conflict, and O'Casey's play centers on an IRA soldier who bears the scars of the 1916 Rising as well as the War of Independence while he participates in the turmoil of the Civil War. Both works use the gramophone as an object that tries to articulate the toll of the violence of those years. But before beginning an analysis of these works, and the ways in which their characters engage with the gramophone, the machine itself must be situated in the broader scope of the global conflict of World War I, as well as its use in describing and treating a larger psychology of the era. Tracking Ireland's experiences of gramophones and war, starting with global conflict then moving to Irish-based conflict, helps pinpoint a specific divergence between the English and Irish experience of shock and how the gramophone was culturally embedded in those experiences.

The Trench Gramophone and Shell-Shock

While the anecdotal references to the gramophone as a form of stress relief for the volunteers in Jacob's biscuit factory might initially seem inconsequential in the context of the larger conflict of the Rising, the machine was actually deeply encoded into soldiers' experiences of armed conflict by the time of the 1916 Rebellion. In the early decades of the twentieth century, the mass production of records and more portable gramophones meant that the machine and its music were more accessible than ever before. In fact, the first truly portable gramophones were patented by Decca in 1914, essentially coinciding with the outbreak of World War I.[8] It follows that portable gramophones became a vital part of soldiers' entertainment in the trenches and recovery in hospitals. In Ireland, as well as other countries, advertisements for gramophones were often targeted for soldiers' use. Decca, for instance, had no qualms about bolstering this connection between soldiers and gramophones as part of its advertising campaigns throughout the war. In one advertisement, Decca depicts soldiers from every branch of the British military benefiting from the portable gramophone, with the ad stating "they shall have music wherever they go."[9] Another Decca advertisement uses similar imagery while emphasizing the benefits of the gramophone for soldiers who are either "well or wounded," and that the machine is "essentially the gramophone for the Hospital, as it is also for the Front": a range of soldiers with visible and non-visible injuries grin cheerily at the commanding officer and his gramophone (see Figure 3.1).[10]

Decca was not alone in promoting the gramophone's suitability for soldiers. Smaller companies, in England and beyond, took up the same

Figure 3.1. Decca gramophone advertisement from *The Tatler*,
13 September 1916, emphasizing the connection between war hospitals
and gramophones. © Illustrated London News Ltd/Mary Evans.

tactic. The strategy was so ubiquitous that the portable machines became known as "trench gramophones." The Dublin-based gramophone sellers G. Butler & Sons, for example, encouraged customers to "Help the War Revenue, Enliven the Home, and Cheer the Soldiers" with the purchase of a "trench gramophone."[11] The ad, published in the *Irish Times* in the fall of 1915, included a note from "A Chaplain at the Front" explaining that "the question of Musical Entertainment as a distraction to the troops will be one of great importance."[12] The same company, a year later, advertised its trench gramophones were as "popular in the home as in the TRENCH, BILLET, and HOSPITAL WARD."[13] This latter advertisement, along with Decca's "Well or Wounded" ad, points to a particular connection to hospitals, where the gramophone was used as entertainment but also as a form of distraction and even treatment for soldiers who suffered psychologically from the shock of war.

By 1915 "shell-shock" was an evolving psychological diagnosis, characterized by severe anxiety and other mental disturbances, often accompanied by somatic symptoms such as rapid heartbeat, nervous tics, and persistent headaches. Despite its prevalence, there was no standard practice for treating this clearly psychological disorder. The gramophone became one of many potential tools for treating and distracting shell-shocked patients. For example, in a two-part exchange in *The Times* called "Gramophones in Hospitals," a "Part Worn Colonel" and a commanding officer of a military hospital disagreed about the gramophone's effects on soldiers. The "Worn Colonel" requested the British public to "give no more" gramophones to hospitals, explaining that the ceaseless playing of records adds to the "distress of their prostrate comrades, too ill to protest, to [*sic*] weary to make a fuss," and who might already be suffering from shattered sleep and inquietude.[14] On the flip side of the debate, the commanding officer of a military hospital wrote, "Only those who live and work among the nerve-shattered wounded can appreciate the joy of the gramophone to patients whose brains are teeming with the screech of shells and the noise of bombs."[15] The C.O. points out that he has witnessed the devastation that soldiers experience when the hospital gramophone breaks and they are left without its comfort or distraction.

This debate, while perhaps little-known to us in the twenty-first century, was depicted in the pilot episode of the 2014 TV mini-series *The*

Crimson Field, in which a British nurse at a field hospital on the coast of France brings her shell-shocked patient, on the verge of a mental break-down, to the C.O.'s quarters specifically to listen to the gramophone. The C.O. winds the machine up and sets it playing ("Un bel dì" from Giacomo Puccini's *Madama Butterfly*), and both C.O. and nurse step out to afford the patient privacy. The music immediately has an effect on the patient as he sobs a release from his mental strain and gradually grows calm. Outside, while the C.O. and nurse wait for the soldier, the former asks the nurse, "Why does it help?" to which she replies, "I don't know. But it does."[16] While this is a fictionalized depiction of the gramophone's potential use for soldiers, it is certainly based on contemporary accounts and debates. The medical questioning of *why* it is effective (or not) is equally accurate.

Despite the gramophone's role as a point of contention in the treatment of soldiers in military hospitals, it remained a fixture in the treatment of shell-shock, even in Ireland, where gramophone recitals featured as recreation and therapy in hospital wards.[17] And even though the gramophone's efficacy as part of treatment remained debatable, a Freudian-based psychoanalysis treatment called abreaction that relied on the gramophonic principles of repetition and release of tension was a much more accepted method of treatment for shell-shock. At the Richmond War Hospital in Dublin, for instance, abreaction was a standard treatment that examined the psychological impact of war and "involved soldiers re-experiencing or reliving traumatic memories in an effort to purge them of their emotional impact" in the present.[18] Essentially, abreaction uses repetition to release tension and wear down the intensity of the traumatic memory.

This release of tension is also a gramophonic principle. When the gramophone plays, the tension stored up in the spring motor unwinds and "performs time" in a way that allows for a reliving of a past recording event in the present.[19] Furthermore, since machines in the early decades of the twentieth century did not have specialized tracking and stylus control, the needle of the machine would gradually wear down and hollow out the vivid imprint of the initial recording event with each playback. As a result, with each replay, the recorded sound would grow weaker and the original clarity would fade.

Through abreaction, a patient temporarily becomes a gramophone: an entity that relives trauma until the trauma is turned into a symbolic worn-down object. When a gramophone's tension releases and the recording begins to wind down, the machine and its physicality, rather than the recording, become the central entity. The gramophone is "transformed," allowing the object's thingness to bleed through the experience.[20] So while abreaction might strive to assimilate trauma—and in the gramophonic parallel, a recording event—the ruts and scars of the event will always remain on the mind and the record after it has been worn down. But the trauma and record will have become a "thing" with no other function than to mnemonically represent the traumas that no longer carry intense emotional impact or are no longer audible. The gramophone and its record, therefore, embody the psychological scars experienced and processed by the trauma patient.

In Dublin, the Richmond District Asylum used abreaction among its myriad other therapies (including non-invasive music therapy) to treat shock, prior to and after its transition in 1916 to the Richmond War Hospital. Interestingly enough, some of the first Irish patients to experience and seek treatment for shock were not, as one would expect, soldiers from the front lines of the Great War. Instead, they were Dublin citizens who were deeply affected by the violence of the Easter Rising. Unlike the volunteers at Jacob's biscuit factory (and their ironic gramophone) who were slightly removed from the heat of the conflict, the patients at Richmond Asylum had been located geographically near the middle of the fighting during that week. One of the doctors at the mental health facility, Resident Medical Superintendent Dr. John O'Conor Donelon, described the conflict that raged just beyond the hospital's grounds as immediate and threatening to the patients: "[T]he belligerents of both sides were constantly firing through the grounds," he writes. "[W]e moved the patients from exposed positions; at night their mattresses were placed on the floor, and, of course, they were confined to the house during the disturbance."[21] The conflict obviously upset routine and the fragile mental health of several patients. The weeks following the Rising saw increased admittance to the asylum, largely as a result of the violent conflict. According to A. Collins, one of the first patients admitted after the Rising was a woman with a diagnosis of "melancholia due to *shock*" on May 1,

1916.[22] This might be the "first occasion that the word 'shock' appears in the admission books" at this hospital, and perhaps in Ireland more generally.[23] Collins goes on to point out that:

> It is reasonable to consider its presence [the diagnosis of "shock"]
> for diagnostic purposes as indicative of an admission where the
> rebellion was deemed to be central to the presentation [...]. There
> were 10 "shock" admissions in all [that May], that is, admission
> that the admitting doctor believed were due to the rebellion [...].
> The individuals [admitted ...] tended to reside in those parts of
> the city most affected by the trouble.[24]

Brendan Kelly identifies other Dublin hospitals, such as St. Patrick's, as also admitting patients with "shock" as well as "shock and terror" as primary symptoms directly after the rebellion.[25]

The Richmond District Asylum was, shortly after the Rising, partially converted into Dublin's Richmond War Hospital (1916–19), which was "explicitly aimed to care for shell shocked and traumatised soldiers returning from the First World War."[26] Because of the chronological proximity between the Rising and the War Hospital's establishment in June of the same year, Richmond serves as a locus for discussion of shock and its treatment in this period, though it is difficult to make exact distinctions between the "shock" of Easter Week and the "shell-shock" of the war. However, the distinct pattern of "shock" in the admissions to psychiatric hospitals in Dublin in the month following the Easter Rising suggest that "shock," or psychological trauma, began to have a divergent meaning for British and Irish culture after the Rising of 1916, when the violence of war shifted from the Western Front to Irish soil. The Irish began to understand shock and trauma as the cultural inheritance of a country with divisive nationalism(s). Similarly, the gramophone—trench models and otherwise—took on divergent metonymic and psychological meanings for British and Irish soldiers and civilians.

To further explore the division of cultural trauma perceptions, we turn our attention to Elizabeth Bowen's *The Last September*, in which Daventry, a British soldier, and Lois, an Anglo-Irish woman, develop different relationships with the gramophone during the Irish War of

Independence. Their different treatment of the object reveals the nationally diverse perspectives on the same war. Daventry's interactions with the gramophone serve as a contrast to Lois's affinity with it, since his relationship with the machine centers on his shell-shock as a result of World War I and his detachment from the current Irish struggle surrounding him. Lois's interactions with the machine are, in contrast, intimate and sustained, revealing her own empathy with the object and her inability to relate to the traumas of a war that conflates the two warring sides of her conflicting Anglo-Irish identity. Both characters are clearly affected by the violence they have endured, but their interactions with gramophones reveal a distinctive difference in English and Irish perceptions of the object in relation to war.

The Death of a Gramophone in the War of Independence

During a dance at the English army barracks in *The Last September*, the dancers upset the gramophone. In the next room, Lois Farquar and the soldier Daventry hear its crash. Daventry bursts out, "Thank God, *they've upset the gramophone!*" and then continues with a laugh, "Done in."[27] His relief and near glee at the gramophone's destruction is in diametric opposition to Lois's reaction. When she hears the machine fall, she seemingly eulogizes the object: "A gramophone passing, a gramophone less in the world; it was not funny."[28] Neil Corcoran observes, "The tone of this is hard to judge. [...] A gramophone less in the world, may not be funny but, even so, [it] hardly deserves elegiac lament."[29] So why is Lois so distressed at the gramophone's destruction? And why is Daventry so unaccountably jubilant? The gramophone seems like an innocuous object for most of the novel, but when it crashes to the floor, drawing attention to itself and to these two characters' reactions, it behaves as a Brownian "thing," asserting its unsuspected complexity and revealing the "story of a changed relation to the human subject."[30] By drawing such specific attention to itself in this scene, the gramophone asserts its role in the novel's wider narrative of both of these characters, forcing us to reconsider its presence in the work.

Bowen's work often reveals the author's fascination with the everyday object. In fact, she once wrote to Virginia Woolf (after Woolf's London flats had both been bombed during the 1941 Blitz), "All my life I have said, 'whatever happens there will always be tables and chairs'—and what a mistake."[31] Though London's destruction during the war seemed to upend her belief in the utter endurability of things, Bowen still stresses the presence of objects in all her fiction. In *The Last September*, the inhabitants of Danielstown go through the motions of routine while the house and its objects are the only things that hint at the repressed tension of war and instability woven throughout the novel. The solidity of objects and the imprecision of the human elements in Bowen's novel suggests that "things" actually "upset any persistent striving toward stable boundaries" between themselves and humans.[32] The narrator describes the Black and Tans, the English soldiers, Irish rebels, and the Anglo-Irish families almost as peripheral in relation to the Big House (a nomenclature that clearly values and even provides proper noun status to an inanimate "thing"), the buried guns on the estate, telephones, umbrellas, books, and other objects that press in upon our attention. While the people in the novel pretend that there is a form of social stability, the anthropomorphized objects belie the façade.

The gramophone's presence in the novel is a continuation of Bowen's fascination with objects in relation to human counterparts. It is possible that she was aware of the machine's psychological connotations through Freud's emerging theories of abreaction and the gramophone's analogous parallels to human memory. At the very least, Maud Ellmann notes, Bowen was particularly interested in "the transferences of human properties to inanimate prostheses, especially to machines that carry bodies and voices across distance," and, as Keri Walsh points out, Bowen had a career-long obsession with "the effects of new technologies on consciousness."[33] In *The Last September*, the gramophone acts as a type of psychological prosthesis, in different ways, for Lois and Daventry.

In Daventry's relationship with the gramophone we have a depiction of an English shell-shocked soldier struggling to cope with the psychological trauma of war. Daventry had led a "company of soldiers in France in 1916, and later on he was an acting-major," even though he is now only a subaltern in the garrison in Ireland.[34] His demotion might be explained by his state of mind, since he is specifically identified as a soldier with shell-shock and his symptoms align with that diagnosis. He is constantly disoriented, disconnected, he has headaches, and struggles to connect thoughts. His behavior is considered rather anti-social by many of the other characters, and he reflects on these attributes in himself:

> He kept shutting his eyes; whenever he stopped dancing he noticed that he had a headache. [... He] had been shell-shocked; he was now beginning to hate Ireland. Lyrically, explicitly; to the very feel of the air and the smell of the water. If it were not for dancing a good deal, whisky, bridge, ragging about the huts, whisky again, he did not know what would become of him, he would go over the edge, quite mad, he supposed.[35]

In his confession that he was "now beginning to hate Ireland," Daventry reveals a certain amount of resentment at being in an armed conflict he cannot understand. He resists defining the current conflict as a war in itself; it is merely "post-war madness" in Ireland, and it infuriates him.[36]

The "post-war madness," according to Daventry, is the current military duty that has him garrisoned in Ireland. His war was supposed to end in 1918 with the Armistice, and technically it had. The War of Independence or Anglo-Irish War (depending on political and historical perspective)[37] was named a war largely in retrospect; Dáil Éireann did not *officially* declare a state of war with England until March 11, 1921, only four months before the ceasefire. From 1919 to 1921, the Irish Republican Army (IRA)—considered by the Dáil as the official state army—engaged in guerrilla warfare against the British presence in Ireland while the British government primarily treated the conflict as a matter for police governance, which explains the primarily mobilized Royal Irish Constabulary (RIC) response as well as the British government's supplementation of the RIC forces with the Auxiliaries and the Reserve Force (Black and Tans). The British army was initially less overtly active in the conflict, though it maintained patrols like those described by both Daventry and Gerald Lesworth in Bowen's novel.

Daventry's frustration at the complicated political conflict and its definition becomes manifest in his conversation with other English soldiers and their associates in Ireland. When one of the soldier's wives comments, "It takes two to make a row, [...] *We're* not fighting," Daventry breaks out in anger: "More's the pity. [...] God, if they'd—."[38] His incomplete sentence implies that "they"—most likely the British government—*should* in fact declare an open war in Ireland, rather than continue in the unofficial conflict that forces him to endure the IRA's guerrilla hostilities without the ability to retaliate with open force and the British army's full support. Gerald similarly, though to a lesser degree, finds the lack of declared war frustrating when he discusses the situation with the Misses Hartigan at the Danielstown tennis party. He starts by saying, "We shall all be leaving you soon, I daresay; all we jolly old army of occupation. [...]—As soon as we've lost this jolly old war," to which Miss Hartigan responds, "Oh, but one wouldn't call it a *war*."[39] Gerald then replies, "If anyone would, we could clear these beggars out in a week!"[40] Later, at the barracks dance, he tells Lois that he rather sympathizes with Daventry's frustrations over the conflict, stating that it "doesn't seem natural."[41]

The implied "peace" of this undeclared war is still more confusing and frustrating to Daventry, since his orders are far from the actions of a resting army. He spends his nights on patrol "searching [...] houses for guns" and on the evening before the barracks dance he had received

special orders to ransack the beds, and to search with particular strictness the houses where men were absent and women
wept loudest and prayed. Nearly all beds had contained very old
women or women with very new babies, but the N.C.O., who
was used to the work, insisted that they must go through with it.
Daventry still felt sickish, still stifled with thick air and womanhood, dazed from the din.[42]

His standing orders render him uncomfortable in his only visit to Daniel-stown later in the novel, when "it seemed to him odd that there should be nothing to search for, nobody to interrogate."[43] He cannot fully disengage from a war mentality in Danielstown, but at the same time he cannot overcome the "dazed" and "sickish" disorder of his mind to assimilate the continued violence in Ireland after his war on the Continent.

Among Daventry's chief coping mechanisms against continued violence after the Great War, as described earlier, are dancing and drinking ("dancing a good deal, whisky, [...] whisky again"). The dance at the barracks incorporates both, and Daventry initially hovers near the gramophone to ensure the continuation of the dancing, silently recalling the previous night's raids while resetting the machine. He then decides to dance:

> Mr. Daventry [...] balanced his cigarette on the rim of the gramophone and came up to Lois and frowned, without speaking. He opened his arms slowly. They danced [...]. At the end of the record Mr. Daventry impassively put back the needle again. [...] They went on dancing. [...] [H]is neck muscles strained. Again, he revived the gramophone. Lois, breathless, said: "Isn't there going to be an interval?" "Not necessarily," replied Mr. Daventry.[44]

His denial of "an interval" might be a reminder of his own lack of a reprieve from armed conflict. And the repetition of the gramophone recording, the retracing of the needle over the scars of sound, the repetitive winding down of the spring motor, could be a form of attempted abreaction. Surely if he continues to play the gramophone, to replay the events of his war and his time in Ireland, things will start to fall into place, start to make sense, and relieve the strain his mind and body perpetually endure. And yet the gramophone's repeated atemporal and asynchronous performance of time could just as likely enhance the effect of replayed trauma for Daventry.

The atemporality of the machine's replay also foreshadows the gramophone's own death in *The Last September*, and perhaps contextualizes Daventry's perpetual resetting of the haunting object.[45] It is anthropomorphized in the scenes leading up to its destruction, enhancing the intensity of the shock when it metaphorically "passes." As Lois and Daventry dance before the ball, the gramophone "spurt[s]" music.[46] Later, the machine "bursts" and "coughs" its sounds, then after a pause in the music, it is "revived."[47] Additionally, the syntactical construction in many of the gramophone's scenes in *The Last September* gives the gramophone active will—no one starts the machine, but it "spurted hoarse music" and "the gramophone in a perceptibly minor key began again."[48] Each of these references is also disturbing, since they suggest that the gramophone's health is deteriorating (coughing, spurting, hoarseness of voice, and reviving), and the "perceptibly minor key" of the music is suggestive of a wearing or winding down of the gramophone's spring motor. It is, as described by Adorno, a "breaking down" of the machine's traditional function and an indication of its "thingness" bleeding through (a dark pun, in this context) the narrative, foreshadowing its own death.[49]

Bowen's choice to write the novel in the historic past tense enhances the spectral feel of the narrative's events, deaths, and images. She wrote the novel nearly eight years after the events of the story. In her 1952 preface to the American edition, Bowen points out that:

> *The Last September* is the only one of my novels to be set back deliberately, in former time [...]. The cast of my characters, and their doings, were to reflect the mood of a vanished time. "All this," I willed the reader to know, "is done with and over." From the start, the reader must look, be conscious of looking, backward—down a backward perspective of eight years.[50]

Bowen further emphasizes the distance between the past and the present of the novel by giving readers what she describes as a "pointer" in the second paragraph, when the narrator states, "In those days, girls wore crisp white skirts and transparent blouses clotted with white flowers; ribbons threaded through [...] appeared over the shoulders."[51] The traditional past tense narrative is punctuated by this embedded backward glance at history. Jessica Gildersleeve aptly observes that Bowen's backward perspective in *The Last September* "anticipate[s] traumas that have always already happened."[52] The gramophone, much like Gerald, is "always already dead,"[53] and therefore its ghost can easily haunt the pages of the novel. Similarly, the trauma and violence of the conflict that surrounds these deaths can temporally swirl around both Lois and Daventry.

So, when Daventry refuses "an interval" between his dances with Lois—repeatedly resetting the gramophone—we can also see a repetition of a haunting unreality settle on Daventry's actions. If the gramophone is always replaying the past, if Gerald is always already dead, then the same could be said of the soldiers lost in World War I. Daventry has not really emerged from the horror of lost friends, and they, too, are always already dead in the dance scenes with the gramophone. A feeling of unreality is pervasive in Daventry's perception of the current armed conflict and possibly becomes conflated with the previous one. His gramophonic abre-action, re-experiencing these moments, is a complex miasma of atemporal memory.

Daventry's perpetual return to the gramophone has at least one literary precedent: Virginia Woolf also depicts a veteran of World War I struggling with ghosts in *Mrs. Dalloway* (1925), when Septimus Warren Smith cannot look away from the gramophone in his own apartment:

> He began, very cautiously, to open his eyes, to see whether a gramophone was really there. But real things—real things were too exciting. He must be cautious. He would not go mad. First, he looked at the fashion papers on the lower shelf, then, gradually at the gramophone with the green trumpet. Nothing could be more exact.[54]

Real things are "too exciting" but are also essential to Septimus as an anchor of stability. But the gramophone also threatens to drive Septimus mad, like Daventry, who also fears madness in these dance scenes. Septimus constantly thinks of and sees his fallen friend Evans throughout the novel. In this particular scene, he hears Evans "singing behind the screen," and is sure he hears "the voices of the dead."[55] The war has indelibly embedded sights and sounds into Septimus, leaving his scarred psyche to replay the voices of ghosts. When he plays back traumas and memories that no one else can hear or understand, he is like a gramophone record himself. And yet the physical presence of the gramophone in his home reminds him that the traumas of the war are real and that "nothing could be more exact" (despite the fact that nothing about the war seems to be "exact" for Septimus). The terrifying trauma of reality is what he initially fears in the gramophone's presence: its physicality and realness. The fact that Daventry is constantly in physical contact with the machine might, in part, be his way of confronting that realness.

In her descriptions of Daventry's reactions to the gramophone's death, Bowen also draws a rather direct literary parallel to Siegfried Sassoon's 1918 poem "Dead Musicians," in which another gramophone is disrupted, only to expose the traumas of World War I. After remembering "dead musicians" like Bach and Mozart who inspired greatness and ideals, the speaker points out how useless those songs are when he is surrounded by memories of friends he has seen die:

> For when my brain is on their track,
> In slangy speech I call them back.
> With fox-trot tunes their ghosts I charm.
> *"Another little drink won't do us any harm."*
> I think of rag-time; a bit of rag-time;
> And see their faces crowding round
> To the sound of the syncopated beat.
> They've got such jolly things to tell,
> Home from hell with a Blighty wound so neat...
>
>   . . . .
>
> And so the song breaks off; and I'm alone.
> They're dead ... For God's sake stop that gramophone.[56]

The gramophone, with its foxtrots and dancing tunes, enables a certain dream-like return to life before war and psychological trauma. Is it any wonder, then, that Daventry keeps the machine running as much as possible?

And yet perhaps it is the unrelenting difficulty of reliving those moments and the perpetual representational abreaction of the machine that informs Daventry's seemingly overblown relief at the gramophone's destruction. Like in "Dead Musicians," the abrupt return to reality occurs when the music "breaks" off. The gramophone in *The Last September* crashes to the ground at the barracks dance and Daventry's "Thank God, *they've upset the gramophone!*" echoes Sassoon's "For God's sake stop that gramophone."[57] Daventry then "smacked his knee, remotely, as though rehearsing the gesture. His look decomposed in laughter. 'Done in,' he said, drawing life from the thought. [... The gramophone] was smashed, finished."[58] This finely honed moment in Bowen's prose creates a swirl of death and life cycles: most overtly, Daventry "draw[s] life" from the fact that the gramophone is "[d]one in"; more subtle is the "decomposed" as an inescapable link with death and decay, but also the compound of breaking from the composure of remoteness, awakening to life. Remoteness has been a defining attribute of Daventry throughout the novel. He does not come to social events at the Big Houses, he is considered an anti-social entity in general, and he lacks the ability to connect to the conflict that he is involved in. This war makes no sense to him. And how could it? He is still reliving the previous war. There has been no interval for him. He is stationed in Ireland, a country considered (by the British government) part of the United Kingdom, and his duties are to raid unprotected houses for weapons that could be used to fight in an undeclared war. When the gramophone breaks, it is uncertain whether Daventry is succumbing to the madness he feels has threatened him since the Western Front, or whether he is emerging from his shock through a (literally) smashing finale of abreaction therapy. Either way, the gramophone's death is a definite action that relieves Daventry of some burden. And it is a distinctly English reso-lution as well; Daventry is coping with the previous war, not the current one. Lois, on the other hand, is trying to pretend that the current war is not happening at all.

Lois's contrasting and profound reaction to the gramophone's death forces a rereading of her interactions with the machine as well. A closer look reveals that Lois is associated with the gramophone *throughout* the novel, not just in this scene. Understanding the relationship between Lois and the gramophone, the changed relation between "thing" and human subject, holds the key to understanding the gramophone as a physical locus of Anglo-Irish trauma in *The Last September*. Lois experiences certain moments of the novel as though she were an extension of a gramophone or vice versa. For instance, one evening when many of the inhabitants of Danielstown cannot sleep, her cousin Laurence conjectures what would have happened if Lois's mother had married Mr. Montmorency instead of Mr. Farquar. In his musings, "Lois, naturally, was not born at all."[59] As if to remind him of her presence, "Lois, child of that unwise marriage, was playing the gramophone" in the darkness.[60] Moments later, when Laurence bangs a chair on the floor to make Lois turn it off, she complies: "[T]he music broke off with a shock, there was a tingling calm as after an amputation."[61] The gramophone is paired with Lois as an extension of her own body; to turn it off is like an amputation.

Lois constantly turns to the gramophone as a source of identity (not just memory) in the novel, relying on it to some extent to stand in as her own voice and physical manifestation. This isn't necessarily an evocation of the automaton as discussed in Chapter 2, but rather an integrated part of her identity (more cyborg than automaton). The more she comes to rely on the gramophonic part of her identity, the more we see how problematic this becomes to her ability to process the violence around her and articulate her own experiences of trauma.

An early example of Lois's reliance on the gramophone (and her own self-doubt) occurs when she tries to provide an account to Mr. Montmorency of a dance on the avenue with Gerald and the gramophone that occurs before the events of the novel. For a bet, she and Gerald dance down the avenue while the gramophone follows behind them, carried by an unnamed man.[62] But in retelling this event, Lois feels a deep inadequacy in the account which bothers her: "She thought how happy that night had been, and how foolish Mr. Montmorency now thought them."[63] The more she thinks about it, the greater seems the discrepancy between the actual event and the description. "[S]he was now unconvinced and anxious but intended to be quite certain" that she was happy in that moment, and is therefore determined to replicate the experience later that evening.[64]

Lois tries to recreate the experience, dancing by herself and to her own internal music rather than have the blaring machine accompany her. Despite the gramophone's absence in this second dance scene, Lois still experiences the subsequent events through gramophonic imagery. While she dances by herself on the avenue, Lois is startled when "[h]igh up, a bird shriek[s] and stumble[s] down through the darkness, tearing the leaves. Silence heal[s], but [keeps] a scar of horror."[65] The sound slices through the silence and Lois feels that, though the momentary shriek passes, the "scar" of the sound will remain, like the scar left behind on Edison's flesh after the experiment that inspired the phonograph, and like the inscribed wake of a gramophone's needle. The violence of the description of the sound and its contextual connection to the recording process suggests that this moment may serve as a type of mental recording of Lois's proximity to the violence of armed conflict and her repressed anxiety about it. Furthermore, the use of gramophonic imagery indicates that what happens next will be ineradicably inscribed on Lois's consciousness.

After the bird shrieks, a "trench-coat" rushes "down from the mountains, making a short cut through their demesne."[66] Lois cannot bring herself to call out to the man and he does not notice her, but in this moment, she witnesses (records) the movements of an Irish rebel and wonders if he has come for the guns supposedly buried on the estate. While she watches him leave, she observes, "[h]is intentness burnt on the dark an almost visible trail."[67] This second use of imagery taken from the gramophone suggests that the recording event has ended. In using recording imagery in relation to her protagonist in this scene and others, Bowen forges a link between the physical traumas of gramophonic recording and the metaphysical and psychological trauma of experiencing or witnessing war in its many iterations.

This is the first instance of Lois encountering the realities of the guerrilla war surrounding her, and it further jars her faith in her ability to accurately represent her experiences. The impetus for this second dance on the avenue is Lois's attempt to recreate and therefore reaffirm the memory of the first dance, reassuring herself of the fidelity of her own account. But the "trench-coat" and the implied violence of the war expose just how out of place, how out of context, a dance down the avenue really is. Her memory cannot possibly be accurate, it seems. The first dance—with an English officer out in the open with a blaring gramophone drawing attention to the event during a guerrilla war—was surely the height of folly. And the second dance—a young woman on her own in the dark and witness to an unknown Irish soldier's movements—is at least equally ill-advised. These overt intrusions of war and Irish guerrilla tactics force Lois to confront—at some level—the idiocy of these decisions. She, therefore, feels the inadequacy of her capacity to accurately recount these experiences, and she begins to question the fidelity of any of her metonymic gramophonic accounts.

Following her encounter with the "trench-coat" on the avenue, Lois's immediate impulse is to "play back" the scene: to report back to the people at Danielstown. But she never does. Her anxiety about accurately sharing her experience with others emphasizes the trauma of her up-close encounter with the movements of the guerrilla war. The "scars" and "burnt visible trail" of the moment have become a part of her, but she does not trust herself to give a report that can withstand closer scrutiny; "It was impossible to speak of [it]. At a touch from Aunt Myra adventure became literary, to Uncle Richard it suggested an inconvenience; a glance from

Mr. Montmorency or Laurence would make her encounter sterile."[68] In believing that others will never be able to understand her experience, Lois isolates herself.[69]

Despite her self-doubt, Lois continues to pair her own experiences of the war with the gramophone, both overtly and through gramophonic imagery. One of her blatant couplings occurs shortly after her experience with the trench-coat on the avenue. She learns that "an R.I.C. barracks at Ballyrum had been attacked and burnt out after a long defense. Two of the defenders were burnt inside it, the others shot coming out."[70] Immediately, Lois makes a direct personal correlation with the events when she confesses, "Do you know that while that was going on, eight miles off, I was [...] playing the gramophone?"[71] And while some critics have read moments like this as a kind of distant and removed reaction to the larger movements of political action around her, Bowen explains that Lois's seeming detachment is in fact "self-defense."[72] "Violence," Bowen writes, "was contained in [Lois's] sense of life, along with dance music."[73] Bowen pairs violence and dance music (played by the gramophone throughout the novel) as compatible and even parallel components of Lois's life. Therefore, when Lois equates the violence of the burning RIC barracks with her own action of listening to the gramophone, it serves as a signal of her own processing of that violence.

When we understand that Lois processes the violence of the war through the gramophone and gramophonic imagery, we can be on alert for further intrusions of the war into Lois's psyche. One of those moments of gramophonic imagery occurs one evening at Danielstown when Lois overhears Myra Naylor and Francie Montmorency discussing her relationship with Gerald. While the two women sit on the steps near Lois's bedroom, Francie begins a sentence that Lois does not want to hear finished. Francie says, "Because Lois is so very—."[74] Before she can finish the sentence, Lois violently uses sound as a distraction:

> [She] lifted her water jug and banged it down in the basin. [...] Later on, she noticed a crack in the basin, running between the sheaf and the cornucopia [...]. Every time, before the water clouded, she was to see the crack: every time she would wonder what Lois *was*. She would never know.[75]

Though Lois insists that she "would never know" what "Lois *was*," the crack still acts as a record of the event. The scars and fissures of gramophone records, easily described as cracks, are also records of trauma. In fact, Bowen draws attention to "cracks" at three highly tense moments in the novel: in this instance of Lois's panic at being defined, at the mill where Lois and Marda are shot at by an Irish rebel, and at the British army barracks, just moments after the gramophone dies. Each of these moments also has its own unique gramophonic signifiers in addition to the cracks. So, when Lois notices cracks throughout the rest of the novel, Bowen is alerting us to additional gramophonic imagery.

But what exactly does this crack in the basin record? Neil Corcoran posits that the crack is a physical representation of the hyphenated Anglo-Irish position in the armed conflict.[76] This makes sense, since the overheard discussion has to do with Lois's relationship to Gerald and the subliminal tensions of that relationship. Lois has a certain affection for Gerald, who is an English soldier. But she also has a cultural connection with and affection for the Irish, as demonstrated in her relationship with the Connors, a local laboring family.[77] Lois's split affection for Gerald and the Connors puts her squarely in the middle of the war raging around her. When she slams the water jug into the basin, she is violently resisting a definition of herself that would force her to identify too much with either the English or Irish half of her identity. The crack serves as a record of her desire to remain passive in her Anglo-Irish identity, her struggle to remain undefined. She uses aggression to remain passive during a war of identity. After all, the term "Anglo-Irish War"—as opposed to Irish War of Independence—suggests that this is in fact *her* war as an Anglo-Irish citizen, and this scene is her most overt engagement with the interiority of that conflict.

Lois's next war recording event is much more overtly violent and occurs when she and Marda encounter an Irish rebel at the run-down mill. Lois notices that "[c]racks ran down [the livid walls]" which signals the beginning of the recording event.[78] The rebel they find sleeping in the mill draws a pistol on the women. The narrative shifts away from the action, describing "a shot, making rings in the silence."[79] Bowen's decision to avoid depicting action fits her general narrative style, while staying close enough to the scene to hear the gunshot lays a heavy emphasis on

sound. The description of the shot also mimics the imagery of a gramophone record when the sound of the shot "makes rings in the silence."[80]
Just like the healed scars upon the silence of the avenue, like the crack in
the basin, left behind after Lois audibly makes her presence known, Bowen
describes the sound visually. This encounter with violence, complete with
an Edison-like physical trauma on Marda's hand as a result of the shot,
drives Lois to her resolution, "I must marry Gerald,"[81] suggesting that the
violence of the Irish in this scene perhaps inclines her toward the English
aspects of her identity.

Lois's next, and final, recording event finds her equally trapped in the
English camp. This occurs at the ball at the English barracks just before
the gramophone breaks, and it is an incomplete recording, as we shall see.
She has been sitting in the kitchen with Daventry when he starts to tell
her something: "About our young friend—[...] Tell me this—"[82] When
the gramophone falls, Daventry fails to communicate something to her.
And in the frenetic flurry of the following moments—her grief for the
gramophone, her distinct awareness of Daventry's shell-shocked mind,
and the whirl of people entering the kitchen—Lois notices cracks in the
barrack walls: "The cracks of the walls that had been straight a minute
ago like bars now seemed to bulge out visibly."[83] These cracks again seem
associated with recordings, since it is after Lois notices these cracks that
she begins her interior speculation about Daventry's meaning. She tries to
replicate Daventry's inflection of the aborted sentence (without success):
"*Our* young friend, our *young* friend, our young *friend*."[84] Without the
gramophone, Lois has become a broken record in more than one sense.
She is stuck on a loop, repeating the same phrase, but she is also incapable
of accurate representation of the original.

The death of the gramophone, in this instance, reveals how deeply
Lois relied on the machine as a prosthesis for processing violence and
the conflict around her. She becomes markedly withdrawn for the rest of
the novel. Days later, she cannot connect with Gerald during their final
conversation: a conversation filled with many similarly aborted sentences
(even more than usual) and oddly stressed words that seem to replicate
Lois's inability to find the right emphasis to make meaning out of Daventry's words. Shortly thereafter Gerald is shot and killed. When Daventry
comes to deliver the news to Lois, it is an oddly cool exchange. Daventry

seems to innately understand that Lois does not have the capacity to process the news through any particular emotional faculty; he has seen her grieve for the gramophone, after all. Lois cannot bring herself to talk to anyone else about Gerald's death after this exchange. She leaves Ireland less than a fortnight later, abandoning any attempt to confront the grief and violence of these events. She chooses to go to France—"for her French, you know"[85]—in what seems a Beckettian decision to leave behind Anglo-Irish identity even through language.

Lois's ultimate abandonment of her narrative of the war can be traced back to the death of the gramophone and her larger personal reliance on it. Perhaps it is because Lois is unable to tell her story during this last September of Anglo-Irish existence that we can understand the belated nature of the narrative structure. The novel emphasizes the pastness of the story even while we read it. Gerald is always already dead, and Danielstown is always already burned. Similarly, the Anglo-Irish are always already anachronistic and obsolete in the Irish Free State of the 1929 perspective from which Bowen wrote (and even before the events of the novel). Bowen's own perspective on the events of the novel reveals that *The Last September* might be her own belatedly assimilated trauma narrative from this particular war. In her preface she wrote, "I *was* the child of the house from which Danielstown derives. Bowen's Court survived—nevertheless, so often in my mind's eye did I see it burning that the terrible last event in *The Last September* is more real than anything I have lived through."[86] And Bowen's use of the gramophone as an object that Lois can at least mourn—unlike Danielstown, for she was "niece always, never child, of that house"[87]—also finds expression in the reality of the Big House burnings in Ireland in the tumultuous early 1920s. The gramophone draws attention to the violence of the war and Lois's solipsistic trauma narrative. She has witnessed guerrilla tactics, Irish violence, and English impotence, but she remains unable to voice these experiences. She doubts her ability to effectively replicate her experiences with absolute fidelity or in an assimilated, linear narrative. In this light, Lois's elegy for the gramophone seems entirely apt and maybe even entirely understated. The death of the gramophone, "one less gramophone in the world," is definitely not funny; it is the only object capable of playing Lois's trauma narrative of the Anglo-Irish War, and it is always already dead.

The Gramophone and Dead Silence in *Juno and the Paycock*

Bowen's use of the gramophone in *The Last September* is not the only literary instance related to the War of Independence. Molly Keane and J. G. Farrell both include gramophones in works based during this same period, and both write from the perspective of the Anglo-Irish Big House. Keane's *Mad Puppetstown* (1931) tells the story of Easter, Basil, and Evelyn as their idyllic youth in the Big House is disrupted when they unwittingly stumble across IRA soldiers in the woods near the estate. Prior to the escalating threat of violence, the three play in the drawing room while Basil rebuilds the gramophone he has previously dismantled. A song "twang[s] shakily on the air from the reconstructed gramophone" when they are joined by Patsy, a semi-reluctant informer for the IRA.[88] Shortly thereafter, Big Houses in the area become targets for burning. The teenagers venture into the woods and are only saved from a violent encounter with the IRA soldiers they come across when Patsy provides them with a pass-phrase that allows them to return home safely. They are then immediately sent to England, for fear of reprisal if the IRA soldiers believe the young people can identify them. Puppetstown is largely abandoned, except for an older aunt who stays as the sole resident, which is the only reason the estate is spared from burning. Six years later, when Basil and Easter return to Puppetstown, it is their gramophone that fills the Big House with echoes of the past: the gramophone's "dreadful tongue was never silent."[89] The youths never seem consciously to process the danger they were in, but the gramophone's recurrence in these crucial moments signals the tension underlying their memories in the Big House.

The gramophone in Farrell's *Troubles* (1970) has a more fleeting appearance, but it combines elements of Bowen's *Last September*, with a shell-shocked (but recovering) British ex-soldier repeatedly winding up a gramophone to prolong a dance. In a novel that "catches with appalling accuracy the brutal yet farcical nature of that war that was never quite a war," Major Archer bemusedly stays at the decaying Majestic Hotel even while the violence escalates beyond the gates.[90] Archer finds the gramophone and dancing with two young women a diversion from the festering unrest—"chang[ing] the needle and [winding] up the gramophone as quickly as he could, so that they would not stop"[91]—but the scene also includes a lecherous older man who watches the young women from the side, ensuring a constant sense of menace. By the end of the novel he has been buried by IRA soldiers up to his neck on a beach at rising tide and the Majestic is reduced to ash.

These connections between the gramophone and the realities of Big House burnings are not confined to fiction. In a moment that aptly combines Bowen's fears for the burning of Bowen's Court—fictionalized in *The Last September*—as well as the fear for Puppetstown and the fate of the Majestic Hotel, a headline in the *Irish Times* from February 17, 1923 read:

SIR BRYAN MAHON'S HOUSE BURNED
INCENDIARIES IN UNIFORM [...]
GRAMOPHONE ACCOMPANIES THE FLAME[92]

The house in Co. Kildare was raided by eight armed men disguised as National Army soldiers and Civic Guards; while it blazed, one of the raiders "took a gramophone from the house, placed it on the doorstep, and set it going to a lively tune."[93] The clash of Irish violence and destruction accompanied by an eerily irreverent gramophone plays out in a real scene to jarring effect. In this fire, taking place during the Civil War that swiftly followed the ceasefire after the War of Independence, the gramophone turns sinister.

Whereas the Big House novels largely bear witness to the fall of a privileged class, Sean O'Casey's works are more concerned with the struggling classes in the heart of Dublin, like the Boyles, and particularly Johnny Boyle, in *Juno and the Paycock*. O'Casey's play follows a family living in a tenement in Dublin during the Irish Civil War. Juno, the long-suffering wife of the drunken and unemployed "Captain" Boyle, tries to hold together her family, which includes her daughter Mary, who is on a union strike and caught between two suitors, and her son Johnny, whose Republican activities in the Rising of 1916, the Irish War of Independence, and the current Civil War have left him maimed. During a brief period of luck, the Boyles learn that the Captain has inherited a small fortune from a distant relative. Upon hearing the news, the family borrow extravagantly from neighbors and creditors to furnish their lodgings.

One of the first purchases they make in the early days of anticipatory wealth is a gramophone.[94] When Mary and Juno carry the gramophone into the lodgings, Juno draws attention to the object's capacity for violent action: "[T]his thing has me nearly kilt with the weight."[95] Moments later, the Captain points out that "what a gramophone wants is dead silence" in order to play its records.[96] And even when it plays those records, the gramophone is considered by Mary to be "destructive of real music."[97] After the introduction of the (violent) gramophone into the family, Johnny's psychological state becomes a primary undercurrent of the play.

Johnny's experiences of the gramophone find parallels with those of the English soldiers of World War I like Daventry and the patients shipped from the Front to the Richmond War Hospital, but his traumas are exclusively incurred by armed actions related to Irish nationalism. Similarly, Johnny and the Boyles have experiences with the machine that parallel Lois's interactions: moments that seem to be recording events that are nearly impossible to articulate. But again, the Boyles engage with the machine from a different political, social, and economic position than Lois. Whereas Lois's experiences of war are tempered by her attempts to distance herself from the violence of the conflict, and her account is considered (by herself as) obsolete due to her status as an anachronistic representative of the Anglo-Irish class, the Boyles' experiences are utterly violent in their compounded repetitions and in their haunting lack of resolution (the play ending "in a terrible state of chassis").[98]

The conspicuous entrance of the gramophone into the Boyles' home signals two simultaneous themes that persist throughout the rest of the play: the physical parallels between the violent machine and the scarred body of Johnny Boyle, and the psychological toll of perpetual war made manifest by gramophonic repetition (gramophony or abreaction) performed by Johnny, Mary, and Juno in particular. All this repetition seems to resonate as a form of abreaction for O'Casey as well, when parallels to his own Civil War experiences inevitably bleed through the telling of the Boyles' war.

O'Casey wastes no time in indicating that his play occurs at the geographical and chronological center of the Irish Civil War. The Boyles live in a tenement building filled with mothers mourning Stater (Pro-Treaty) and Diehard (Anti-Treaty) sons alike. The play commences with

Mary Boyle reading out an account of an IRA soldier's death from the newspaper: "On a little by-road, out beyant Finglas, he was found."[99] Johnny's commitment to the IRA is tested and found wanting when it becomes clear that he has betrayed a fellow officer and friend to his death. He is ultimately executed for his betrayal, becoming the second soldier's body in the play to be found and reported to the Boyles.

It was, in fact, the idea of the traumatized body of an IRA soldier that first inspired O'Casey's play. In his biography *Sean O'Casey: The Man I Knew* (1965), Gabriel Fallon points out that "[O'Casey] had been telling me for some time about a play he had mapped out, a play which would deal with the tragedy of a crippled I.R.A. man, one Johnny Boyle. He mentioned this play many times and always as the tragedy of Johnny."[100] Fallon's recollection clearly places the physically maimed body at the center of the play's conception. And that body has a visual impact in the first act. Mary and Johnny are both present on the stage when the play begins, but Johnny is hunched over the fire while his sister reads about the dead soldier on Finglas road. It is only after the first few minutes of dialogue between Mary and Juno that he stands, and the audience see his entire body:

> [H]e is a thin, delicate fellow, something younger than Mary. He has evidently gone through a rough time. His face is pale and drawn; there is a tremulous look of indefinite fear in his eyes. The left sleeve of his coat is empty, and his walks with a slight halt.[101]

Immediately after Johnny's appearance, Juno's dialogue explains her son's physical traumas: "The bullet he got in the hip in Easter Week was bad enough; but the bomb that shatthered his arm in the fight in O'Connell Street put the finishin' touch on him."[102] And now that he's "goin agen the Free State," Johnny's political position as a Diehard in the current struggle is made clear.[103]

This young man—younger than his 22-year-old sister Mary—has been involved in armed conflict in Dublin for the past six years, taking a bullet during the 1916 Rising as a 14- or 15-year-old boy (his mother describes him as a "only a chiselur of a Boy Scout" during the Easter Week).[104] His physical body also documents the violent division between the Pro- and

Anti-Treaty forces after the War of Independence; the "fight in O'Connell Street" refers to the Battle of Dublin (June 28 to July 5, 1922)—generally considered the first battle of the Civil War—when the Four Courts building was bombed and, later that week, bombs were set off again by the Free State forces against the Diehards holed up in a block of buildings near the head of Parnell Street. Johnny's implied presence in the battle that started the Civil War suggests his prolonged embattlement in the Irish nationalist cause. Even though both of these conflicts (the Rising and the Battle of Dublin) were known to have a high number of civilian casualties, Johnny erases our doubts as to whether his presence in both cases was deliberate or the bad luck of a bystander: "I'd do it agen, ma, I'd do it agen; for a principles a principle."[105] Unlike the initially unwitting Donal Davoren of O'Casey's *The Shadow of a Gunman* (1923), who allows others to believe he is an IRA gunman on the run and consequently embroils those around him in the violence of the War of Independence, Johnny's engagement in the skirmishes of this period is the result of his conscious and "principled" participation as an IRA soldier.

Johnny's scars are the literal manifestations of recorded violent traumas; the scars/grooves on a record equate to the scars on his body. And Johnny's traumas are physical mnemonics for Ireland's cultural scars. His arm and hip are testaments of war that his family and neighbors comment on. They seem to largely overlook his concomitant psychological trauma. Johnny's physical descriptions, however, are often combined with reminders of his psychological state; his "tremulous look of indefinite fear," for instance, makes it clear that the mental strain of the Civil War is present and ongoing.[106]

Perhaps as a result of his psychological trauma, Johnny has developed a linguistic habit of repetition. When Juno asks Johnny what he thinks of the family's new gramophone, his initial response is "['t]isn't gramophones I'm thinking of," but then he begins to respond to all her subsequent inquiries in triplicate (like a skipping gramophone).[107] When she asks what he *is* thinking of, he responds, "Nothin', nothin', nothin'."[108] When she suggests he needs rest he declares, "I can rest nowhere, nowhere, nowhere." And when she pushes the issue further he cries out, "Let me alone, let me alone, let me alone, for God's sake!"[109] In other scenes, Johnny also has a tendency to repeat the list of his injuries, "Haven't I done enough for

Ireland? I've lost me arm, an' me hip's desthroyed so that I'll never be able to walk right agen! Good God, haven't I done enough for Ireland?"[110] His recitations take on the tone of a shock patient's abreactions in an attempt to assimilate the psychological trauma of violence and war.

Johnny certainly shares the symptoms of the shock patients treated at Dublin's Richmond Asylum in the month following the Rising, as well as symptoms of shell-shock as diagnosed by the War Hospital under the same aegis. Johnny's sullen moodiness corresponds with the "melancholia" of the first shock patient admitted to the Richmond after the Rising; the "tremulous look of indefinite fear in his eyes" matches the "terror" of another patient; and his vivid imaginings of the appearance of ghosts, the reliving of the tearing pain of bullets, and his obsession with the lighted candles on the altar in his room mirror the "mania secondary to shock" of yet another Richmond patient.[111] Additionally, Johnny mentions that the sounds of an upstairs neighbor are "like thunderclaps in my brain,"[112] which was a primary indicator of shell-shock in soldiers, who had inexplicable intense head pains and sensitivity to sound. Johnny's psychological state is a recognizable replication of Ireland's definition of shock as a result of nationalist conflict; as such, it is perhaps not surprising that his mental state is underscored in his interactions with the gramophone.

A strong undercurrent of death accompanies the gramophone in this play, which again highlights Johnny's war-torn psychological state. Several times, Captain Boyle insists that the gramophone requires "dead silence" before it can be played, and shortly after his first pronouncement to that effect, Charlie Bentham places technology and the dead together in his discussion of theosophy. Juno abruptly asks, "You don't believe in ghosts, Mr. Bentham?"[113] Bentham responds by positing that technology and science may account for some people's sensitivity to ghosts:

Scientists are beginning to think what we call ghosts are sometimes seen by persons of a certain nature. They say that sensational actions, such as the killing of a person, demand such great energy, and that energy lingers in the place where the action occurred. People may live in the place and see nothing, when someone may come along whose personality has some peculiar connection with the energy of the place, and, in a flash, the person sees the whole affair.[114]

Bentham's description of lingering ghosts after a "sensational" or traumatic event may seem supernatural, but the gramophone can be viewed in a similar light, as discussed in Chapter 1. Just as, according to Bentham, a place may have lingering energy that is unintelligible without the right apparatus or sensitivity, the gramophone is similarly embedded with the ghost of sound, "a delicately scribbled, utterly illegible writing," from the violence of recording.[115] Johnny's proximity to the gramophone at this moment, and his shocked reaction to Bentham's proposal of the reality of haunting apparitions, suggests another reinforced connection between ghosts and gramophones.

Johnny reacts with horror at this description of ghosts—"Is there nothin' betther to be talkin' about but the killin' o' people? My God, isn't it bad enough for these things to happen without talkin' about them!"— and, after leaving the room, he immediately rushes in again, screaming of Tancred's ghost that only he can see:

I seen him ... I seen Robbie Tancred kneelin' down before the statue ... an' the red light shinin' on him ... an' when I went in ... he turned an' looked at me ... an' I seen the woun's bleedin' in his breast ... Oh, why did he look at me like that? ... it wasn't my fault that he was done in ... Mother o' God, keep him away from me![116]

What the rest of the Boyles do not know at this point, and what we are piecing together, is that Johnny betrayed Tancred to his death, and that the dead IRA man almost literally haunts Johnny already. He relives his guilt repeatedly (through his triplicate recitations, for instance), wearing himself down at the same time. The descriptions of Johnny, apart from those that dwell on his maimed body, point out that he is often pale, affected, and frightened. He glides in and out of the main room of the family's lodgings, and, as Susan Harris points out, "[M]any of Johnny's lines are cries of pain in one form or another and he seems to respond somatically to intangible stimuli."[117] He is practically a ghost in his own right.

As it turns out, Robbie Tancred's death is made relevant through Johnny's haunted and traumatized body. Harris suggests that "Johnny functions primarily as a way of making that violence accessible by embodying its consequences."[118] The audience must confront a sensation-alized and palpable performance of suffering in order to be jolted out of complacency about violence during this turbulent era. As a result, John-ny's physically and psychologically maimed body has more impact than the forensic newspaper description of Tancred's body that Mary reads out somewhat dispassionately: "[S]even wounds he had—one entherin' the neck, with an exit wound beneath the left shoulderblade; another in the left breast penethratin' the heart and, an'..."[119] Not even Mrs. Tancred's maternal description—"he was lyin' for a whole night stretched out on the side of a lonely counthry lane, with his head, his darlin' head, that I often kissed and fondled, half hidden in the wather of a runnin' brook"[120]—can move audiences as clearly as Johnny's pain and fear throughout the play.

Furthermore, Johnny's haunted vision of Tancred bears a potential connection to some of O'Casey's own lingering experiences during this violent period. O'Casey told his friend Joseph Holloway of one particular instance of violence that sounds similar to the fictional Robbie Tancred's experience:

> [O'Casey] knew of a young fellow, a member of the I.R.A., who was on the run, being taken in the middle of the night by the C.I.D. men and brought out towards Finglas and brutally beaten with the butt end of their revolvers, and then told to run for his life while they fired revolver shots after him, taking bits off his ears, etc., and catching up on him again renewing their beating.[121]

Christopher Murray asserts that this particular IRA man's experience "was the germ of *Juno and the Paycock*,"[122] which opens with the news-paper report of Tancred being found "out beyant Finglas" and Juno's later account that he was "found, e'er yestherday, lyin' out beyant Finglas riddled with bullets, be all accounts."[123] Murray's assertion initially seems to go against the grain of Gabriel Fallon's avowal that it was *Johnny's* body that was the central focus for *Juno and the Paycock*. But it is Johnny's body that makes Tancred's all the more accessible and gives life to O'Casey's own account of violence for an otherwise potentially jaded contemporary audience.

For instance, just before the Boyles are about to turn on the gramophone, Mrs. Tancred visits the lodgings, after which the Boyles and their guests spend a short time listing all of the casualties of war in their own tenement building:

> Hasn't the whole house, nearly, been massacred? There's young Dougherty's husband with his leg off; Mrs. Travers that had her son blew up be a mine in Inchegeela, in County Cork; Mrs. Mannin' that lost wan of her sons in an ambush a few weeks ago, an' now poor Mrs. Tancred's only child [...].[124]

Tancred's death has been so far removed from their thoughts that Juno admits to "forgettin' about him being brought to the church tonight" and counts it as luck that she and her guests hadn't already set the gramophone playing.[125]

Perhaps it is to be expected that after an intensely emotional encounter with Mrs. Tancred, it is Johnny who ultimately calls for the gramophone to be played; it is a way to try to escape the realities of the war, as Daventry and Lois demonstrated. Before the machine plays, the Captain reminds the room once more that what a gramophone wants is "dead silence."[126] He unwittingly stresses the particular violence of gramophonic functions, since, in the final moments of the second act, the gramophone and Tancred's funeral struggle for prominence. The song "If You're Irish Come into the Parlor" blares out for less than a minute before the Boyles' neighbor Nugent bursts in and shouts above the noise, "Are yous goin' to have that thing bawlin' an' the funeral of Mrs. Tancred's son passin' the house? Have none of yous any respect for the Irish people's National regard for the dead?"[127] The "dead silence" Boyle calls for is pierced by the gramophone, but more overtly by the reminder of the dead IRA soldier passing by the window. O'Casey forges a connection between the gramophone and violence through the proximity of these parallel events.

When Nugent interrupts the gramophone, demanding respect for the dead, Juno counters with, "Maybe [...] it's nearly time we had a little less respect for the dead, an' a little more regard for the livin.'"[128] This moment forces an examination of the disparity between the "dead silence" and the "regard for the living" that seems to plague O'Casey's depictions of Johnny. When the evening is interrupted by the "darlin' funeral,"[129] the Boyles and their guests all leave the room to get a better view of the spectacle. All except Johnny, that is. He and the gramophone sit alone in the room.

Though Johnny does not touch the gramophone, the ghost of the jarringly jaunty tune played on the machine, "If You're Irish Come into the Parlor," still hangs in the air, and the recently voiced object reminds us of its function as a recording and replaying device. This song is exclusionary in its invitation and implies that only the truly Irish have a place in the tenement. But during the Civil War, Irishness is particularly difficult to define. Johnny's own turmoil is, in some respects, based on his inability to determine his loyalties (is he still a Diehard after he has betrayed a man to the Staters?) and therefore his Irish identity. The invitation into the parlor might also extend to the dead Irish soldiers of these conflicts, since that is where they would have been displayed before their burials. Tancred's passing funeral makes this particularly tangible.

As a result, the final few moments of the second act are implicitly imbued with the gramophone's physical presence and its role as a ghostly observer, but also as a recorder. And the silent object is the only witness to the exchange between the Mobiliser and Johnny, when the latter is exhorted to attend an IRA meeting to give information about Tancred's death. The gramophone's presence at this poignant, chilling moment between Johnny and the IRA's representative forces us to recognize that we are witnessing a traumatic recording (like Bentham's concept of embedded trauma, and Lois's encounters with violence). This recording is also the ghost of things to come. While the body of the bullet-ridden Tancred passes in the street, Johnny tells the Mobiliser he won't attend, saying "I won't go! Haven't I done enough for Ireland! I've lost me arm, an' me hip's desthroyed so that I'll never be able to walk right agen! Good God, haven't I done enough for Ireland?"[130] As the young IRA man leaves, he tells Johnny, "no man can do enough for Ireland!",[131] and Johnny is again alone with the gramophone. His gramophonic repetition of his physical traumas hangs in the air as the funeral crowd in the distance begins to pray: "Hail, Mary, full of grace, the Lord is with Thee."[132] The scene ends with Johnny and the gramophone again sitting alone in the apartment while the lights fade and the portentous violence swirling around his world, manifested in his wrecked body and unsettled mind, imprints itself on our consciousness.

The final act of the play is filled with echoes and distorted resonances of what has occurred since the gramophone was introduced into the Boyles' home. The gramophone, carried in by Juno and Mary as a signifier of wealth, is removed by Mrs. Madigan as a signifier of a debt unpaid. The Boyles' fortunes and prospects are all in reversal. And the scene with the Mobiliser is repeated, but with much greater force. Two armed Irregulars come to claim Johnny's body as forfeit in the case of Tancred's betrayal and death:

> SECOND IRREGULAR. Poor Tancred was an oul' comrade o'
>   yours but you didn't think o' that when you gave
>   him away to the gang that sent him to his grave.
>   […] Have you your beads?
> JOHNNY.   Me beads! Why do you ass me that, why do
>   you ass me that? […] Are yous going' to do in a
>   comrade?—look at me arm, I lost it for Ireland.
> SECOND IRREGULAR. Commandant Tancred lost his life for
>   Ireland.[133]

The repetitions and echoes of Johnny's earlier speeches are nearly impossible to miss, even as the grim reality of his fate sets in.

In an important moment of gramophony, this scene is also an abreactive repetition of one of O'Casey's personal experiences of war. In his autobiography, *Inishfallen, Fare Thee Well*, O'Casey describes a young and frightened IRA man who was tracked down by three Free State officers, one of whom was a former friend of the IRA man. This encounter, as O'Casey describes it, mirrors the text for Johnny's final moments:

> —I'm an old comrade of yours, Mick, the young man pleaded.
> —Sure I know that well, said the Colonel heartily, and I'll say this much—for the sake of oul' times, we won't let you suffer long.

—Jesus! Whimpered the half-dead lad, yous wouldn't shoot an old comrade, Mick!

The Colonel's arm holding the gun shot forward suddenly, the muzzle of the gun, tilted slightly upwards, splitting the lad's lips and crashing through his chattering teeth.

—Be Jasus! We would, he said, and then he pulled the trigger.[134]

Johnny's final scene on stage when he pleads for mercy demonstrates so many verbal parallels to this graphic death that it is clearly an echo of O'Casey's memories. And in this moment, we also realize that when Fallon suggested that Johnny's body was always the center of the play, it was likely a form of abreactive gramophony for O'Casey as much as for Irish culture. The scene is all too familiar. Johnny echoes the young man's rhetoric, crying "I'm an oul' comrade—yous wouldn't shoot an oul' comrade."[135] And though we never see or hear the gunshots that kill Johnny, we are assured of the results of this encounter when we later hear secondhand reports from the police and the doctor who recognizes Johnny's arm injury. These reports are the unspoken "Be Jasus, we would" to Johnny's questions about his fate. The ghostly echoes remind us that Johnny's body has been the central traumatic focus of the play, and that the impact of trauma is largely felt through repetition.

The rest of the play is echoes. We hear Johnny repeat his rote account of what he's lost for Ireland. When he realizes he is a dead man, he sobs out, "Hail, Mary, full o' grace … the Lord is … with Thee…" and the curtain falls,[136] reminding us of the prayers said for the dead Tancred. The echoes continue when we hear a second report of an IRA soldier's body: "Some poor fella's been found."[137] Another mother mourns for her son: Juno cries out, "It's my turn to say it now: […] Mother o' God, Mother o' God, have pity on us all!"[138] Juno and Mary have even caught Johnny's abreactive habit of repetition: Mary cries out "Oh, it's thrue, it's thrue […]—there isn't a God, there isn't a God!" while Juno exclaims, "Blessed Virgin, where were you when me darlin' son was riddled with bullets, when me darlin' son was riddled with bullets?"[139] The gramophonic imagery spins slower; the play winds down until we hear—much like the drooping whirr of a wind-up gramophone on its last rotations—another disconnected and dissonant account of Boyle's philosophy: "th'whole worl's … in a terr …

ible state o' ... chassis!"[140] The play fades away, reminding us that what a gramophone wants is dead silence.

The final moments of the play, with their gramophonic echoes of Ireland's cultural violence and trauma brought home (both literally and figuratively) to the Boyles, denotes the pervasive and inescapable trauma culture of a nation perpetually at war. The gramophone's intrusion into the home, temporary though it is, brings to the foreground its relevance to the war-torn country. It shows itself capable of a violent, murderous action—having Juno "nearly kilt" by its mere "destructive" presence and establishing its "want" for "dead silence." The machine, like Johnny, bears scars as a testament to the violence it has endured—the record and needle serving as constant reminders of trauma's scars, which are bound to find expression through repetition, like Johnny's perpetual refrains. Those gramophonic scars are manifest in Johnny's own psychological perceptions of Tancred's haunting presence throughout the play. In the final scene, Juno, Mary, and Boyle are all transformed into traumatized gramophonic echoes. The Boyles subside into a silence that fills the stage. The "dead silence" that the gramophone demands is filled with the ghosts of the Diehards and Staters, those who have died for Ireland, willingly or not. In that moment, the silent gramophone embodies Ireland's dead and its stunned and traumatized living.

Conclusion

The gramophone's connections to war in a global context become much more nationally based with the armed conflicts in Ireland. The traumas of the British soldiers of World War I, though tangible and present in Ireland, as represented particularly by Daventry, are distant and removed from the Irish nationalist struggle. Irish national cultural traumas of this era, beginning with the Easter Rising, denote a distinct difference between the Western Front's shell-shock and the national shock of home-based conflict. Lois sees herself as associated with the gramophone in her struggle for Anglo-Irish identity. Johnny sees himself as a gramophonic object whose scars, when replayed, give voice to his own psychological and physical engagement with Ireland's nationalist struggles. The gramophones in both *The Last September* and *Juno and the Paycock* point to traumas experienced by Irish citizens during a period of intense national violence. Both gramophones exit before the finales, but their echoes are felt up until the final moments and resonate beyond the texts. The resonances of these two conflicts—their deeply embedded traumas not only for the protagonists of the stories, but for the peripheral characters and their perception of Ireland—fade into the "dead silence" where ghosts and scars of war can speak. And in the post-war decades that followed the conflicts of the Irish revolutionary period, the consequences of events such as these continued to echo in depictions of jarring, blaring gramophones.

CHAPTER FOUR

Gramophonic Strain
Residual Tension in Post-War Literature

By the 1920s the gramophone had hit its commercial stride in Ireland and was a ubiquitous part of daily life for the post-war generation. In the July 24, 1923 edition of the *Irish Times*, an article on gramophone maintenance makes the assumption that "every home possesses a gramophone of sorts."[1] The article serves as a reminder of the mechanics of gramophones and how to get the best playback results. Along with advice to store records flat to avoid buckling and to remove dust from both needle and record before playing to avoid impairing the playback quality, the article also reminds readers not to "wind the machine to its full extent at any time" and to "[n]ever leave the spring wound" for long periods.[2] To do so strains the motor and could ultimately result in a weakened, fractured, or even broken mainspring. The fracturing of a mainspring would release its coiled potential energy in a sudden and violent outburst that could destroy the larger mechanism of the gramophone motor. This release could be so violent that enthusiastic gramophonists were actively discouraged from trying to fix issues related to the mainspring; the sudden release of tensile pressure could result in terrible lacerations for the would-be repairer.

The article's cautious strictures about the consequences of an overly strained gramophone mainspring were timely, not only because of the popularity of the machine but also because of the article's potential to be read as allegorical in a larger, less obvious cultural context. Only two months prior to the article's publication, the Civil War had officially ended, concluding what amounted to nearly a decade of armed conflict in what was now the Irish Free State. But an official political peace did not automatically resolve the tensions that had propelled the conflicts. For instance, the Free State's borders were still in a certain amount of flux (the Boundary Commission had yet to be formed to determine the border with Northern Ireland); the Indemnity Act that restricted the pursuit of "legal proceedings in respect of certain acts and matters done during the suppression of the state of armed rebellion" during the Civil War[3] was days away from being enacted; and there were still reports coming in from across the country of post-ceasefire violence and executions. The same newspaper issue that discussed gramophone maintenance also had an article on "Irish Questions in Parliament" in which questions of amnesty, damages, and the constitutional status of citizenship in the Free State were still under discussion.[4]

All this points to a culture of psychological strain and trauma that had wound up the larger Irish populace for an extended period and in which post-war tensions were still very palpable. In this light, the article's warning about the consequences of prolonged tension extends beyond the gramophone and into the post-war culture of Ireland. Whereas the previous chapter discussed the gramophone's connections to war *during* the violence of conflict, this chapter points to the strain left behind *after* those encounters had been formally resolved. In the literature written after the ceasefire of the Civil War, gramophones act in ways that force a focus on the residual tension left in the spring motor of the cultural collective.

To fully appreciate the advice in the *Irish Times* article, more familiarity with and context for the gramophone's motor might be in order. The power source of the gramophone motor (dating from the mid-1890s) was the mainspring, an adaptation of the horological or clockwork mechanism. Instead of a minuscule spring residing in a wound pocket watch, however, the gramophone's mainspring was created on a larger scale and housed in the machine's motor. The mainspring is a spiraled ribbon of tempered steel as represented in Figure 4.1. Inside the gramophone, the exterior extremity of the spring, or pin joint (A), is attached to a fixed point in the motor while the arbor or axle (B) is attached to the center of the spiral. The arbor is wound up with the machine's crank mechanism.

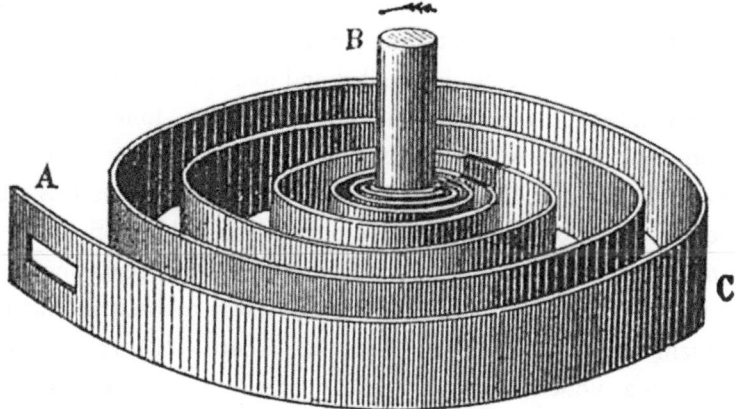

Figure 4.1. Mainspring mechanism. Illustration by Dionysius Lardner,
Common Things Explained (London: Walton and Maberly, 1855), 23.

The spring then uncurls itself to recover its original shape while rotating
the arbor. The motor (and thereby, the turntable) of the gramophone is
propelled by a mechanically regulated release of the coiled tension in the
mainspring.

The mainspring stores a great deal of potential energy, even while at
rest. Les Pook explains that even during manufacturing, "material near the
surfaces [of the mainspring ribbon] is stressed beyond the elastic limit."[5]
So even in its relaxed state inside the gramophone motor, there is always
residual stress on the coil's inner and outer surfaces. The end result of
this perpetual stress, over time, is the breakdown of the mainspring. The

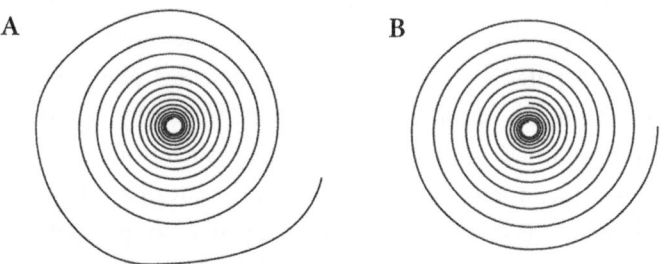

Figure 4.2. Representations of (A) a "tired" mainspring and
(B) "fatigue failure" in a mainspring.

mainspring might become "tired," meaning that it can no longer maintain its initial tight coil and loses torque force; this usually occurs when the outer coils closest to the pin joint relax and lose their tensile dynamism (see Figure 4.2A). Or the spring might crack near the inner coils closest to the arbor where the tensile stress is greatest. The initial fracture might cause a slight jump in the spring tension. In a gramophone this would manifest in a temporary stall in the motor or cause the machine to stop working until wound up and caught on the mechanical gears once more. These fractures, however, almost always give way to what is called full fatigue failure or breakage in the coils (see Figure 4.2B). Fatigue failure can result in a sudden and violent release of the spring's coiled potential energy and, in extreme cases, can destroy the gramophone on a larger scale.[6]

The gramophones of Irish literature, post-Civil War, have a tendency to manifest a certain anxiety about the spring-powered motor, seemingly enacting the residual psychological stress in the cultural psyche of the era and belying the official post-war peace. The gramophone maintenance article essentially predicts the neuroses of literary gramophones over the following two decades. The delicate stability of the mainspring's potential energies expresses the larger cultural struggle to cope with the stressed tensile opposition of the official peace and the internal discontent of post-war culture.

A relatively quick (and by no means exhaustive) survey of Irish literature written or set between the ceasefire and the end of the 1930s produces over twenty-five texts that include gramophones functioning beyond their traditional instrumental uses and exhibiting neuroses (see Table 4.1). While an in-depth exploration of each would be ideal, it would also be prohibitively lengthy, so instead I have selected two representative texts for detailed analysis. The first is the short play *Portrait* (1925) by Lennox Robinson, set in 1925 Dublin and meant by its author to be a "portrait of the times" in post-war Ireland;[7] as such it depicts the difficult psychological adjustment of shifting out of a decade of armed conflict. The gramophone accompanies a shockingly violent act of passivity by a character who cannot seem to reconcile the violence of the previous decade with the supposed peace of daily Dublin life. The second is the novel *At Swim-Two-Birds* (1939) by Flann O'Brien, which represents generational

Table 4.1. Works published or set between the Civil War ceasefire and the end of the 1930s that feature gramophones

Text	Author	Genre	Publication date
Portrait	Lennox Robinson	Play	1925
The Knight of Cheerful Countenance	Molly Keane	Novel	1926
Taking Chances	Molly Keane	Novel	1929
Ever the Twain	Lennox Robinson	Play	1929
"Her Table Spread"	Elizabeth Bowen	Short Story	1930
The States through Irish Eyes	Edith Somerville	Novel	1930
Friends and Relations	Elizabeth Bowen	Novel	1931
To the North	Elizabeth Bowen	Novel	1932
Conversation Piece	Molly Keane	Novel	1932
Dream of Fair to Middling Women	Samuel Beckett	Novel	1932
Church Street	Lennox Robinson	Play	1934
Devoted Ladies	Molly Keane	Novel	1934
The End of the Beginning	Sean O'Casey	Play	1934
Eclogue for Christmas	Louis MacNeice	Poetry	1934
Storm Song	Denis Johnston	Play	1935
Killycreggs in Twilight (Bird's Nest)	Lennox Robinson	Play	1937
The Rising Tide	Molly Keane	Novel	1937
"More Pricks than Kicks"	Samuel Beckett	Short Story	1937
The Death of the Heart	Elizabeth Bowen	Novel	1938
At Swim-Two-Birds	Flann O'Brien	Novel	1939
Leinster, Munster and Connaught	Frank O'Connor	Memoir	1950
Black List, Section H	Francis Stuart	Memoir	1971
Farewell Companions	James Plunkett	Novel	1977
Dancing at Lughnasa	Brian Friel	Play	1990
Nightlines	Neil Jordan	Novel	1994
"Five Entries from a Fictional Diary"	Angela Power	Short Story	2011
Jimmy's Hall	Paul Laverty	Screenplay	2014
"The Boy Who Swapped a Bog for a Gramophone"	Moya Cannon	Poem	2019

tension between a student and his uncle. In the text, the gramophone is overtly linked to war by the protagonist's uncle, but the unnamed student protagonist sees the gramophone as antiquated and sees violence as more academic and literary than tangible.

All of the texts set in this period, and specifically *Portrait* and *At Swim-Two-Birds*, focus on gramophonic tension as a manifestation of cultural unease—a culture that no longer struggles against an oppressive colonial force, but, rather, struggles with the competing values left behind in its absence. What does it mean to be the Irish Free State? What happens when there is no longer an overt force to push against to assert nationalism? What happens when gaps between a revolutionary generation and a post-revolutionary generation highlight these tensions? In gramophonic terms, the answers essentially come down to matters of torque and tensile strength.

Fatigue Fractures

Lennox Robinson's *Portrait*, "a play in two sittings," was first performed at the Abbey Theatre on March 31, 1925. *Portrait* was considered to be a play that "captured something of the attitude of the post-war generation," represented by the four young characters: Peter, his fiancée Maggie, his brother Charlie, and Tom, their new acquaintance. Over the course of the play, they discuss the spirit of the age, Tom explains his philosophy of always toting a gun, Maggie breaks her engagement in light of her confessed attraction to Tom, and Peter commits suicide with Tom's gun. These events are accompanied by Charlie's inconsistent gramophone: a machine that breaks and re-breaks due to a malfunction with its spring-based motor and blares in stops and starts in order to draw our attention to the very real physical strain on the machine.

On opening night, the play and its dramatic final scene were met with great approval. According to a review in the *Irish Times*, "The author was loudly called for and cheered at the end of the play."[8] But while the first-night audience of *Portrait* "strongly applauded the rather bizarre ending," Robert Hogan and Richard Burnham write, "the critics had many reservations."[9] Andrew Malone from the *Dublin Magazine* pointed out:

It is a portrait of our time in two sittings, and, of course, a finished portrait could not be expected in such a hurry. [...] However, Mr. Robinson does succeed in sketching in black and white the main features, and the sketch suggests that its features are blurred and indistinct.[10]

The most "blurred and indistinct" aspect of the play, according to Malone, was the finale, which he described as "the crudest of melodrama."[11] He went on to write, "The theories of Freud and the practices of D.W. Griffith have gone to [*Portrait's*] making, and the interest of the resultant play depends largely upon the proportions, and the way in which they are mixed."[12] Malone's allusion to Freud and the psychological nature of the play were picked up by other reviewers, like H.N.K. from the *Manchester Guardian* who wrote, "Perhaps it is old-fashioned, but Dublin still prefers *The Whiteheaded Boy* [an early comedy] of Lennox Robinson to his essay in psychoanalysis."[13] And while other reviewers similarly took pains to identify the play as a type of "essay in psychoanalysis," almost none bothered to identify what the psychoanalysis revealed.

Susan Mitchell from the *Irish Statesman* provided one of the most in-depth contemporary analyses of the play and also attempted to understand its larger psychology. "To me," she wrote, "it seems that *Portrait* is the strongest of Mr. Lennox Robinson's plays. The very narrowness of this stage seems to deepen the emotion pressed into it, and how admirably it was played."[14] She continues:

When one thinks over it, the suicide in which the play culminates is an amazing development, but as the drama evolves under our eyes, we are amazed at nothing. Everything is natural; in order. Peter finds no reassurance in himself; no answer to any of his questions. He steps back from the scene of life as he stepped back from [a] swarming tram.[15]

And while Mitchell admires the "natural" progression of events that culminates in Peter's suicide, she does pause to puzzle over the gramophone's role in the climactic final moments:

The extraordinary invention of Maggie's dance with the dying
man, designed to prevent his mother seeing the tragedy, as,
aroused by the shot, she peers into the room, with its horrible
accompaniment on the gramophone, "For to-night we'll merry,
merry be," gives the play the crowning touch of the fantastic. *I
cannot understand why Maggie, as she leaves the room where the
dead man is stretched on the floor, turns on the gramophone.*[16]

Mitchell's confusion about the gramophone's role in the final moments of
the play is perhaps understandable. The finale is admittedly rushed and
intensely dramatic (or melodramatic, if one adopts Malone's perspective).
But Robinson's use of the gramophone *throughout* the second act makes
the machine's physical and aural presence inescapable.

The gramophone is almost literally the beginning and end of the
play's second act. The first words are from Charlie when he bursts out
"Damn the thing!" in reference to his temperamental machine.[17] And the
play ends with the stage directions, "*The gramophone declares that to-night
we'll merry, merry be...*"[18] The gramophone is also the object that brings
together the main characters on this climactic evening, since Maggie has
come to hear Charlie's new records. By tracing the gramophone's presence
throughout the act, an answer emerges to Mitchell's question; in *Portrait*,
the gramophone breaks and re-breaks, blaring in stops and starts in order
to draw our attention to the strain of a post-war culture, the psychological
toll on the characters in the wake of long-standing violence.

Portrait points to the residual psychological wear *after* overt physical
traumas have passed. We are now witnessing the wearing down of the
components that propel the mechanism. And Robinson was attuned to
the gramophone's evolving cultural mnemonics for trauma. He was clearly
fascinated with the machine during this period. In his capacity as manager
of the Abbey, he facilitated "gramophone recitals" at the theater, like the
one held on December 9, 1924, in which recordings of popular singers were
played for a full house while a gramophone agent provided clarification on
the gramophone's functions and variations in recordings.[19] Robinson also
used the gramophone in at least five of his plays in the 1920s and 1930s.[20]
His particular attention to gramophonic detail in *Portrait* implies a deep
interest in representing the mechanics of the machine in a play with deep

psychological impact for its contemporary audience. And when Robinson uses the gramophone to represent a culture under tensile stress, he not only capitalizes on his mechanical knowledge of the machine, but builds upon previously established analogies between the gramophone and the mind, adding nuance to the machine's capacity to represent the human psyche.

By frequently drawing attention to the wear on the gramophone's spring, Robinson creates a "portrait" of the traumatized mind. He does not overtly venture into discussions of shell-shock in *Portrait*, but Peter and Tom both show a keen awareness of previous violence and display different manifestations of residual stress and trauma in this new peace. Tom remains constantly armed and Peter becomes unstable, committing unexpected violence. So, when Robinson adopts the established gramophone and human mind parallel, he enhances this metaphor by representing the potential for breakage that a mind manifests *after* sustained stress, violence, and trauma. The gramophone's playback abilities are directly impacted by the stressed mainspring. The music is frequently interrupted, not allowed to flow seamlessly to a natural conclusion at any point during the action of the play. Instead, the mechanism malfunctions, wears out, threatens to fracture. It is voicing its own narrative of tensile limits.

The machine's evolving cultural connection to war, as discussed in Chapter 3, and Robinson's adaptation thereof, make *Portrait* a significant development in depictions of post-war mnemonics. In the play, the gramophone's stops and starts signal that its "flow within the circuits of production and distribution, consumption and exhibition, has been arrested, however momentarily," and therefore, in this scene of perpetual gramophonic disruption, "[t]he story of [the] object asserting [itself] as [a] thing, then, is the story of a changed relation to the human subject and thus the story of how the thing really names less an object than a particular subject–object relation."[21] In the case of Robinson's play, the subject–object relation being named by the gramophone is that between Tom, Peter, and the machine, but more broadly, between post-war Ireland and the gramophone.

Robinson's play takes as its material the spirit of the age, understood by Mary, Maggie's sister, as an age of "harder stone and harder iron,"[22] and forces audiences to confront what that age might cost when Peter takes

his life. The play, set less than two years after the ceasefire of the Civil
War, comes at a developmental and therefore defining period for both
Irish national and cultural identity in the newly minted Free State. Mary
describes the age as follows:

> We're in the iron age—or it is the stone age?—action, strength,
> brute force. It began with the suffragettes, bless them, smashing
> their way through franchise. Then the war—bless it—carried on
> that spirit. The mollycoddles thought it would die as the remem-
> brance of the war faded; it might have died if the remembrance of
> the war hadn't faded but thank goodness society is getting every
> year harder stone and harder iron.[23]

Her description of the age as hard as stone and iron seems apt from the
perspective of someone who has endured a decade of war.[24] And yet it
raises the question of what is driving society to become harder every year
if Ireland is no longer enacting the militant nationalist ideals of "action,
strength, and brute force"? The Irish Free State was seen as provisional,
essentially a placeholder until the underlying issues that brought on the
Civil War were more substantially resolved. Bill Kissane describes this
early period as one in which a "common national identity existed but
intense competition over its ethos and telos continued."[25] And because of
this perpetual competition—a debate exemplified by *Portrait*'s discussion
of Ireland's new "iron age—or it is the stone age?"[26]—the tension of the
previous war-fraught era was never fully dismantled.

It is this tension between peace and "action, strength, and brute force"
that drives the "portrait of our times." In 1922 Norreys Jephson O'Conor
wrote in the *Sewanee Review* that "[n]o Irish writer more faithfully interprets this time" than Robinson;[27] in that same vein and seventy-five years
later, Kurt Eisen wrote that "Robinson had a keen sense of what kind of
plays and which themes were worth trying at crucial points in the development of Irish drama."[28] It therefore comes as no surprise when Hogan
and Burnham conclude that *Portrait* "capture[s] something of the attitude
of the post-war generation" that Mary describes.[29]

Peter and Tom serve as particularly apt manifestations of this era of
strain, with Tom serving as the Fortinbras to Peter's Hamlet. Peter even

makes several allusions to *Hamlet*, including a direct quotation of Hamlet's assessment that "something is rotten in the state of—."[30] The omission of the state's name suggests Peter's inability to fully express ideas represented in the Free State and a discontent with a state that is not really at ease with itself in its newfound peace. Tom further exemplifies this discomfort during peacetime, first by report, then in person.

Before Tom even appears on stage, we are told what to expect. "Tom Hughes. Now there's a man!" says Maggie's sister. "[He is a]rmed, literally armed, always."[31] Furthermore, we are meant to understand that this accoutrement is still appropriate since "[g]oodness knows you'd need to be armed now-a-days. [Tom] got into the habit when he was fighting, [and now] says he wouldn't feel dressed now without his automatic."[32] When he appears in the second act, even his costume reflects his continued war mentality. He is rigged out for a fancy dress party with his loaded gun, and attired in "genuine cowboy's kit, belonging to a pal of mine in the West [who was] killed in a saloon shoot-up."[33] He even offers to "show [Peter] the hole in the shirt the bullet made."[34] Furthermore, Tom encourages his reputation for being perpetually armed, saying, "It's a jolly good reputation to have these times."[35] The *preceding* years of violence make Tom's habit of wearing a gun seem natural enough, though the belief that "you'd need to be armed now-a-days" and the need for such a reputation in "these times" undercuts the assumed stability of an Ireland at peace. Tom's general reputation, it would seem, hardly needs "bolstering up" either, according to Charlie: "[Not] after all you've done."[36] Following Charlie's oblique reference to fighting in the wars with an overt declaration of his own violent involvement, Tom asks if he is referring to "[a]ll the poor beggars I've done in?" and then shrugs off the suggestion that he is still haunted by that violence.[37] Though there is enough braggadocio in Tom's character to suggest that his feats and involvement in past armed conflicts are not exactly as people believe, he does not hesitate to embrace the fighter persona. He tells Peter that he "always fight[s] to win," and that "I'm on the side of the gun-men every time."[38]

Robinson's use of the term "gun-men" in 1925 would have had strong contextual links to the previous violence and trauma of wartime, specifically for Abbey patrons. Sean O'Casey's *The Shadow of a Gunman*, set during the War of Independence, was already a popular play, first performed (and produced by Robinson) in 1923. Furthermore, the November 1925 performances of *Portrait* were paired with *The Shadow of a Gunman*—both plays on the same ticket—making this instance of cultural allusion even more overt. The reference to the "gun-men" also adds credence to the possibility that Tom might be embellishing some of his involvement in the wars, or at the very least encouraging his reputation as an armed man, since, in *The Shadow of a Gunman*, Donal Davoren allows individuals in his tenement to erroneously believe that he is an IRA gunman on the run.[39]

Tom's wartime mentality, swearing ongoing fealty to the gunmen (and the gun) during an official time of peace, enacts the spirit of the post-war age, described in the play as an "iron age" and defined by "action, strength, brute force."[40] But Peter despises what this culture is shaping into. He hates the idea of having to continue to struggle and fight in this new country, not just on the larger political scale, but even in smaller daily occurrences. He reveals to Maggie his hesitation to struggle against his fellow creatures in any aspect of his life: "It's hateful, it's horrible. [...] This pushing past, this shoving, hustling."[41] He sees this "pushing" in several aspects of his life. As a youth, he boxed, but constantly "let [Charlie] off easy" to avoid beating his brother and creating a rivalry.[42] At school, examinations meant "having to beat someone or else be beaten."[43] At the office it's "straining" and "pushing" for prominence, promotion, and pay.[44] But, as Peter tells Maggie, "I'm not much of a fighter [...]. I won't push. [...] I can't. I—I almost physically can't."[45] It is therefore characteristic of Peter that, after Maggie asks him to "keep me in spite of myself," he can only admit "I shall never try to do that."[46]

And where Tom's "gun-men" allusion evokes O'Casey's *The Shadow of a Gunman*, Peter's psychological turmoil bears a slight resemblance to Johnny Boyle's in *Juno and the Paycock*. Though not physically maimed like Johnny, Peter demonstrates a similar psychological wearing down to O'Casey's character. Perhaps most tellingly, Johnny and Peter must both confront intrusive gramophones as part of their internal struggles. Johnny finds the gramophone distressing for its ghost-like allusions when the gramophone's song is interrupted by the funeral procession for Tancred. Peter, on the other hand, sees the gramophone as essential to articulating his state of mind.[47] When the spring motor's malfunctions intrude into the action of the play, they create a space for Peter to voice and demonstrate his deep-rooted anxieties.

Whereas O'Casey's works famously depict the gun and the gramophone as having an impact on events during armed conflict, Robinson quietly embeds both these images in different iterations in his post-conflict play. Both the gun and the gramophone are still very relevant and revealing of the Irish psyche. While the Free State struggles to find an identity that does not rely implicitly on the gun or the gunmen, the young generation of Robinson's play seem to find the gramophone a suitably harmless substitute. But guns and gramophones both largely function on spring-based principles. The gun's potential for violence is overt and purposeful, whereas the gramophone's is incidental, but the coiled tension in the springs enable both actions. And in an Irish context, the parallel between the gramophone and the gun is closer still. Frank O'Connor observed first-hand the post-ceasefire tensions manifest via a gramophone in Sligo. His landlord, an ex-soldier, would engage in symbolic battle with a gramophone as his weapon:

> Occasionally of an evening [...] a window at the opposite side of the street would open and a neighbor's gramophone would play "God Save the King." Almost at the first insulting bars my landlord, ordinarily the placidest of men, would burst into my bedroom with a portable gramophone, throw open my window, thrust out the gramophone and put on a record of "A Soldier's Song." It was merely a matter of gramophones instead of machine-guns.[48]

In this instance, the "gramophones instead of machine-guns" play out the tensions that remain after the Civil War and demonstrate how frighteningly easy it might be to escalate from gramophones to weapons upon provocation. In *Portrait*, Robinson picks up on these telling similarities as the gun and the gramophone fight for supremacy in the final act.

The play comes to its climactic gramophonic scene after Maggie breaks off her engagement to Peter because she has fallen in love with Tom. Tom then pushes into the room with Charlie, who winds up the gramophone to play "Come, Landlord, Fill the Flowing Bowl." The record is a traditional song that vows that "tonight we'll merry merry be," drinking copiously, "for tomorrow we'll be sober."[49] It also hints at the underlying tensions of the play, since it suggests a postponement of current pressing issues, choosing to drink now and address life's problems another day. It is a song of waiting, of holding out, delaying the resolution of a greater conflict. During the song, Maggie asks Peter to dance. Soon, however, Tom cuts in, taking Maggie away from Peter. Suddenly, the gramophone stops. Charlie again curses at the gramophone, then explains that "[t]here's something wrong with the winding spring."[50] This is the second intrusive mainspring fault, signaling a fatigue fracture and forewarning those who are familiar with the mechanism of the spring's impending failure. And yet Charlie seems oblivious. He immediately winds the machine up again, but doesn't set it going, neglecting the advice of the *Irish Times* article. The fractured spring is now wound to its limits and held in tension. Something must give. And while the gramophone has already alerted us to the stressed tautness and its potential for an abrupt rupture, it is not the gramophone but Peter who sees that potential through.

Once the gramophone is wound, Peter announces the terminated engagement as well as the news that, though he has earned a promotion at work that would have financially enabled his marriage to Maggie, he might now decline it. Tom describes this last bit of news as "against all commonsense" while Maggie calls Peter a coward.[51] And yet, the more Tom and Maggie goad him, the more Peter resists:

> You can't sting me into fighting for you [Maggie]. You can take her, Mr. Hughes: [...] she's yours for the asking. That won't please you because you like to fight for everything; but I give her to you without a struggle. You needn't have tried to terrify me tonight by wearing that violent dress; I'm cowed. You needn't have stuck your gun in your belt. (*He darts at him and snatches it from the belt. He holds it aloft like a crucifix.*) The symbol of your faith— and Maggie's! Nearer my God, to Thee![52]

The use of the gun as a substitute crucifix is a jarring condemnation of the gunmen and the diehard mentality that has driven much of the violence in Ireland's recent history. And when Tom grows alarmed, warning Peter that the gun is loaded, Peter responds:

Loaded? I should hope so. Of what use is an impotent God? Even
I, now that I have it in my hand, feel its terrific power. I—the
meek one ... of course, that's it! Do you remember, Maggie, my
saying that all the meek shall inherit the earth, and wondering
how the devil they could if they *were* meek? Why, of course, it's
true, it's all they can inherit—six feet of it—like this. (*He shoots
himself.*)[53]

Once Peter shoots himself, it is as if an excessive pressure on the gramophone spring has been removed. It functions perfectly in the ensuing
chaos.

Tom, the gunman, takes charge of the gramophone in what is perhaps
Robinson's most revealing use of the machine. In the confusion after the
shot, Tom directs the others: "It may be nothing—I can't make it out—wait
till we know."[54] To hide Peter from his mother, whom they hear coming
to the room in reaction to the sound of the gunshot, Tom runs to the
pre-wound gramophone and sets it playing. "Dance, damn you," he says
to the others, seizing Charlie and dancing while Maggie supports the still
upright Peter.[55] In this moment, the gramophone's mainspring smoothly
propels the record, blaring its jolly tune as accompaniment to Peter's
death dance. We do not know for sure that Peter is actually dead before
this dance begins, suggesting that the mainspring is gradually uncoiling
its tension while Peter expires. When Peter's mother leaves, Tom turns
the gramophone off; he and Charlie examine Peter's body, and after a
time during which they "mak[e] little exclamations, giving directions to
each other," Tom declares, "He's done for. [...] I've seen it too often not
to know."[56] Tom's expertise with guns and violence make his interactions
with the gramophone and Peter's body all the more meaningful.

In the original manuscript of the play, it is Charlie, not Tom, who turns
on the gramophone to disguise Peter's death scene.[57] Robinson's revision
underscores the author's evolving understanding of the gramophone's
specifically Irish capabilities to carry psychological meaning. He had used
a gramophone in one of his plays three years earlier. In *The Round Table*
(1922), a character plays Alexander Scriabin's music on the gramophone
to accompany his calisthenic exercises.[58] There is no overt connection
to violence in this depiction of the machine. However, only a year prior

Figure 4.3. The set for Lennox Robinson's *Portrait* and the gramophone used in the Abbey Theatre during the 1925 season. Abbey Theatre, *Portrait*, 31 Mar 1925 [Stage Management Files]. Abbey Theatre Digital Archive at National University of Ireland, Galway, 2990_SM_0001, P1. (n.d.).

to the premiere of *Portrait*, Robinson produced O'Casey's *Juno and the Paycock* in which the previously mentioned gramophone enters the play having "nearly kilt" Juno and plays during Tancred's funeral procession. In all probability, the same physical gramophone was used in all three plays: *The Round Table*, *Juno and the Paycock*, and *Portrait* (see Figure 4.3). And perhaps because of this very tangible Abbey-based connection, Robinson's play underwent the shift to emphasize Tom's handling of the gramophone. Robinson highlights the tensions between Tom and Peter through their physical interactions with the psychological symbol. Tom releases the literal gramophone's tension at the same time that Peter releases the metaphorical tension by using the gun to end his life.

The final moments of the play depict one last interaction with the gramophone, the interaction that sparked Mitchell's confusion about the play in her review. Maggie, left alone with Peter's body, decides to play the gramophone one last time and run from the room:

> [she] goes near Peter and looks very steadily at him ... There is complete silence ... Suddenly, violently). No, no, no, it's impossible. (She puts her fingers to her ears ... The silence is still unbroken.) Say something, Peter! Say something, someone! (She rushes to the gramophone, switches it on, and runs out. The gramophone declares that to-night we'll merry merry be.)[59]

For those unfamiliar with the spring motor, this finale might seem a bit overwrought. But the fact that the gramophone functions perfectly for this last performance of Peter's jaunty death dirge defies mechanical logic and provides the answer to Mitchell's question of why we need this last moment. After multiple demonstrations of mainspring fatigue fracturing and the gramophone's continued tensile stress once Charlie winds it up and leaves it, the logical conclusion of the scene would be a complete and violent fatigue failure in the gramophone. But instead, Peter has experienced *psychological* fatigue failure, has snapped and lashed out with self-destructive violence. The gramophone, on the other hand, no longer bears the symptoms of its threatened rupture and instead blares its jarring tune. The tableau or "portrait" emphasizes the parallel between the gramophone and the mind that Robinson has so deftly woven throughout the play.

Though *Portrait* has not been performed at the Abbey since 1925, it remains a revealing glimpse into the war-strained psyche of the young generation in the new, at peace, Irish Free State. Robinson's work capitalizes on established analogies between the gramophone and the mind, building upon them, and using Abbey-based allusions to tie them all together. His "essay in psychoanalysis" relies heavily on a contemporary understanding of the gramophone's inner mechanism to unlock our understanding of the tensions that pull at Peter and Tom throughout the play. It is Robinson's answer to the post-ceasefire *Irish Times* article that cautions against winding a gramophone too tight for too long. A mainspring, like the Irish psyche, can only withstand so much strain.

Held in Tension

If the gramophone in *Portrait* serves as a warning of the wear on a gramophone spring wound too tightly, then the literature of the next several years depicts gramophones and characters trying to find outlets for unresolved tensions. Frank O'Connor sees the men in Sligo venting their frustrations through a gramophonic war. In *Farewell Companions*, one of James Plunkett's protagonists has an aunt who morphs into a gramophone "full of diehard republicanism," which alienates her from much of her family and community.[60] And in Louis MacNeice's poem "An Eclogue for Christmas," the weary speaker finds no solace in a country that "will not yield you any sanctuary"; all that is left to them is to "wind your gramophone and eavesdrop on great men" from the past.[61] The speaker's respondent agrees and adds that stagnant nationalism has "made of me pure form, a symbol or a pastiche, / Stylised profile, anything but soul and flesh" that is now internalized by "turn[ing] this jaded music on / to forswear thought and become an automaton."[62]

Grappling with residual gramophonic political tensions wasn't confined to fiction, either. In 1932 in County Leitrim, Jimmy Gralton and his gramophone became a lightning rod for Church and State tensions. Gralton had fled Ireland ten years earlier due to his involvement in the War of Independence, specifically his involvement in the Direct Action Committee which was a Republican court held in defiance of British rule in the community hall built on his land. When he arrived back in Ireland, "he brought with him a gramophone and some records" and he reopened the hall.[63] Paul Laverty, who wrote the screenplay for *Jimmy's Hall* (2014) which was inspired by Gralton's life, collected stories of people who came from "over 30 miles on their bicycles to hear the latest new record from across the Atlantic" played on that gramophone. The machine was, Laverty imagines, "Jimmy's secret weapon in the battle against drabness."[64] (Notice the gramophone/weapon connection even in Laverty's contemporary perspective.) In the film, the unpacking of the gramophone, complete with a beautiful ornate horn and wind-up motor, gets its own scene, with onlookers whispering in fascination before a jazz record plays. And as the community dances begin to take off, so does the ire of the local parish priest, Father Sheridan, who sees the gramophone as a specific threat that can be weaponized: "With a gramophone … he'll have the[m] dancing first, then reading … he'll work up from their feet to their brains […]. I'm going to get one too."[65] Soon enough, Gralton was targeted by both Church and State for his communist politics. In February 1933 the de Valera government ordered Gralton to be deported as an "undesirable alien," and he is, thus far, the only Irish citizen ever to have been deported from the country. The film ends with the young people that Gralton inspired saying "Send more records … We'll keep dancing!" as proof of the gramophone's role in Gralton's community presence.[66]

As the decade continued, gramophones seemed to point to an ever-widening gap between those who had fought in the wars of the 1920s and the new generation. It was as though the post-war generation was anxious to participate in any kind of demonstrative nationalism, whether it was specific to Ireland or not. As a result, the Spanish Civil War attracted many Irish soldiers on both sides of the conflict. In *Dancing at Lughnasa*, for instance, Gerry is a gramophone salesman who has enlisted as a Republican soldier in the Spanish Civil War. He doesn't know much about Spain—"Not a lot. A little. Enough, maybe"[67]—but he commits anyway. He describes his enlistment interview in comical terms:

GERRY.   "Do you offer your allegiance and your loyalty
          and your full endeavours to the Popular Front?"
CHRIS.   What's the Popular Front?
GERRY.   The Spanish government that I'm going to keep
          in power. "I take it you are a Syndicalist?" "No."
          "An Anarchist?" "No." "A Marxist?" "No." "A
          Republican, a Socialist, a Communist?" "No." "Do
          you speak Spanish?" "No." "Can you make explo-
          sives?" "No." "Can you ride a motor-bike?" "Yes."
          "You're in. Sign here."[68]

When Chris asks Gerry why he decided to enlist, he responds, "Who wants [gramophone] salesmen that can't sell? And there's bound to be *something* right about the cause, isn't there?"[69] If he can't sell gramophones, he might as well pursue war. Gerry's distinct lack of political conviction reveals what might be considered the post-war generation's desire for something larger than what seems available after the polarizing decisions made during the previous wars in their country.

In Neil Jordan's *Nightlines*, the protagonist Donal is also involved in the Spanish Civil War and the novel opens with him as a Republican prisoner of war. Donal's reasons for enlisting were rooted in a generational tension between himself and his father: a need to get his "hatreds in perspective."[70] His father was a part of the Protestant Ascendancy, who converted to Catholicism and the Republican cause during the War of Independence, but then joined the Pro-Treaty side in the Civil War; after the war, he worked as a civil servant in W. T. Cosgrave's first Free State government, an administration in which Cosgrave enacted a Public Safety Bill that allowed for the execution of those bearing arms against the Free State as a means of asserting the new government's authority. His father therefore "presided, in part, over the incarceration and decimation of his former comrades."[71] Donal turns on his gramophone on the night that he shatters his tattered relationship with his father by sleeping with the older man's young wife, Rose.[72] After this betrayal, Donal tries to reconcile his "hatreds" of his father's personal and political choices in order to sort out his own loyalties in the looming world war.

Though Ireland would remain neutral during World War II, it would be impossible not to be aware of the tense political climate in Europe. In Francis Stuart's semi-autobiographical *Black List, Section H*, the protagonist spends the years of the war in Germany rather than in Ireland, "abandoning" his portable gramophone during the Berlin bombings in a scene reminiscent of the newspaper account of the burning Big House and gramophone from Chapter 3: "Before abandoning the portable gramophone, they put on a record and left the flat, with its doors all open, to the music of one of the popular tunes of the moment."[73] Samuel Beckett, who, in contrast to Stuart, was part of the French Resistance, famously stated that he preferred France at war to Ireland at peace. And Flann O'Brien once joked that Adolf Hitler hated his novel *At Swim-Two-Birds* so much that he started the war just to interfere with sales.[74]

The Fear of Breakage

O'Brien's novel, though not a commercial success when it was first published, is now considered a central work of Irish modernism, bridging the works of James Joyce and Samuel Beckett.[75] In the novel, a student at University College Dublin boards with his uncle. The student is an aspiring author and his novel—which makes up over half of the text of *At Swim-Two-Birds*—is a tangled mass of plot lines that sounds like the beginning of a particularly odd joke: did you hear the one about the devil, the Irish hero, and the author who walked out of a student's notebook? In broad strokes, the student's story depicts a novelist, Dermot Trellis, who is writing a story about "wrong-doing."[76] While Trellis expects his characters to commit horrible acts—his character Furriskey, for instance, is meant to assault the young woman Sheila Lamont—he as their creator also commits horrific violence: "Trellis creates Miss Lamont in his own bedroom and he is so blinded by her beauty [...] that he so far forgets himself as to assault her himself."[77] Trellis's characters randomly encounter figures from Irish mythology who then also get integrated into the novel. These figures include Finn MacCool, the Pooka (a species of human Irish devil endowed with magical powers), a Good Fairy, and Mad King Sweeny. The characters discover that when Trellis is asleep, they can act on their own volition. They drug Trellis to assure themselves as much freedom as possible and concoct a plan to gain violent retribution on their creator through their own story, written by Trellis and Lamont's offspring, Orlick. After putting Trellis through a hellish physical and literal trial, his characters are thwarted in a final judgment when the pages of their existence are burned by Trellis's maid and Trellis is therefore unexpectedly released from his characters' clutches. The novel ends with the student earning good marks at college and, for the first time, being on good terms with his uncle.

The tapestry of narratives constantly switches between the perspectives of the student, Trellis, his myriad creations, and the Irish mythic figures. When told from the student's perspective, there is a large amount of narrative dedicated to the generational tension between him and his uncle, which comes to the fore when the uncle brings home a gramophone and draws parallels between the spring motor and war. While the uncle sees war and violence as something tangible for his generation—the generation of Peter Brandon and Tom Hughes in Robinson's *Portrait*—the student takes a more academic and literary perspective, which is not surprising given his vocation as both student and aspiring author. The disparity between the uncle's war experiences and the student's academic and literary perceptions of violence creates a driving tension in their relationship and the larger work.

Both uncle and student limit their perspectives on violence (nationalist or otherwise) to Ireland's history, rather than looking beyond their country to the brewing European war. This insular shift might be indicative of the country's political neutrality throughout the war, but it might also point to the larger wounds and costs of Irish nationalism even seventeen years after the Civil War's ceasefire. The uncle and the student refer to gramophones in this text with a distinct generational gap in perspective on post-war Irish nationalism, but both with a certain anxiety about the possibility of the machine's breaking.

The gramophone appears only three times throughout the course of the novel. The first gramophonic intrusion—and the most worthy of explication—occurs when the uncle brings a gramophone into the room where the student has been working on the narrative of Mad King Sweeny for his novel. The second appearance occurs within the student's novel, when mythic figures converge (one being mistaken for a miniature gramophone in the Pooka's pocket) and the physical Sweeny enters. The final mention of the gramophone occurs in the last scene between the student and his uncle, followed directly by the final scene of the entire book in which Sweeny sits in a tree contemplating psychology. The repeated intrusion of the gramophone into contemplations of Sweeny's madness becomes central to our understanding of these explorations of generational nationalism.

The gramophone enters the novel when the uncle, with his friend Mr. Corcoran, intrudes on the student's writings, carrying "a weighty object covered with a black water-proof cloth" which he places on the table before beginning the conversation.[78] The unknown object remains on the table while the uncle asks the student about his studies (much to the latter's annoyance). When the conversation becomes uncomfortably tense, Mr. Corcoran creates a diversion by revealing the concealed object. The black cloth is removed "in a priestly manner" to reveal a gramophone.[79] Immediately, the two older men set up the machine. The uncle "tak[es] a small canister [of needles] from his pocket" and then

> the two of them bent together at the adjustment of the machine, extracting a collapsible extensible retractable tone-arm from its interior with the aid of their four hands. [...] Mr. Corcoran opened a small compartment at the base of the machine by pressing a cleverly hidden spring and brought out a number of records, scraping and whistling them together by a careless manner of manipulation. My uncle was occupied with the machine's side and winding it with the meticulous and steady motion that is known to prolong the life and resiliency of springs.[80]

The student observes that "the records were old and not of the modern electrical manufacture," and moments later, the uncle "placed a needle finely on the revolving disk and stepped quickly back" and a "tune came duly, a thin spirant from the *Patience* opera."[81]

O'Brien dedicates several pages to this scene and the meticulous descriptions of the gramophone. This sustained focus on a single object stands out among the novel's general tendency to flit in rapid succession between myriad scenes, characters, and narratives. Additionally, this scene pays particular attention to the gramophone as an object rather than an instrument—in fact, while the gramophone itself seems to intrigue the student, it is the music, described as "thin" and "hollow," that ultimately drives the student from the room (that and a grotesque sneeze from Mr. Corcoran which is accompanied by a "spattering [of] mucus discharge" that triggers the student's gag reflexes).[82]

The gramophone is regarded by the older men with reverence: Corcoran's "priestly manner" when removing the machine's black waterproof shroud is paralleled by the image of the uncle setting the machine going but keeping his "meticulous hands held forth without motion" as if in rapturous, prayer-like devotion. The conversation preceding the gramophone's unveiling is decidedly religious—"Name the seven deadly sins. Name the one that begins with S."—and the conversation that occurs directly after the machine's unveiling initially continues in a similar vein:

the uncle points out that "there is little respect for the penny catechism in Ireland to-day and well I know."[83] In this context, the "priestly devotion" given to the gramophone flows naturally enough from one topic to the next, but at second glance it makes the gramophone's position in the scene take on greater significance, since this is clearly not a religious object. It is a bit like Tom Hughes's gun becoming a crucifix in Robinson's *Portrait*—a jarring shift from traditional Catholicism to the mechanized and violent.

The conversation then shifts again when the uncle begins cranking the gramophone's spring motor. He fears his "meticulous and steady" motions might go unnoticed and therefore points out that "fast winding will lead to jerks, jerks will lead to strain and strain to breakage."[84] He then makes the curious remark, "Moderation in all things [. . .], that is the trick that won the war."[85] "Moderation" is not a likely description of war in any respect. And yet the uncle sees a parallel between his methodical winding up of the spring motor and "moderation" in war that makes a winning combination. The steadiness with which he winds up the motor is also meant to "prolong the life and resiliency of the springs"—an admirable goal and one that the *Irish Times* article would applaud on behalf of all gramophone owners, but hardly an overt parallel to war. In fact, a more apt parallel between the spring motor and war is the consequences outlined if one were to wind the motor quickly: the lack of moderation leads to jerks, strain, and breakage. It is the strain and breakage in relation to war, rather than moderation, that rings true in the uncle's oration.

When the uncle explains that moderation is the trick that "won the war," the ambiguity regarding which war implies a resistance to identifying a single conflict, as well as an amplification of the difficulty, in an Irish context, of singling out a specific war in recent memory. This makes the allusion a powerful reminder of the decade of violence that brought about the Irish Free State. By 1939, the year of publication of *At Swim-Two-Birds*, three wars had occurred in the uncle's lifetime (technically, it is possible that the wars also occurred during the student's lifetime, but he would not likely have the same kind of vivid memories, since he would have been only an infant during World War I). Is the uncle referring to World War I, the War of Independence, or the Civil War? One might be initially inclined to take the phrase "the war" as a descriptor of World War I, considering that the definite article was generally applied to that conflict in that era. However, at different points in the book, characters refer to "pre-War" fashions and events that happened "before the War"—with the capitalization indicating its status as a proper noun—and in these other instances, the phrase definitely refers to the international conflict.[86] In the gramophone scene with the uncle, the proper noun signifier is absent. And yet to eliminate World War I as a possible allusion here might be an overly hasty assumption.

There is additional ambiguity to this war allusion when the uncle refers to "*winning* the war." He is potentially making a polarizing political comment, but his vagueness blunts the impact. If he *is* referring to World War I, then he aligns the victory with the forces of Great Britain; if he is referring to the War of Independence, he aligns with Ireland's nationalist forces; if he is referring to the Civil War, he aligns with the Pro-Treaty forces. Each of these wars (and victories) marks a nuanced but definite shift in Irish politics. Even alignment with Pro-Treaty forces is an outdated political position in the novel's setting, since after the 1932 election of Éamon de Valera and Fianna Fáil, a political party that, apart from being Anti-Treaty during the Civil War, in 1937 essentially ended Ireland's dominion status in the United Kingdom with the implementation of a new Constitution. The fact that the uncle makes no distinction between these wars suggests *intentional* ambiguity on O'Brien's part—pointing to *all three* wars and their combined traumas.

The uncle also draws attention to repetition when he states that "fast winding will lead to jerks, jerks will lead to strain and strain to breakage."[87] In *Portrait*, the strain of repeated wars and a cultural resistance to a post-war peace ultimately leads to a gramophone's malfunction and a man's "breakage" and violent death. It is likely that the uncle in *At Swim-Two-Birds*, who lived through the repeated wars as well as the post-war strain, is sensitive not just to the trauma of war, but the trauma of repetition. The student then points out that his uncle's phraseology is a particular figure of speech—"Anadipolsis [*sic*] (or Epanastrophe)."[88] Anadiplosis is the repetition of the last word or phrase of a preceding clause at the beginning of a new sentence or clause. This repetition is a rhetorical device for emphasis (to which the naming of the figure of speech draws attention) and the words that we are meant to notice in this instance are "jerks" and "strain" that ultimately lead to "breakage." The uncle is concerned about the wearing down of the spring motor in the machine, the possible "breakage" that comes from repeated winding and strain. His anadiplosis requires us to see the parallel between gramophonic terminology and violent imagery in the wake of Ireland's wars.

This Irish tendency for reflection on historical violence is represented again in the physical description of the uncle's gramophone. The machine consists of a "collapsible extensible retractable tone-arm from its interior" as well as a "small compartment at the base of the machine [...] cleverly hidden [by a] spring" that holds records, and, of course, a crank for winding up the machine.[89] Each of these elements, along with the machine's portability and waterproof cloth, are an exact description of the HMV portable gramophone, Model 102, which was first introduced in 1931, and was simultaneously the pinnacle of what could be achieved by the wind-up gramophone and the machine that signaled the imminent decline of the age of the wind-up (see Figure 4.4). The uncle's wind-up gramophone is a bit of an antique in 1939, when gramophones were more and more frequently designed to operate electrically or to plug into wireless receivers, further emphasizing the generational gap between him and his nephew.

In addition to the gramophone's implied antiquity, O'Brien draws attention to the anachronistic nature of the record that the uncle puts on the machine: "the records were old and not of the modern electrical manufacture."[90] Electronic recording, using microphones to funnel the sound waves rather than a horn, began in the mid-1920s.[91] The music the uncle plays on the machine is from the 1881 Gilbert and Sullivan comic opera *Patience*, and the only pre-electronic version of that opera was recorded by HMV in 1921. *Patience* is primarily meant as a satire of the aesthetic movement of the late 1800s; it does, however, also satirize military bravado, as evidenced by songs like "When I First Put This Uniform On." It is likely that this is the song that the uncle and Mr. Corcoran happily sing along with, "stressing the beat with manual gesture."[92] This chorus provides a jarring connection to the romanticism of war and its accoutrements. Furthermore, the recording is from the same year as the signing of the Anglo-Irish Treaty that signaled the end of the Irish War of Independence and instigated the subsequent Civil War. And this isn't the only instance of a musical allusion connecting to war tropes in the

Figure 4.4. HMV portable gramophone, model 102, 1931.
Science Museum Group Collection Online, 1962-154S.

novel. Later on, when the uncle's committee debates the waltz's lack of nationalistic heritage (which seems typical of anxious, self-conscious, post-revolution Ireland), Mr. Connors of the committee points out that many members present have previously danced the waltz without detriment to the national character. Mr. Hickey seems dubious and asks, "When did I dance it?", to which Mr. Connors responds, "Twenty-three years ago at the Rotunda gardens."[93] Declan Kiberd points out that "twenty-three years earlier would have been 1916; and the Rotunda gardens was the place in which the republican insurgents were rounded up by the British enemies before being marched off to prison."[94] The committee's debate about the waltz's (un)Irishness serves to highlight the lapse of the revolutionary spirit of the nation, according to Kiberd.

O'Brien's meticulous details provide a backward glance at the violence that gripped Ireland in the first two decades of the twentieth century. And while "wound-up gramophones produced abundant sound, particularly when they were playing the electronically produced records that were marketed by the late 1930s,"[95] the pre-electronic recordings played in *At Swim-Two-Birds* are described as sounding "thin" and "spirant."[96] The ghostlike voices of the past are merged with contemporary voices when the uncle and Mr. Corcoran "joined in" during the chorus.[97] The war memories of the previous generation are still present, and the older Irish generation are still singing the same old songs. The machine, music, and allusions here all speak to the uncle's generational disparity with his nephew.

The student certainly seems uninterested in the revolutionary spirit, but he does have an intense obsession with violence as part of Irish history. Kiberd points out that the student and his comrades seem to stagnate to a certain extent, having "no natural outlet for their energies of youth" in comparison to the previous generation.[98] "Had those youths been born twenty years earlier," Kiberd explains, "they might have found an alternative expression of their vitality on the streets of Dublin that witnessed the Easter Rebellion," but instead "one has a sense of a post-heroic society" in 1930s Dublin. The death of revolution leads the student to look, not to the conflicts of recent memory for his novel's materials, but even further back, to a largely violent Irish heritage spanning centuries of myth, legend, and history. The end result is the student's novel, which essentially embraces violence as an Irish inheritance, and which explicates violence beyond the nationalist and revolutionary perspective.

When the student is interrupted by the gramophone's intrusion into the narrative in *"Biographical reminiscence, part the sixth,"*[99] he has been working on the narrative of Mad King Sweeny, as told by Finn MacCool to three of Trellis's characters, who only occasionally interrupt. This section on Sweeny is one of the longest sustained passages of narrative in the entirety of *At Swim-Two-Birds*, spanning nearly thirty-five pages without a break.[100] The depictions of Sweeny throughout O'Brien's text are worth particular notice, since they relate to an embodiment of violence in Irish cultural consciousness (as part of the nation's mythology) through Sweeny's connection to war, and, in the larger narrative of the novel, they are frequently accompanied by references to the gramophone.

O'Brien took as inspiration for his Mad King Sweeny the text of *Buile Suibhne*, which was published by J. G. O'Keeffe in a bilingual edition in 1913.[101] O'Keeffe based his translation on a manuscript written between 1671 and 1674 in which Sweeny (O'Brien's preferred spelling) is a legendary King of Ireland who—after provoking the clergyman Ronan by throwing his psalter into a lake, slaying one of his fellow clergymen, and breaking the bell of his church—is cursed by Ronan to madness and bird-like flight. It is from Sweeny's tale that we get the novel's title (he stops in *Snámh dha Én*, the Irish placename that translates as Swim-Two-Birds). O'Brien also considered *Sweeny in the Trees* as an alternative title, further emphasizing Sweeny's impact on the larger text.

Many versions of the *Buile Suibhne* text have been published since O'Keeffe's 1913 edition, including Seamus Heaney's 1983 translation *Sweeney Astray*,[102] but O'Brien's translation is still considered a notable and impressively stylistic rendition. O'Brien's version was also the first detailed translation of *Buile Suibhne* to appear after an emerging standardized vocabulary for the trauma of war was established after World War I.[103] O'Brien's translation seems to set a trend for later translations (like Heaney's) wherein the curse is overtly contextualized as a reaction to the violence of the battle scenes. As a result, the "fright-fraught fear" that comes over a soldier like Sweeny, sometimes driving him to attempt to flee in the face of war, no longer seems something as simple as a debate over courage and cowardice.[104] In the *Report of the War Office Committee of Enquiry into "Shell-Shock"* which was published after World War I, a section was dedicated specifically to the distinctions between cowardice and shell-shock. The committee concluded that if an individual is capable of self-control, but will not face the situation, he is a coward. However, "[i]t is here that difficulty arises in cases of war neurosis for it becomes necessary to decide whether the individual has or has not crossed that indefinite line which divides normal emotional reaction from neurosis with impairment of volitional control."[105] In Sweeny's case, the curse accounts for his "impairment of volitional control" when he flees battle, but O'Brien's text takes Sweeny's torment to new physical and psychological heights as a type of explication of the toll of long-standing violence on an Irish cultural icon, really prodding the culture's war-curse and the "breakage" that drives this particular version of national identity. Sweeny's tale is not just a story of initial madness, but of the king's continued psychosis after the battle. It is about living with the "eye-mad and heart-quick" curse "in craze and madness [left over] from the battle."[106]

In Finn's telling of the story (the part of O'Brien's novelistic use of Sweeny that most literally translates from *Buile Suibhne*), the drawn-out physical and psychological torment of Sweeny is inescapable. Denell Downum highlights this translation work when she explicates the scene after Sweeny falls from a thorny thicket, when he is described as having "not one inch of him from toe to crown that was not red-prickled and blood-gashed, the skin to his body being ragged and flapping and thorned, the tattered cloak of his perished skin."[107] The account in *Buile Suibne* is less graphic: *co nach raibhe méd n-orlaigh ann o a bhonn go a bhathais gan fhuiliúgudh, gan forrdergudh fair.* Downum points out that "[w]hile 'red-prickled and blood-gashed' is a reasonable rendering of '*gan fhuiliúgudh, gan forrdergudh fair*', there is nothing in the Irish in this passage that corresponds to O'Brien's vivid image of Sweeny's skin as a ragged and flapping cloak."[108] Sweeny's physical hardships are graphically enhanced in O'Brien's text, and as Downum further observes, it makes selective omissions that remove "moments of respite" from Sweeny's tale, therefore leaning heavily into the perpetual trauma.[109] As a result, Sweeny's post-traumatic psychological state deserves further examination.

In Finn's (and therefore O'Brien's) telling of the story, Ronan curses Sweeny in the following terms:

The holy bell that thou hast outraged
will banish thee to branches,
it will put thee on a par with fowls—
the saint-bell of saints with sainty-saints.

Just as it went prestissimo
the spear-shaft skyward,
you too, Sweeny, go madly mad-gone
skyward.[110]

As a result of the curse, Sweeny, the warrior king, can no longer tolerate the clamor of battle; therefore, when his armed forces engage in battle shortly after the curse, Sweeny goes mad:

[W]hen the hosts clashed and bellowed like stag-herd and gave three audible world-wide shouts till Sweeny heard them and their hollow reverberations in the sky-vault, he was beleaguered by an anger and a darkness, and fury and fits and frenzy and fright-fraught fear, and he was filled with a restless tottering unquiet a desire to be where he never was, so that he was palsied of hand and foot and eye-mad and heart-quick in craze and went from the battle.[111]

O'Brien's translation of the text uses phrases like "madly mad-gone" and the alliterative "fury and fits and frenzy and fright-fraught fear" to describe Sweeny's "eye-mad and heart-quick" mental state in the face of battle.[112] The repetition of words and sounds recalls the student's previous identification of anadiplosis for emphasis; O'Brien is not using anadiplosis specifically, but he *is* drawing our attention to his narrative process, much like the uncle while he winds the gramophone. And it is the repetition of violence, the lack of moderation, that ultimately brings on the "breakage" in Sweeny's mind.

It is no coincidence, therefore, that O'Brien interrupts his narrative of Sweeny with a gramophone, a discussion of war, and the fear of "breakage." O'Brien's translations of *Buile Suibne* implicitly belong to the student, delivered by Finn MacCool in the student's novel. The younger generation to which the student belongs has inherited a legacy of mythological violence wrapped up in nationalist rhetoric. Oliver Sheppard's bronzed sculpture *The Death of Cúchulainn* (1911) serves as an apt example. It was unveiled with great fanfare by de Valera at the General Post Office in Dublin in April of 1935 as a memorial to the 1916 Rising, embedding the mythic narrative of violence and death in the Free State's identity. Connections between the violent Mad King Sweeny and the uncle's evocation of "the war" are similarly embedded in the presence of a dated gramophone, given the network of literary and cultural gramophonic references that O'Brien drew upon.

The student seems to have subliminally taken this connection into his writing when, later in in the work, the mythic characters of Trellis's novel are characterized as finding voices through magic, like a "small gramophone in your pocket,"[113] and almost immediately afterward the physical Mad Sweeny enters Trellis's growing list of characters (no longer just part of Finn's oral tale). Sweeny briefly picks up the recitation of *Buile Suibne*—"Grey branches have hurt me / they have pierced my calves, / I hang here in the yew-tree above, / [...] I will not come down"—to which another character responds, "His is not all in it" (meaning Sweeny is not mentally stable).[114] When Sweeny finally leaves the tree, his descriptions again emphasize the physical and psychological torment he has endured:

There came the rending scream of a shattered stirk and an angry troubling of the branches as the poor madman percolated through the sieve of a sharp yew tree, a wailing black meteor hurtling through green clouds, a human prickles. He came to the ground with his right nipple opened to the wide and a ruined back that was packed with thorns and the smallwood of the trees of Erin, a tormented cress-stained mouth never halting from the recital of inaudible strange staves.[115]

Sweeny's "breakage" seems absolute in these descriptions, and yet the fictional and mythological characters of the student's novel begin to care for his physical needs and are not particularly off-put by his psychological state, treating him with their normal roll-with-it attitude. He seems to heal, to some extent, both physically and psychologically during the time that he spends with Trellis's characters. He then largely disappears from their narrative.

In the final pages of *At Swim-Two-Birds*, both the gramophone and Sweeny reappear, providing one last chance for the exploration of generational cultural traumas. The student, having completed his exams with aplomb, is congratulated by his uncle and Mr. Corcoran. After a time, "on the pretext of requiring tea, I made my way from the room. Glancing back at the door, I noticed the gramophone was on the table under its black cover."[116] Though the student does not provide any further commentary on the gramophone, it is one of the last images we get from the student's perspective in this "[b]iographical reminiscence part the final."[117] And yet it seems to evoke Sweeny's presence, when in the "[c]onclusion of the book, ultimate,"[118] Sweeny controls the narrative. He has somehow survived the destruction of Trellis's characters and now seems to be sitting in a tree outside the student's home in contemporary Dublin: "The eyes of the mad king upon the branch are upturned, whiter eyeballs in a white face, upturned in fear and supplication. His mind was but a shell."[119] This reference to the "shell" in connection with madness draws a parallel to shell-shock, and in the next sentences he considers his madness as viewed by famous (fictional) European psychologists. A Professor Unternehmer, "the eminent German neurologist," pronounces diagnoses of lunacy, whereas Doctor Du Fernier, a Professor of Mental Sciences and Sanitation at the Sorbonne, finds lunacy to be only an extension of bad hygiene. Sweeny then concludes, "Which of us can hope to probe with questioning finger the dim thoughts that flit in a fool's head" since there is a legitimate fear "of breakage" in that fragile psyche.[120] The reiteration of "breakage" in this final paragraph recalls the uncle's meticulous winding of the gramophone to avoid jerks and strain. And mental breakage is made clear in the last image of the novel when an anonymous and mentally disturbed man commits suicide.

Though the student and the uncle in *At Swim-Two-Birds* never fully reconcile their generational perspectives, the final scenes tie together all the threads of influence that have gone into the tension of their relationship. The uncle's mildly antiquated gramophone is a parting image for the student. He can, through his own writings, better appreciate his uncle's postwar anxieties and how the gramophone embodies them. He is capable of depicting Sweeny's madness in a contemporary context; it is brought out of the past and converted from a mythic curse into a psychological condition. He understands "breakage" as a consequence of mental strain and fatigue from the residual tensions in a post-war and post-heroic culture.

Conclusion

When the *Irish Times* published its 1923 article on gramophone maintenance, warning of the consequences of residual tension in the machine's spring motor, the newspaper essentially predicted how gramophones would be represented in Irish literature for the next fifteen years at least. The 1920s and 1930s represented the height of gramophone production and consumption in Ireland, resulting in a proliferation of literary depictions. The works discussed in this chapter depict the tensile strength of a culture being tested over and over again while the country must recover from war, adapt to peace as a Free State, adopt a new Constitution and a revised position in the United Kingdom, and remain neutral in a second world-wide conflict, all within a short span. *Portrait* and *At Swim-Two-Birds* depict some of the most overt tensions of the post-war literature, namely the acclimation to peace and the cultural (and nationalistic) gap between the revolutionaries and the younger post-war generation.

The stress load on the gramophone in *Portrait* violently erupts. The gramophones of the 1930s become focal points of generational tension. The gramophone in *At Swim-Two-Birds* is treated with delicacy so as not to exacerbate any existent fractures and to "avoid breakage." But the residual tensions discussed in these texts are only postponed or delayed, not fully resolved. After the 1930s the gramophone dipped in popularity (with the rise of the wireless). Gramophones become more antiquated, their appearances become more infrequent, and their mainspring motors grow tired. The tensile strength of the springs is sapped and exerts less consistent, more chaotic torque as the era of the gramophone winds down. And yet the machine continues to appear in works long after its heyday. In the coda of this book, the chaos of the anachronistic gramophone culminates in a violent outbreak that echoes the unresolved tensions in the post-war decades.

Coda

Gramophonic Echoes

The gramophone's presence in Irish literature from the 1800s through the 1930s, as discussed in previous chapters, seems natural enough, given the object's popularity and relevance during these decades. But by the late 1930s the wind-up gramophone was beginning to be an outdated technology. Record players, with electric power and fly-wheel friction, were replacing the spring-motor mechanism. And these new machines could be integrated into the popular wireless sets. Brian Friel's *Dancing at Lughnasa* (1990) serves as a particularly apt depiction of Ireland's media evolution away from gramophones. The play follows the five Mundy sisters in 1936 who, at a climactic moment, dance with abandon to their wireless set, which intermittently erupts into song. Prior to the pivotal dance, Gerry, who is Chris Mundy's love interest and the narrator's father, tries to repair the temperamental wireless. Gerry is a traveling gramophone salesman. The contrast between the wireless and the gramophone speaks to one of the larger themes of the play: the advance of modernity and those who are left behind in its wake. The Mundy sisters struggle to make ends meet when the town's new knitwear factory effectively eliminates the income brought in by Agnes and Rose, who knit mittens as part of Ireland's traditional cottage industry. Similarly, Gerry tries to sell the slightly dated gramophone technology in an area that already has the progressive wireless set. He initially describes, with bravado, his successes as a gramophone salesman in Ireland:

GERRY: This country is gramophone crazy. Give you an
           example. Day before yesterday; just west of Ough-
           terard; [...] Out comes this enormous chappie
           [...]. I show him the brochures; we talk about
           them for ten minutes; and just like that he takes
           four—one for himself and three for the married
           daughters.

CHRIS: He took four gramophones?

GERRY: Four brochures! (*They both laugh.*) But he'll buy. I
           promise you he'll buy. Tell you this, Chris: people
           thought gramophones would be a thing of the
           past when radios came in. But they were wrong.
           In my experiences...[1]

All of his assertions about the gramophone's success in Ireland are
undercut, however, by his comment shortly thereafter: "Maybe this week
I'm going to sell a gramophone or two after all."[2] Ultimately, if even the
poverty-stricken Mundys have a wireless, we can see precisely the relevance of the outdated gramophone in Ireland.

And yet the gramophone continued to crop up in Irish literature
long after the machine's decline. By the 1950s and 1960s the gramophone,
with its signature horn and spring-driven motor, was almost a novelty
item, since the turntable, radio, and even magnetic tape had become the
commercial mainstays of recorded sound. Even so, during the decades
subsequent to the gramophone's commercial peak, Ireland's gramophones
continued to intrude. The machine takes on slight valences of memory
and tension. More muted, perhaps. But it still acts as a witness or agent
in correlation to memory and trauma, usually in connection with established motifs of the early twentieth century, rather than as a mere prop
piece to establish setting. This coda traces these echoes throughout the
decades, noting the evolving motifs, until the gramophone is once again
revived, and the unresolved strain left in the machine, discussed in the
previous chapter, breaks free in unexpected violence.

The gramophones of the 1940s tend to create echoes of past memories
and pain, but with a growing distance and a progressive numbness. This
is especially true when recalling previous violence and war while Ireland

remains neutral in "The Emergency" of World War II. Elizabeth Bowen is particularly effective at evoking these themes. In her short story "Songs My Father Sang Me" (1945), the protagonist remembers that, when she was a child, her father repeatedly sang snippets of songs from "last war's pre-war,"[3] as she now sits in a bar, listening to the band playing one of those tunes. She also remembers that her mother discouraged his singing, until after a while the "tune" became "now and then asking when there'd be something to eat, as unmusical as a gramophone with the spring broken."[4] There are compounding motifs of an old trauma throughout the story: the broken gramophone spring, the incomplete melodies on repeat, the father's history as a soldier, the fact that the protagonist insists that her father is perpetually 26 years old. It culminates in a new and compound trauma for both father and daughter. He is broken from his experiences in World War I—"he was a man in the last war until that stopped; then I don't quite know what he was, and I don't think he ever quite knew either."[5] And as a result of this brokenness, he nearly kidnaps but ultimately abandons his daughter, who is remembering, retelling, and reliving their story years later to the accompaniment of his pre-war songs.

In Bowen's *The Heat of the Day*, the gramophone continues its ghostly theme when it plays after the death of Stella's cousin Francis—an Irishman whose "death had returned him to life" in Stella's memories.[6] Francis dies from a simultaneous heart attack and stroke as he tries essentially to force his way into a mental health facility; the ambulance that comes to pick up his body is "greeted by music from gramophones wafted out of the windows of the patients' rooms."[7] Resonances of memory, soldiers, and the psychological abreactive sounds of gramophones during World War II fit well with Bowen's perception of the gramophone as established in *The Last September*.

Ireland's gramophones of the 1940s also depict the dark humor of a problematically insular Free State in a time of global crisis. Similar to Gerry's gramophone in *Dancing at Lughnasa*, in Flann O'Brien's *The Poor Mouth* (1941), the gramophone's novelty in the Irish *Gaeltacht* is satirized, since the machine serves as a contrast between modernity and the impoverished and backward, but oh-so-Gaelic inhabitants of Corkadoragha. It signals the incompatibility of a metropolitan and Dublin-based Irish culture that can romanticize the Irish language (which is supposedly recorded on the machine in *The Poor Mouth*) at the expense of its half-starved western citizens. In this parody of the Blasket biographies, which had gained popularity in Ireland in the previous decade, the narrator of the tale, O'Coonassa Bonaparte, describes the gramophone as "a wonderful instrument" capable of "memorizing all it heard if anyone narrated stories or lore to it."[8] And like the collectors from the Irish Folklore Commission who were highly active in the 1940s—and still carrying the Ediphones discussed in Chapter 1, rather than the more contemporary magnetic wire recorders[9]—an Irish language scholar comes to Corkadoragha to collect the most authentic Gaelic available. The gramophone, however, frightens most of the villagers, so the scholar has difficulty recording any stories, until one night a drunk man stumbles into his rooms and begins speaking:

> It really was rapid complicated stern speech—one might have thought that the old fellow was swearing drunkenly—but the gentleman did not tarry to understand it. He leaped up and set the machine near the one who was spewing out Gaelic. It appeared that the gentleman thought the Gaelic extremely difficult and he was overjoyed that the machine was absorbing it; he understood that good Gaelic is difficult but that the best Gaelic of all is well-nigh unintelligible.[10]

The recording session lasts for an hour and the scholar is thrilled with the results. The villagers later learn that the scholar was "highly praised for the lore which he stored away in the hearing machine," traveling to Berlin and playing it before the cognoscenti of Europe: "These learned ones said that they never heard any fragment of Gaelic which was so good, so poetic and so obscure as it and that [they] were sure there was no fear for Gaelic while the like was audible in Ireland."[11] Furthermore, the scholar earns a "fine academic degree" for his work, and a small committee is appointed to analyze the record.[12] And then comes the punchline of the whole episode: "I do not know whether it was Gaelic or English or a strange irregular dialect which was in the old speech which the gentleman collected from us here in Corkadoragha but it is certain that whatever word was uttered that night came from our rambling pig."[13] The scholar's gramophone satirizes the troubling trope of devaluing those who speak the language, often considered the "[anachronistic] backward peasants," despite the fact that the Irish language was "constitutionally enshrined" in 1937.[14] And O'Brien, at least, is deeply suspicious of an Ireland that is becoming obsessed with Irishness for Irishness's sake, as demonstrated by the celebration of the gramophone's physical encapsulation of the Irish language, while the conditions of those who speak it are ignored.

The gramophone's slightly *passé* presence in the 1940s also signals rote repetition and a progressive numbness. In Sean O'Faolain's short story "The Faithless Wife" (1947), for instance, the protagonist plays the gramophone repeatedly while having an affair with the "beautiful Mlle Morphy, whose real name was Mrs Mehawl O'Sullivan."[15] And yet, while the gramophone is most overtly visible and audible during their illicit moments together,[16] it is clear that the Irish beauty is much less engaged (both physically and emotionally) in the relationship than he is, creating echoes of Molly Bloom's gramophonically repetitious "yes" in the final scene of *Ulysses*, and a continued play on the sexual and gendered undercurrents of the machine.[17]

By the 1950s the gramophone more overtly signals antiquity and a sort of paralysis in the past, as the country grew even more insular in the first full decade of the established Republic. As an example, James Plunkett's 1951 short story "The Eagles and the Trumpets" includes "an old fashioned gramophone complete with sound horn" that makes a group of drunk revelers in rural Ireland quarrel over who gets the chance to wind up the machine; afterwards, they "laugh uproariously at the thin nasal voices and the age of the records."[18] But the antiquity of the machine does not mean the gramophone cannot still recall the possible mental violence inherent in it. The protagonist—named Sweeney, perhaps as a nod to Mad Sweeny of O'Brien's novel—twice describes the gramophone as "shatter[ing]" a burgeoning epiphany that might lead to an escape from his stagnant, city-based paralysis: "the gramophone rasped out again and the moment of quietness and awareness inside him was shattered to bits."[19] He expresses his frustration at not being able to collect his thoughts, since "[t]hat always happened. [...] He has been on the point of touching something and it had been knocked violently away from him [...], a spinning globe which shot forward and shattered about him. A new record whirled raspingly on the gramophone."[20] And the cycle continues. Even when the gramophone begins to wind down, Sweeney is denied a respite since someone in the group winds the machine up again "without bothering to lift off the pick-up arm," which results in "a nerve-jarring ascent from chaos to pitch and brightness."[21] Sweeney is doomed to constant disruption of thought, it would seem, since "[o]nce again the composite globe spun towards him. Sweeney held his head in his hands and groaned."[22] He is denied his epiphany and returns to his stagnant city life.

Samuel Beckett also picks up on this paralysis near the end of the decade. The radio play *Embers* (1959) evokes the gramophone in a work that is largely about the haunting sounds and presences that refuse to let Henry exist in the present. Beckett's use of competing media technologies in *Embers* came only a year after he wrote and produced the more popular *Krapp's Last Tape* (1958), which also problematizes the recorded voice and living in the present.[23] In *Krapp's Last Tape*, the tapes physically embed the act of recording and tangibly bring Krapp closer to death with each playback; he essentially plays out an entire (repetitive) lifetime on the cassettes. The play's title uses ambiguity to enforce the connection to death. Krapp records his "last" tape, implying that this might be a (metaphorically) dead man talking, and this is what recording does: preserve ghosts. Similarly, in *Embers*, Henry clings to his past in the form of a physical gramophone while speaking to us via the radio. Carrying such an antiquated machine is, of course, absurd, but that is Beckett's *métier*, and, according to Sarah Keller, "[i]n Beckett's oeuvre, technology plays a role both within the diegesis of the work and outside of it, as part of the work's formal mechanisms. Media chez Beckett specifically mediates memory."[24] Henry plays this idea out when he implies that the machine is meant to ward off the "dead silence" and lack of sound in "the embers, sound of dying, dying glow" that haunt him as he tries to commune with his dead father.[25] It is, after all, only after Ada reminds Henry that "Underneath all is as quiet as the grave. Not a sound. All day, all night, not a sound" that we finally learn about Henry's gramophone.[26] The "dead silence" paired with a gramophone and ghosts in this play inescapably recall the machine in *Juno and the Paycock*. But Beckett disrupts the connection when Henry admits, "I forgot [the gramophone] today," and therefore is largely unsuccessful in conversing with his father.[27]

By the 1960s the gramophone takes on a kind of threatening antiquity, especially in gendered terms. Edna O'Brien's works from this period make this particularly visible. In *The Country Girls* (1960), the gramophone provides cover for young Kate when she first realizes that her friend Baba knows about her evolving relationship with the older and predatory Mr. Gentleman.[28] The machine later plays "Silent Night" while Kate remembers Mr. Gentleman's first physical advances in a parked car during a snowstorm.[29] In the second book in *The Country Girls* trilogy, *The Lonely Girl* (1962), Kate stares at the silent, antiquated wind-up gramophone in Mr. Gentleman-turned-Eugene's bedroom after he tells her "[M]y dear girl, I haven't seduced you yet," and she shakes in fear.[30] Later in the novel, when she spends the night in his bed, he "put[s] a record on the wind-up gramophone" to soothe himself and her.[31] And even though they do not consummate their relationship that night, the machine sparks an uncomfortable conversation about the possibility of her living with him. The motif also appears in O'Brien's short story "Irish Revel" (1968) when the young protagonist Mary is not only used as a drudge at a party where she had assumed she was to be a guest, but is also subjected to the older man O'Toole's threatening advances. The old gramophone blares out with "rasps and scratchings" at the beginning of the evening's dancing, and after O'Toole kisses Mary, the machine makes "crackling noises [as] Mary ran from the landing, away from O'Toole."[32] She then spends the night barricaded in the guest bedroom to prevent the man from entering. In each of these instances, O'Brien highlights how outdated the gramophones are, with their big horns and wind-up mechanism, and they serve as a rather overt gesture toward the age of the men. Both Kate and Mary are frightened by the men, and the machine's intrusions in these scenes highlight the psychological stress of these threatening sexual situations.

In Patrick McCabe's *The Butcher Boy* (1992), also set in the 1960s, the gramophone crops up on multiple occasions in conjunction with Francie Brady's mental instability. Near the end of the novel he notices a shop with "a dog hanging over the door looking into a trumpet, trying to find his master's voice. I'm in here get me out Fido says the master. How says Fido. How do I know says the master just do it will you my best little pet dog?"[33] This stream of consciousness moment in which Francie explicates the HMV logo echoes Paddy Dignam's ghost enacting Nipper's plight in

Ulysses.[34] Shortly after this scene, the police pursue Francie for violently murdering his neighbor Mrs. Nugent. In his frantic effort to evade capture, Francie returns to his home and sets the stage for his suicide by bringing an old gramophone out of storage. He then sets a record of "The Butcher Boy" playing: the song his mother sang perpetually to him as a child before she also commited suicide.[35]

From the 1940s to the 1960s the Irish gramophone tends to present itself as an object that no longer acts with the vibrancy and violence of the early twentieth century, but it still asserts itself in tense moments as a mnemonic of memories and tensions unresolved. It is as though the machine has been wound up and held in tension, as in the previous chapter, and then put up on a shelf. Still visible, occasionally adjusted or dusted off, but largely ignored as a relic of uncomfortable memories better left alone for fear of what the volatile machine might revive. By the late 1960s those cultural tensions were manifest in the outbreak of sectarian violence in Northern Ireland. And when the Troubles began to wind up, Brian Friel's play *The Gentle Island* (1971) literally revived an old gramophone in a scene of shocking violence that finds parallels, yet again, in the cultural moment.

Friel—who was born in Omagh, Co. Tyrone in Northern Ireland in 1929, lived in Derry during his formative years, and moved, in the late 1960s, from Derry to Co. Donegal in the Republic of Ireland where he lived the rest of this life—is just one Irish author who personally identified with the struggles of Northern Ireland from both sides of the border. Many of his works—*Philadelphia Here I Come* (1964), *Translations* (1980), and *Dancing at Lughnasa* among them—are set in a fictional Donegal town called Ballybeg (from the Irish *Baile Beag*, meaning "Small Town"), where Northern Ireland's political anxieties are often tangible from the Republic's side of the border. *The Gentle Island*, as one of the Ballybeg plays, uses a gramophone in a scene of intense violence to embody many of the concerns of the Troubles.

The Gentle Island has often confused critics with its violence. In a climactic scene, an "ancient gramophone" is repaired, and, when it begins to play, the characters on stage begin a performance that drastically escalates in violence until a man lies beaten on the ground, one onlooker is delighted, and another is so frightened by what has happened that he snatches the record from the machine and smashes it. The scene is unsettling for its bizarre escalation of intense violence with no obvious impetus. Frank McGuinness describes the play as "the most threatening [and] the most perplexing" of Friel's works.[36] And yet this violence in conjunction with a gramophone holds a certain logic, considering the gramophone's history of violent associations in the Irish literature of the past, and the weight of mnemonic representation the object carries with it into the 1970s. Fintan O'Toole describes the work as a play that "reads badly," with a framework that is "too rickety for the burden of symbolism which it must bear."[37] And yet the gramophone's presence bolsters the "rickety symbolism," as O'Toole describes it, in this time of conflict.

Since Friel later emphasizes the gramophone's irrelevance in the 1930s in *Dancing at Lughnasa*, its appearance in *The Gentle Island*, a play set on an island just off the coast of Ballybeg in the 1970s, is a particularly revealing media choice. The play depicts the relationships between the Sweeney family—Manus, his two sons Joe and Philly, and Philly's wife Sarah—and two Dublin travelers—Peter and Shane. The Sweeneys are the only people left on the island after a voluntary evacuation at the play's opening, and the travelers have come to view what Peter deems an idyllic village in order to appreciate the simplicity of life in the west of Ireland. While the Sweeneys and the travelers initially strike up a friendship—Peter works with the men in the fields and Shane repairs machinery at the house— the end of the second act erupts in gramophonic violence. This bizarre scene foreshadows greater violence in the third act, after Shane is accused of having sex with Philly. Manus and Sarah hold Shane at gunpoint and Sarah ultimately shoots him in the back. Shane and Peter leave the island; it is unclear whether Shane will survive, but he will certainly never walk again. The Sweeneys, minus Joe who is appalled by Manus and Sarah's actions, remain. And Philly, who never learns why Shane and Peter left, settles back into life with Manus and Sarah on the "gentle island."

The play's title is an obvious misnomer, but one that allows for word-play and contemporary parallels to islands that can embody such violence. At one point, Peter asks Sarah the meaning of Inishkeen (an anglicized form of the island's name); she explains that it means "the gentle island." But Shane has already provided his own fictional etymology, which is perhaps more accurate in its nuanced acknowledgement of the sinister feel of this (mostly) abandoned island: "Apache name: Means scalping island."[38] The island's name and its potential meanings have sparked speculation. Sarah's definition translates from the Irish *Inis Caoin*. But Frank McGuinness has pointed out that "Inishkeen" in its anglicized form (as it exclusively appears in the play) can also translate as "island of lamentation" (island of keening).[39] José Lanters points out that there could be another Irish translation of Inishkeen as *inis scian* or "knife island," which would perhaps account for Shane's suggestion that the name is the Apache for "scalping island."[40] These alternative interpretations point to the inherent irony of Sarah's translation. The violence of the incongruously titled "gentle island" is apparent throughout the play. Chu He points out that "[v]iolence and brutality [...] are pervasive on the island" and the play includes references to war, disaster, drownings, shootings, mutilation, torture, and ultimately xenophobia.[41] Seamus Deane describes it as a "savage play" about lives which are "brutal, squalid, beset by sexual frustration and violence."[42] And Lanters describes the violence as a form of sacrifice or scapegoating. It is a scathing critique of the in-fighting and violence inherent to the place and its inhabitants. And it is not difficult to understand that we are meant to read the Gentle Island as a parallel for the larger island of Ireland.

At the beginning of the second act, Shane sets about repairing the "ancient gramophone," which seems to anchor the violence of the ensuing scene.[43] The phrase "ancient gramophone" forces a backward perspective on the object's history. We see all of Ireland's gramophones in this backward glance: the burning phonograph cylinders in Seward's office, the gramophone that Eliza Doolittle declares her independence from, the "political gramophone" of Home Rule, the gramophone Lois mourns, the gramophone that Johnny remains wary of, the blaring gramophone that accompanies the burning of a Big House, the one that accompanies Peter's suicide, and the gramophone that a post-revolutionary Frank O'Connor sees as replacing machine guns. The "ancient gramophone" of *The Gentle Island* bears the mnemonic weight of all of these and many other Irish gramophones.[44]

To this cultural heritage, Friel adds nuance by delineating the provenance of the Inishkeen gramophone. Shane observes that the majority of the objects on the island have an off-putting source, since they are usually remnants of shipwrecks or even plane crashes. The opening of the play describes Manus "sitting in an airplane seat," which is just one of his many treasures pulled out of the sea in the wake of wreckage and destruction. Manus tells Shane and Peter the history of his chair: "It came out of a German airplane that crashed into the side of this hill. [...] It was flung out in the explosion and the pilot was still in it."[45] Joe then adds a catalogue of other items that have come to Inishkeen in a similar manner:

> That clock came off a Dutch freighter that broke up on the Stags; and that table came off a submarine; and those lamps came off a British tanker; and these binoculars came off a French mine-sweeper. My father used to sit up all night waiting for the wreckage. All the men did. And they got bales of rubber and butter and tins of cigarettes and timber and whiskey and whatnot. Tell them about the night the Norwegian lifeboat floundered below the cliffs, Father, when the men were screaming and the—[46]

Here Manus cuts Joe off, fearing that Shane and Peter "will think we're a race of scavengers"; but "they were bad times. We had to live."[47] It appears that Manus's fears are justified, given Shane's incisive and cutting imitation later in the scene where he repairs the gramophone. Shane parodies Manus's previous account of how many of the objects found their way to the island:

> D'you see that bed you're lying on, sir? Three hundred and forty-seven sailors went down with the ship that bed came off. And that ring on your finger was on the finger of a young airman when his plane plunged down on the very spot you're standing on. We're poor people, sir. We survive only because of other people's disasters – musha, God help them.[48]

Shane concludes that the island is ultimately "a war museum."[49] The gramophone seems part and parcel of that heritage when Peter asks, "What's wrong with it anyhow? [...] It looks like a collector's item to me."[50] This gramophone's provenance as a relic in the "war museum" provides partial context for the abrupt violence on stage following its revival.

And oddly enough, Manus's description of the objects that wash ashore on Inishkeen is almost exactly like the account in Muiris Ó Súileabháin's autobiography of Blasket life, *Twenty Years A-Growing*. The parallels with the Blasket Island biographies are fairly overt in *The Gentle Island*, especially in the exodus from the island at the play's opening.[51] But the catalogue of washed-up items on the island is a stunning piece of verisimilitude. In *Twenty Years A-Growing*, Ó Súileabháin gives an account of wreckage that washed up on shore during World War I:

> There was good living on the island now. Money was piled up. There was no spending. Nothing was bought. There was no need. It was to be had on the top of the water—flour, meat, lard, petrol, wax, margarine, wine in plenty, even shoes, stockings, and clothes [and every sort of riches]. Not a house on the Island but a storeroom was built beside it to keep the gatherings.[52]

Wealth and supplies came from the sea, but more significantly, from the violent, war-driven destruction of ships. Even wreckage from the *Lusitania* made its way to the Blaskets, including the body of one of the sailors.[53] On Inishkeen, as well as the Great Blasket, the detritus of war is essential to life and even glorified, as we see with Manus and Joe's litanies. It is also reflected in Ó Súileabháin's autobiography, when he hears one of the islanders exclaim, "War is good" after some of the wreckage washed ashore; another islander responded, "If it continues, the Island will be the Land of the Young."[54]

But Shane's description of where the gramophone and other objects on the island have come from is only the beginning of the violence of this scene. While he works to repair the gramophone, Sarah offers herself to Shane—"I want to lie with you, engineer"—and explains that Philly "is no good to me" as a husband.[55] Shane turns her down, finishes fixing the gramophone, and winds the machine up. By this time, Peter has joined the scene and Shane prepares to play a record on the gramophone, asking, "If you were going to end your days on a barren island, Sir Peter, what record would you choose?"[56] Shane selects a record at random from the Sweeneys' collection and continues: "[M]y first choice would be an ancient Gaelic folk-song that I first heard sung by an old man on an island off the west coast of County Donegal."⁵⁷ The record is "Oh! Susanna." Before the music starts, Philly and Joe enter the scene. Shane sets the music going and sings and dances, inviting others to dance with him, being rebuffed more and more violently by each person he approaches. First Peter waves him off, then Joe says, "You're doing great by yourself."⁵⁸ When Shane catches Philly's hand, Philly shakes it off roughly saying "Go to hell!"⁵⁹ Sarah then re-enters the room:

	([... SHANE] catches [SARAH] and swings her round. She slaps his face viciously—howls of laughter from JOE and PHILLY.)
JOE:	Jaysus, that's a quare uppercut, Sean!
PHILLY:	Give him another! Another! Another!
JOE:	Beat the head off him, girl!
PETER:	Stop it! Stop it! (*SHANE pretends the slap has sent him reeling. [...] PHILLY trips him at the door. He falls. The laughter rises. He gets up—without breaking his song—and pretends to stagger after her. PHILLY shoves him roughly back. He falls against JOE. JOE pushes him away. He falls against PETER. PETER shies away from him and looks around in rising panic. He lurches toward PHILLY. PHILLY punches him. He falls heavily. He makes no effort to rise. He just lies there, singing. PHILLY punches him again and again.*)
PHILLY:	Dance, you bastard! Dance! Dance!
JOE:	Yip-eeeeeeeeee!⁶⁰

The violence only stops when the shocked and frightened Peter takes the record off the gramophone and smashes it.

The scene's violence seems to escalate erratically and inexplicably, but historical context for when *The Gentle Island* was written and first produced helps inform the violence in this scene. In her article "Brian Friel's Gentle Island of Lamentation," Helen Lojek provides a detailed and sobering background for the first performance of Friel's play:

Brian Friel's *The Gentle Island*, [...] premiered at Dublin's Olympia Theatre on 30 November 1971. The opening came two days after a weekend *The Irish Times* described as "the most violent since internment was introduced in August." It was the same day the British Army announced its intention to arm its Northern Irish helicopters with machine guns. It was only two months before Bloody Sunday shattered what remained of calm in Friel's own city, Derry. On 1 December *The Irish Times* both reviewed Friel's new play and lamented the Dáil's "detachment" concerning deaths in the North.[61]

Lojek goes on to point out that less than a year later, when the Belfast Lyric Theatre first performed *The Gentle Island* on October 18, 1972, "[t]he next day, 19 October, the front page of *The Irish Times* announced that forty-eight hours of rioting between British troops and Belfast Protestants had left four dead and many injured."[62]

The connections between Friel's play and the violence of the Troubles don't end there, since the gramophone was also being revived in political discussions surrounding the escalating conflict. In February of 1971, when Friel was still writing *The Gentle Island*, journalist Denis Ireland pointed out that, even in the "glare of petrol bombs," the "confused situation in the Six Counties" was a perpetuation of a long-standing tension between unionist and nationalist loyalties:

"In Ireland the extreme party is always right." [...] Right for more than three-quarters of Ireland. [... R]ight in 1971 and the glare of petrol bombs on the Falls. It is also right in the present confused situation in the Six Counties as long as the official viewpoint at Stormont remains a mere reproduction 55 years later of Dublin Castle: that is, as long as the *gramophone* record of official "Ulster" Unionism keeps on blaring, "forward with the help of the British troops, not to mention the British royal family, to 1916."[63]

Ireland's account draws from a clearly Republican perspective, citing both the 1916 Rising and the current Troubles in Northern Ireland, with the "petrol bombs on the Falls" referring to the Falls curfew in July 1970 when the nationalist Lower Falls area of Belfast was placed under curfew and subjected to violent searches conducted by hundreds of troops, and which resulted in four nationalists' deaths. The journalist characterizes the problem as gramophonic in its repetition, expressing disgust with "official Unionism's gramophone record" that calls for British aid in Ireland's affairs (comparing Northern Ireland's Stormont parliament to the loyalist Dublin Castle before the War of Independence). And while this creates an interesting inversion of the "gramophone campaign" of Home Rule as discussed in Chapter 2, it simultaneously reminds us how anachronistic a gramophone reference would be in the 1970s without the mnemonic cultural context behind it.[64] However, when the *Irish Times* mentions gramophones in coverage of the Troubles and places that allusion against the historical backdrop of political debates and conflicts that have roots at least a hundred years earlier with the first Home Rule bills, the antiquated, Victorian-era technology becomes an apt referent.

Despite all these parallels, Friel resisted putting too much emphasis on connections between the violence of his play and the Troubles in Northern Ireland. In an interview with the *Irish Times* he insisted "that it has nothing to do with the present situation in the North."[65] However, the connections between the two, particularly with the added weight of the gramophone's centrality in the escalating violence, rather overwhelm his protests. It would seem that when Shane repairs the old gramophone, winding it up and setting it playing after years of disuse, he is essentially (and unwittingly) bringing Ireland's historical grievances to the foreground and releasing the political tensions and violence that have largely been held at bay for nearly forty years. Friel's gramophone, contextualized by the literary heritage of the Irish gramophones that have gone before, also shoulders much of the burden of symbolism that O'Toole finds so cumbersome in *The Gentle Island*. By contextualizing the violence of the play against a political backdrop, much of its "rickety" symbolism stabilizes. The very anachronism of the gramophone, and many of the other objects on the island, indicates that "time is out of joint, that past, present and future are blurred and undetermined" on Inishkeen.[66] The asynchrony serves as an indicator of a revived or unresolved cultural trauma narrative, identified in this book as an event that exists out of joint with a linear/chronological timeline and which is belatedly assimilated.

Not only does the gramophone in Friel's play visually recall the historical gramophones of previous eras, but the Inishkeen machine traces its mnemonic ancestry in the way it is incorporated into the plot and action, since with a little prodding, further connections between the gramophones of the previous chapters and that on the "gentle island" emerge. Like Dr. Seward's asynchronous phonograph diary which signals the collective trauma of the vampire hunters in *Dracula*, this "ancient gramophone" is a signifier of the past, of unhealed grievances that have not been fully addressed, which will be relived over and over until assimilated and resolved in the larger cultural narrative. Furthermore, the machine in *Dracula* mnemonically represents the physical and psychological traumas of a culture, when "ancient Gaelic folk-songs" were committed to wax cylinders generations after the Famine, one of Ireland's greatest cultural traumas. This belated action undermines belief in the historical or cultural authenticity of those records, much like Shane's faulty and bastardizing assertion of the cultural heritage of "Oh! Susanna" (which is out of time *and* place). The song's origins reveal yet another layer of the gramophone's coded history, since it was first published in 1848, at the height of the Famine and in the year of a failed rebellion.

Friel's gramophone also serves as accompaniment for the physical altercation. Peter seems almost to view it as an accomplice to the violence, since he thinks that destroying the record will stop Philly from beating Shane further. The destroyed record recalls the "death" of the gramophone in Elizabeth Bowen's *The Last September*. Additionally, in *Juno and the Paycock*, the gramophone is capable of embodying the scars and brutal violence of war-torn Ireland, and in *The Gentle Island*, Philly repeatedly beats Shane while the latter sings along with the gramophone until the record is abruptly and violently destroyed. Shane is cut on the hand in this altercation—"it looks deep. [...] Put this (*handkerchief*) round it in the meantime"[67]—creating a physical scar. And there is another parallel visual signifier of trauma in the plays: Johnny Boyle and Manus Sweeney are both missing their left arms. Johnny's arm was blown off during nationalist fighting, whereas Manus's arm might have been lost in a mining accident in Montana. Or was it cut off by the brothers of Manus's wife as retaliation for seducing their sister? While the text never confirms which of the two stories is in fact the case, we are inclined to believe the latter account of Manus's injury, indicating internal violence on a small island that parallels the fighting of the Civil War (in Johnny Boyle's case) and the escalating violence in Northern Ireland for Friel and his contemporaries.

On Inishkeen, the gramophone accompanies Shane's violent dance, recalling the death dance in Lennox Robinson's *Portrait*. In Robinson's play, the gramophone provides accompaniment to a macabre dance of violence and even death for Peter, a man worn down by the psychological stress of striving to fit into a post-war culture that seems to hold no place for those unwilling to struggle and fight; Shane's dance is similarly sinister since he is "almost hysterical" before the music even starts, and the dance becomes an exponential escalation of physical violence against him. The war-weariness of Robinson's play and the hysteria of Friel's work are also present in Flann O'Brien's *At Swim-Two-Birds*: Mad King Sweeny's battle fatigue is signaled by a gramophone with nationalist implications, reminding us that in *The Gentle Island*, Manus Sweeney—described by Joe as "king of the whole bloody island"[68]—views the island as a bastion of Irish authenticity, despite the clearly negative implications of what reductive nationalism might lead to. Manus and, in fact, all the Sweeneys may be a little war-mad like Ireland's mythic hero, given their island's perpetual turn to violence. The gramophone in each of these works signals the tensions left unresolved in the wars of the early twentieth century, and in *The Gentle Island*, that tension "shatters fragile peace," making "war imminent."[69]

The culminating violence of Friel's play occurs when Manus and Sarah revile Shane for his alleged sexual liaison with Philly, which threatens the "barren island."[70] In *Dracula* and *Pygmalion*, the gramophone's coded gender and political implications make resistance to accepted gender roles necessary for political and individual autonomy. Mina Harker's ameliorative conformation to gender expectations as a mother at the conclusion of *Dracula* is belied by her subversive sexuality and use of the phonograph throughout the text. And *Pygmalion* prescribes certain sexualized gender roles for the gramophone and for women, which Eliza ultimately defies to gain independence. Heteronormative gender expectations are also bent in *The Gentle Island* when Shane solicits primarily male dancing partners and, later, when Philly beats Shane as a potential "expression of [...] subconscious sexual attraction" toward him, since directly after ascertaining that Shane is not badly hurt, he invites him to go out on his boat later that evening.[71] In *The Gentle Island*, gender roles are challenged during the gramophone scene, but the final act when Manus and Sarah attack Shane indicates that a continued cultural stranglehold on restrictive gender roles can lead to even greater violence.[72]

Shane too seems to understand that the incident with the resuscitated gramophone is only the beginning of the violence to come when he reports at the end of the scene, "Single yelp shatters fragile peace. Acute unease on paradise island. War thought imminent."[73] Friel uses the gramophone to highlight the ghosts and unresolved tensions of the past and how they are renewed in the present with flashes of parallel violence. They may be anachronistic and "ancient," but they are revived nonetheless against the backdrop of the Troubles. The Troubles themselves initially manifest as cultural traumas being belatedly assimilated, which, as a process, is traumatic in its own right.

✳✳✳

In conclusion, I have argued throughout this book that the gramophone functions in Irish literature as a signifier of the country's cultural memories, tensions, and traumas through the decades. It is not merely an object that sits quietly in the background as a setting piece nor is it an inconsequential prop. Its seeming inconspicuousness is exploded by its perpetual presence and action. This phenomenon is what drew me to this project in the first place. After noticing the gramophone in one Irish work, I couldn't help but see it cropping up over and over again in prominent works of Irish modernism. I couldn't unsee the work the gramophone was doing. This book examines over a dozen works in which the gramophone is not only present, but active in some way. These gramophones are agents of, assistants to, and witnesses of violence in myriad forms. As both a mute and voiced object, the gramophone not only embodies memories through its physical function, but it also replicates the belated assimilation of trauma in its asynchronous replay function. These gramophones are products of the Irish culture that surrounds them, and are also capable of influencing the culture that constructed them.

The gramophone functions as an irrepressible thing in a culture riddled with the symptoms of problematic memories, unresolved tensions, and unhealed traumas. The approach taken here reconsiders the potential for "thing theory" and media studies by contextualizing them against a specific culture's traumas. And if, as Ann Kaplan writes, "trauma theory is more about recovered referentiality [...] than about recovered memory,"[74] then a codified referent like the gramophone may be a more effective way of exploring cultural trauma than retracing history or literature in isolation. The gramophone collates and refers to cultural memory from its myriad strains. By explicating the gramophone's presence and actions in Irish literature, we become more attuned to the latent threads of cultural influence that shape these works. We understand that the mnemonics of a single object can be traced through time, accommodating shifts in cultural perception. We learn that a specific culture can subconsciously adopt an object to signify a latent cultural theme. The gramophone, as a media object, might speak through its records, but as a cultural object of memory and trauma in Ireland, it might speak even more loudly. This is the gramophonic echo.

Notes

Introduction

1   James Joyce, *Ulysses*, ed. Declan Kiberd (London: Penguin, 2000), 144.
2   Sebastian D. G. Knowles, "Death by Gramophone," *Journal of Modern Literature* 27, no. 1 (2003): 1–13, https://doi.org/10.1353/jml.2004.0060.
3   Joyce, *Ulysses*, 606.
4   Joyce, *Ulysses*, 625.
5   Joyce, *Ulysses*, 598.
6   Paul K. Saint-Amour, "Ulysses Pianola," *PMLA* 130, no. 1 (2015): 15, https://doi.org/10.1632/pmla.2015.130.1.15.
7   Many critics focus on the gramophone as a voiced object in *Ulysses*, a cyborg-ish mechanism that, through its audio, asserts a kind of human–object relationship. Angela Frattarola, for instance, argues that the gramophone in modernist literature, and in *Ulysses* in particular, demonstrates an effort to negate a filtration of experience through audio; the gramophone represents "a drive to present reality without a sense of mediation; an attention drawn to the subjectivity of hearing; an aesthetics of fragmentation; an association with the repetitious workings of the mind" (Angela Frattarola, "The Phonograph and the Modernist Novel," *Mosaic: An Interdisciplinary Critical Journal* 43, no. 1 (2010): 144). Chih-Hsien Hsieh points out that there is a "gramophone motif" throughout the novel, while explicating the "Proteus" episode in particular. Hsieh finds gramophonic imagery throughout the scene: a dog digging in the sand recalls Nipper the terrier from the His Master's Voice record labels while also recalling the scratching of the needle on a record; Stephen sorts through memories like archival recordings; time becomes an abstract

construct rather than a linear progression (see Chih-Hsien Hsieh, "Hark the Written Words: The Gramophone Motif in 'Proteus,'" in *Polymorphic Joyce*, ed. Franca Ruggieri and Anne Fogarty (Rome: Edizioni, 2012): 51–62). Other critics have pointed to the fact that Joyce actually recorded a portion of *Ulysses* as another point of interest; he recorded the "Aeolus" episode and chose it for its oratory qualities. See Adrian Curtin, "Hearing Joyce Speak: The Phonograph Recordings of 'Aeolus' and 'Anna Livia Plurabelle' as Audiotexts," *James Joyce Quarterly* 46, no. 2 (2009): 269–84; see also Damien Keane, "His Remastered Voice: Joyce for Vinyl," in *Science, Technology, and Irish Modernism*, ed. Kathryn Conrad, Cóilín Parsons, and Julie McCormick Weng (Syracuse, NY: Syracuse University Press, 2019), 144–59.

8   Walter Benjamin, "The Work of Art in the Age of Its Technological Reproducibility," in *The Norton Anthology of Theory and Criticism*, ed. Vincent B. Leitch, 2nd ed. (New York: W. W. Norton, 2010), 1051–71.

9   Jacques Derrida, "*Ulysses* Gramophone: Hear Say Yes in Joyce," in *Derrida and Joyce: Texts and Contexts*, ed. Andrew J. Mitchell and Sam Slote (New York: State University of New York Press, 2013), 56.

10   Jean-Marie Guyau, "Memory and Phonograph," in Friedrich A. Kittler, *Gramophone, Film, Typewriter* (Stanford, CA: Stanford University Press, 1999): 30–33. Kittler's work on gramophones starts with his 1984 essay "Dracula's Legacy" in which he describes the gramophone (and its predecessor, the phonograph) as a hardware in literature and culture that connects physical bodies to bodies or institutions of information and power. See Friedrich A. Kittler, "Dracula's Legacy," in *Literature, Media, Information Systems: Essays*, ed. John Johnston (Amsterdam: GB Arts International, 1997): 50–84.

11   Sam Halliday, *Sonic Modernity: Representing Sound in Literature, Culture and the Arts* (Edinburgh: Edinburgh University Press, 2013); Julian Murphet, Penelope Hone, and Helen Groth, eds., *Sounding Modernism: Rhythm and Sonic Mediation in Modern Literature and Film* (Edinburgh: Edinburgh University Press, 2017).

12   David Trotter, *Literature in the First Media Age: Britain Between the Wars* (Cambridge, MA: Harvard University Press, 2013).

13   Theodor W. Adorno, "The Curves of the Needle," trans. Thomas Y. Levin, *October* 55 (1990): 55, https://doi.org/10.2307/778935.

14   Bill Brown, "Thing Theory," *Critical Inquiry* 28, no. 2 (2001): 3.

15   Elaine Freedgood, *The Ideas in Things: Fugitive Meaning in the Victorian Novel* (Chicago: University of Chicago Press, 2010), 4.

16   Celia Marshik, *At the Mercy of Their Clothes: Modernism, the Middlebrow, and British Garment Culture* (New York: Columbia University Press, 2017), 9.

17   Jeffrey C. Alexander, *Trauma: A Social Theory* (Cambridge: Polity, 2012), 1.

18 Jeffrey C. Alexander, "Toward a Theory of Cultural Trauma," in *Cultural Trauma and Collective Identity*, ed. Jeffrey C. Alexander et al. (Berkeley, CA: University of California Press, 2004), 11.

19 This largely reinforces Marshall McLuhan's assertion that "the medium is the message." Marshall McLuhan, *Understanding Media: The Extensions of Man* (Cambridge, MA: MIT Press, 1994).

20 The gramophone sculpture was six meters tall and played music from the era through embedded speakers. The sculpture also created a sense of interactivity and community during the event. The plinth of the machine was designed purely as structure, "but it turned into basically seats and it would attract; it was like, I would say, bees landing on a flower" (Donnacha Cahill, RTÉ Gramophone Sculpture, Zoom Interview, March 13, 2021). This unintended outcome largely replicates the sense of community that gramophones created in that time period. The cover image for this book visually represents a community of listeners around the gramophone on Inishbiggle, Co. Mayo in 1900. The image is, of course, also capturing a certain sense of novelty attached to the machine. All the same, a single gramophone could serve as community entertainment for an entire village in the early twentieth century (see Hilary Bracefield, "Gramophone or Radio: Transatlantic Effects on the Development of Traditional Music in Ireland," *Irish Journal of American Studies* 13/14 (2004): 115–21). Cahill also points out that there is something "hypnotic" about the gramophone's combination of audio and visual presence: "I can imagine […] in the 1920s sitting down and imagine if they had a Bose or JBL or something like that, you know. You wouldn't look at it. But [with the gramophone] there was almost this piece of art to engage with." Cahill also has a smaller-scale gramophone, commissioned by National University of Ireland Galway, that has travelled throughout Ireland at events like the 2016 Galway Arts Festival and continues to create moments of memory and place. One of the primary experiences Cahill wants people to encounter with the sculpture is embedded memory: "Do know what was in that space? Do you remember the time that giant gramophone was there and occupied that space? That's the kind of conversation I want to hear about it."

21 F. S. Lyons, *Culture and Anarchy in Ireland, 1890–1939* (Oxford: Oxford University Press, 1979), 177.

22 William Butler Yeats, "Remorse for Intemperate Speech," in *The Winding Stair and Other Poems* (New York: Scribner, 2011), 58–59, lines 11–13.

23 Yeats, "Remorse," line 14.

24 Brendan Bradshaw, "Nationalism and Historical Scholarship in Ireland," in *Interpreting Irish History: The Debate on Historical Revisionism, 1938–1994*, ed. Ciaran Brady (Dublin: Irish Academic Press, 1999), 205.

25   Robert F. Garratt, *Trauma and History in the Irish Novel: The Return of the Dead* (New York: Palgrave Macmillan, 2011), 3.

26   Queensland Brain Institute, "Types of Memory," University of Queensland Australia, December 2, 2016, https://qbi.uq.edu.au/brain-basics/memory/types-memory.

27   Sean O'Casey, *Juno and the Paycock*, in *Modern and Contemporary Irish Drama*, ed. John P. Harrington, 2nd ed. (New York: W. W. Norton, 2009), 197–246.

28   Andrew E. Malone, "From the Stalls," *Dublin Magazine* (May 1925), 633.

29   Flann O'Brien, *At Swim-Two-Birds* (Normal, IL: Dalkey Archive Press, 1998), 99.

Chapter One: Gramophonic Trauma: Shattered Narratives and Undead Oralities

1   Our Special Correspondent, "The United States," *The Irish Times*, November 21, 1877.

2   Bram Stoker, *Dracula*, ed. Maurice Hindle (London: Penguin, 2003), 63.

3   Seward also contributes via telegrams, letters, and written journal entries while the vampire hunters chase Dracula beyond London. These varied media platforms make up less than 20 percent of Seward's overall contribution.

4   Stoker, *Dracula*, 68–69, emphasis original.

5   Stoker, *Dracula*, 6. The note has no attributed author, though the common assumption is that Harker is the author since he also writes the final note to the novel. Alyssa Straight, however, proposes that Mina might just as easily be the author. See Alyssa Straight, "Giving Birth to a New Nation: Female Mediation and the Spread of Textual Knowledge in *Dracula*," *Victorian Literature and Culture* 45, no. 2 (2017): 385, https://doi.org/10.1017/S1060150316000668.

6   Stoker, *Dracula*, 402.

7   Jean-Marie Guyau, "Memory and Phonograph," in Friedrich A. Kittler, *Gramophone, Film, Typewriter* (Stanford, CA: Stanford University Press, 1999), 30.

8   Guyau, "Memory," 30–31.

9   Guyau, "Memory," 30.

10   Stoker, *Dracula*, 235.

11   Mícheál Briody, *The Irish Folklore Commission 1935–1970: History, Ideology, Methodology*, 17 (Helsinki: Finnish Literature Society, 2007), 244.

12   Stoker seems to underestimate this storage issue as well, when he has Seward store these cylinders in a "large drawer" (*Dracula*, 236). Large indeed.

13 Joseph Finnamore, "The Latest Scientific Wonder," *The Irish Times*, May 27, 1878.

14 John Picker takes the connection to vampirism even further when he points out that Edison used to bite into musical instruments, including the phonograph, to accommodate his progressing deafness. See John M. Picker, *Victorian Soundscapes* (New York: Oxford University Press, 2003), 133–34.

15 The novel also discusses the "mind" on several occasions. The Victorian perception of the brain (biological organ) versus the mind (social construct) makes this distinction particularly interesting. By focusing on the references to the brain, however, I am following Seward's suit, since his interest is primarily scientific and concerned with the psychology of the physical brain.

16 Stoker, *Dracula*, 44.

17 Stoker, *Dracula*, 145.

18 Stoker, *Dracula*, 275.

19 Rob Boddice effectively summarizes Victorian theories about the gendered brain, explaining that the "man's brain" of this period was based on the idea of intellectual gentlemen, rather than the broader gender. Furthermore, "non-manly men, determined by race or by class ('brutes' or 'savages'), women ('emotional', 'childlike' and 'intuitive') and animals ('brutes' who were 'emotional', 'childlike' and 'intuitive', or 'sagacious')" were all generally compared with the animal mind, rather than the "man." Therefore, Dracula's "child brain" is much more animalistic than contemporary audiences might understand, and Mina's "man's brain" gives her both intellectual and social standing with her male counterparts. See Rob Boddice, "The Manly Mind? Revisiting the Victorian 'Sex in Brain' Debate," *Gender & History* 23, no. 2 (2011): 335, https://doi.org/10.1111/j.1468-0424.2011.01641.x.

20 Stoker, *Dracula*, 363.

21 Stoker, *Dracula*, 204.

22 Bram Stoker, *Personal Reminiscences of Henry Irving*, vol. 2 (Cambridge: Cambridge University Press, 2013), 316.

23 Friedrich A. Kittler, "Dracula's Legacy," in *Literature, Media, Information Systems: Essays*, ed. John Johnston (Amsterdam: GB Arts International, 1997), 56.

24 Stephanie Moss, "Bram Stoker and the Society for Psychical Research," in *Dracula: The Shade and the Shadow*, ed. Elizabeth Miller (Westcliff-on-Sea: Desert Island Books, 1998), 89. Moss goes on to point out that the distinction between these two consciousnesses are represented in Dracula by the "two Lucy Westenras" (alive and undead) and the Van Helsing/Dracula opposition.

25 Frederic W. H. Myers, "Das Doppel-Ich," *The Proceedings of the Society for Psychical Research* 6 (1889), 207, emphasis original.

26 Moss, "Bram Stoker," 90.

27 Nathan Oppenheim, "Why Children Lie," *Popular Science* 47, no. 2 (1895): 386.

28 Oppenheim, "Why Children Lie," 386.

29 Stoker, *Dracula*, 32–33.

30 Stoker, *Dracula*, 184.

31 Stoker, *Dracula*, 184.

32 Stoker, *Dracula*, 184.

33 Stoker, *Dracula*, 201, emphasis original.

34 Stoker, *Dracula*, 68.

35 Stoker, *Dracula*, 77–80, 152.

36 Stoker, *Dracula*, 80.

37 Stoker, *Dracula*, 69.

38 The flat-disk gramophone was largely in use in 1897 when Stoker published *Dracula*. The phonograph was still preferred by those like Seward who wanted to record *themselves*, since the gramophone disks largely dispensed with that function, placing a greater emphasis on duplicating sound production and playback. While the gramophone provides a more apt demonstration of centripetal and centrifugal forces in this particular scenario, those forces *are* still at play in the phonographic technology being used by Seward, particularly in the spring motor. Chapter 4 provides a closer examination of this particular aspect of the machinery.

39 Gramophone disks were much easier to duplicate than phonograph cylinders; it was in part because of the impracticality of duplication of cylinders that Berliner invented gramophone disks. Berliner's duplication process and the disks' durability largely account for the gramophone's commercial success over the phonograph in the twentieth century.

40 Stoker, *Dracula*, 111, 113, 167, 241, 265, 298.

41 When the gramophone company purchased the rights to the painting, they required the artist, Francis Barraud, to paint a gramophone instead of the competing phonograph.

42 Patrick Feaster interprets Nipper's "fidelity" to his master as a parallel to the idea of oral fidelity. See Patrick Feaster, "'Rise and Obey the Command': Performative Fidelity and the Exercise of Phonographic Power," *Journal of Popular Music Studies* 24, no. 3 (2012): 395, https://doi.org/10.1111/j.1533-1598.2012.01341.x.

43 Stoker, *Dracula*, 296.

44 Stoker, *Dracula*, 293.

45 Kittler, "Dracula's Legacy," 67.

46 Cathy Caruth, "Introduction," in *Trauma: Explorations in Memory*, ed. Cathy Caruth (Baltimore, MD: Johns Hopkins University Press, 1995), 8.

47 Caruth, "Introduction," 9.

48 Sigmund Freud, *Beyond the Pleasure Principle* (New York: Dover, 2015), 12, emphasis original.

49 Jamil Khader, "Un/Speakability and Radical Otherness: The Ethics of Trauma in Bram Stoker's *Dracula*," *College Literature* 39 (March 1, 2012): 74, https://doi.org/10.1353/lit.2012.0021.

50 Stoker, *Dracula*, 6.

51 Stoker, *Dracula*, 251, emphasis added.

52 Stoker, *Dracula*, 68.

53 The Penguin Classics edition of *Dracula* (2003) draws particular attention to some of these idiosyncrasies in its "Note on the Text." The text is based on the first edition of the novel, but the editors make "emendations" to the dates of four specific entries in order to assimilate these accounts accurately into the timeline of events. It is worth noting that other critical editions (including Oxford and Norton) make no mention of these errors, nor do they correct the dates. The impossible timelines stand.

54 Stoker, *Dracula*, 306.

55 Freud, *Beyond the Pleasure Principle*, 12, emphasis original.

56 Jennifer Wicke argues that Mina's typewriter is also like a vampire, consuming all of the narrative and all of the other media platforms to create a homogenized account. The phonograph, however, has several more physical features in common with the vampire. See Jennifer Wicke, "Vampiric Typewriting: *Dracula* and Its Media," *ELH* 59, no. 2 (1992): 467–93, https://doi.org/10.2307/2873351.

57 Christopher Morash, *A History of the Media in Ireland* (Cambridge: Cambridge University Press, 2010), 98.

58 "Classified Ad 103—No Title," *The Irish Times*, August 24, 1878.

59 "The Phonograph," *Dublin Evening Mail*, August 17, 1878.

60 "The Phonograph," *Weekly Irish Times*, August 24, 1878, emphasis added.

61 Stoker, *Personal Reminiscences*, vol. 2, 220.

62 Stoker, *Personal Reminiscences*, vol. 2, 220.

63 Cited in Picker, *Victorian Soundscapes*, 125.

64 See Chapter 2 for a discussion of "phonographysteria" in gendered terms.

65 Stoker, *Dracula*, 237.

66 Stoker might also have learned to appreciate oral folklore beyond his home through sources like his friendship with Oscar Wilde's family. Sir William and Lady Jane "Speranza" Wilde collected and published works of Irish folklore in the latter part of the nineteenth century. William Wilde took his sons with him on trips to the west of Ireland in order to collect oral iterations of these stories. Both Speranza and Oscar were famous for their oral delivery of stories and narratives, and Speranza in particular had a clear nationalistic fervor, since her pen name was a remnant from

her days as a fiery poetic contributor to the 1840s nationalist journal *The Nation*. Stoker was personally familiar with all of this history and he spent time at the Wilde household enjoying Speranza's hospitality and public salons.

67   Joseph Valente, *Dracula's Crypt: Bram Stoker, Irishness, and the Question of Blood* (Urbana, IL: University of Illinois Press, 2002), 16.

68   Valente, *Dracula's Crypt*, 16.

69   Robert Augustin Smart and Michael Hutcheson, "'Negative History' and Irish Gothic Literature: Persistence and Politics," *Caliban* 15, no. 1 (2004): 112, https://doi.org/10.3406/calib.2004.1509.

70   Charlotte Stoker, "Appendix II: Charlotte Stoker's Account of 'The Cholera Horror' in a Letter to Bram Stoker (c. 1875)," in Stoker, *Dracula*, 418.

71   Bram Stoker, "The Invisible Giant," in *Under the Sunset* (London: Sampson Low, 1881), 71.

72   Stoker, "The Invisible Giant," 66–67.

73   See Valente, *Dracula's Crypt*; Seamus Deane, *Strange Country* (Oxford: Clarendon Press, 1998); Terry Eagleton, *Heathcliff and the Great Hunger* (London: Verso, 1996); and Declan Kiberd, *Irish Classics* (Cambridge, MA: Harvard University Press, 2001).

74   *Dracula* includes its own examples of embedded folklore: the Transylvanians have significant lore about how to ward off vampires (which Harker dismisses as cultural superstition) and Dracula himself takes great pains to deliver an oral history of his ancestry and heritage, telling stories of battles and campaigns that utterly captivate Harker.

75   Stoker, *Dracula*, 9.

76   Deane, *Strange Country*, 89.

77   Cathal Póirtéir, ed., *Famine Echoes* (Dublin: Gill and Macmillan, 1995), 16.

78   Póirtéir, *Famine Echoes*, 11.

79   Stoker, *Dracula*, 6.

80   Briody, *Irish Folklore Commission*, 244.

81   "Feis Ceotest," *The Irish Times*, July 30, 1897.

82   Stoker, *Dracula*, 235.

83   Briody, *Irish Folklore Commission*, 245. The process of folklore collection via phonograph—and its "enticement"—is wonderfully satirized by Flann O'Brien in his 1941 novel *An Beal Bocht* (*The Poor Mouth*), which is explored further in the Coda.

84   Kittler argues that *Dracula* "is no vampire novel" but is rather "the written account of our bureaucratization [which a]nyone is free to call […] a horror novel as well" ("Dracula's Legacy," 73).

85   Stoker, *Dracula*, 237.

86   Stoker, *Dracula*, 237.

87   Cited in Briody, *Irish Folklore Commission*, 73, emphasis added.
88   Stoker, *Dracula*, 356.
89   Leanne Page, "Phonograph, Shorthand, Typewriter: High Performance Technologies in Bram Stoker's *Dracula*," *Victorian Network* 3, no. 2 (2011): 108.
90   Page, "Phonograph," 107. She compares Seward's adapted speech on the phonograph to Holmwood's abbreviated language in telegrams as well as our current text messaging abbreviations (e.g., BRB instead of "be right back").
91   Stoker, *Dracula*, 69.
92   Stoker, *Dracula*, 69.
93   Stoker, *Dracula*, 402.
94   Briody, *Irish Folklore Commission*, 237.
95   Briody, *Irish Folklore Commission*, 244.
96   Sean O'Sullivan, "The Work of the Irish Folklore Commission," *Oral History* 2, no. 2 (1974): 15.
97   Cited in Briody, *Irish Folklore Commission*, 245, emphasis added.
98   Stoker, *Dracula*, 304.
99   Stoker, *Dracula*, 6.
100 Stoker, *Dracula*, 402.

Chapter Two: Gramophonic Gendering: Women, Phonographysteria, and the Political Machine

1   "Phonogra[p]hysteria," *Weekly Irish Times*, April 15, 1899.
2   "Phonogra[p]hysteria."
3   "Phonogra[p]hysteria."
4   Barbara Engh, "Adorno and the Sirens: Tele-Phonographic Bodies," in *Embodied Voices: Representing Female Vocality in Western Culture*, ed. Leslie C. Dunn and Nancy A. Jones (Cambridge: Cambridge University Press, 1994): 120–35.
5   Kyle S. Barnett, "Furniture Music: The Phonograph as Furniture, 1900–1930," *Journal of Popular Music Studies* 18, no. 3 (2006): 315, https://doi.org/10.1111/j.1533-1598.2006.00096.x. The physical machine was assimilated into the domestic (and generally considered feminine) sphere as an object that men still controlled—advertisements of this period depict men supervising the use of the machine while women remained passive listeners (Barnett, "Furniture Music," 316)—and that women considered a potential source of aesthetic embarrassment, given its gendered implications.
6   For an overview of popular representations of the metropolitan marriage during the nineteeenth century, see Carol Schloss, "Molly's Resistance to the Union: Marriage and Colonialism in Dublin 1904," *Modern Fiction*

Studies 35, no. 3 (1989): 529–41; Julie Anne Miller, "Acts of Union: Family Violence and National Courtship in Maria Edgeworth's *The Absentee* and Sydney Owenson's *The Wild Irish Girl*," in *Border Crossings: Irish Women Writers and National Identities,* ed. Kathryn J. Kirkpatrick (Tuscaloosa, AL: University of Alabama Press, 2000): 13–37; Jane Elizabeth Dougherty, "An Angel in the House: The Act of Union and Anthony Trollope's Irish Hero," *Victorian Literature and Culture* 32, no. 1 (2004): 133–45, https://doi.org/10.1017/S1060150304000403.

7   Gendered taxonomy of race was a popular motif in the late nineteenth century, and most definitely in Ireland. See L. Perry Curtis, "The Four Erins: Feminine Images of Ireland, 1780–1900," *Éire-Ireland* 33, nos. 3–4 (1998): 70–102, https://doi.org/10.1353/eir.1998.0007.

8   "Home Rule: Resolution at Derby Conference Militant Irish Unionists," *The Irish Times*, December 2, 1911.

9   George Moore, *Modern Painting*, in *The Collected Works of George Moore* (New York: Boni and Liveright, 1923), 144.

10   John M. Picker, *Victorian Soundscapes* (New York: Oxford University Press, 2003), 129.

11   George Du Maurier, "Suggestions," *Punch*, no. 74, April 20, 1878, 179.

12   Picker, *Victorian Soundscapes*, 130.

13   Jennifer Forrest describes the sexual implications of female performance in the late nineteenth century and the anxiety over those same sexual implications in the recording of the female voice (Jennifer Forrest, "Scripting the Female Voice: The Phonograph, the Cinematograph, and the Ideal Woman," *Nineteenth-Century French Studies* 27, nos. 1/2 (1999): 71–95).

14   Bram Stoker, *Dracula*, ed. Maurice Hindle (London: Penguin, 2003), 68.

15   "The Possibilities of the Phonograph—By an Imaginative Artist," *Pall Mall Budget* 36 (August 16, 1888): 19. Picker also uses this comic image (*Victorian Soundscapes*, 121) to point out a different section of the illustration and the phonograph's potential for the "Criminal Voice Detection" department, which our modern voice recognition partially realizes. The illustration is a densely packed trove of seven different possibilities for the phonograph and voice recording—fanciful and practical—that have modern technological counterparts.

16   "Possibilities of the Phonograph," 19.

17   Stoker, *Dracula*, 153, 164.

18   Picker, *Victorian Soundscapes*, 135.

19   During Lucy's illness, Seward records at least two entries on her phonograph as part of his documentation of her illness and death (his September 18 and 19 accounts). Seward's phonograph is the primary record of Lucy's fatal illness, largely outweighing Lucy's own contribution to her narrative. Leah Richards points out that Lucy's contribution

to the overall narrative is limited in quantity and is largely imitative in quality (Leah Richards, "Mass Production and the Spread of Information in *Dracula*: 'Proofs of so Wild a Story,'" *English Literature in Transition, 1880–1920* 52, no. 4 (2009): 447, https://doi.org/10.2487/elt.52.4(2009)0047). For instance, Lucy only has nine identified entries in the overall account (three letters to Mina, five diary entries—meant to "imitate Mina" (*Dracula*, 119)—and one memorandum). Her authorial contribution to the novel equals less than 2.5 percent of the entire work.

20　W. J. McCormack, "Irish Gothic and After (1820–1945)," in *The Field Day Anthology of Irish Writing*, ed. Seamus Deane, vol. II (New York: W. W. Norton, 1992), 843.

21　Joseph Valente, *Dracula's Crypt: Bram Stoker, Irishness, and the Question of Blood* (Urbana, IL: University of Illinois Press, 2002), 16.

22　Valente, *Dracula's Crypt*, 17.

23　Bram Stoker, *Personal Reminiscences of Henry Irving*, vol. 2. (Cambridge: Cambridge University Press, 2013), 31.

24　While at Trinity College, Stoker was involved in the Historical Society's debates, in which he voted and spoke approvingly of Daniel O'Connell's political career (which culminated in a struggle for the repeal of the Act of Union) and argued and voted in favor of abolition of the viceroyalty in Ireland. And yet he also voted repeatedly against the dissolution of British imperial rule (Valente, *Dracula's Crypt*, 22).

25　Valente, *Dracula's Crypt*, 22.

26　See Carole Pateman, *The Sexual Contract* (Stanford, CA: Stanford University Press, 1988).

27　Joseph Valente, *The Myth of Manliness in Irish National Culture, 1880–1922* (Urbana, IL: University of Illinois Press, 2011), 27.

28　Valente, *Myth of Manliness*, 27. Valente's work points to several examples of political illustrations from this period in which illustrators resisted the tendency to simianize the Irish Parnell, instead depicting him as a strong masculine character. His self-restraint and lack of emotional response in Home Rule debates added to his aura of masculinity (as opposed to the effusive, "effeminate" responses generally attributed to Irish figures). His self-restraint and masculinity seemed like "something akin to Home Rule of the soul" (*Myth of Manliness*, 34).

29　Cited in Joe Joyce, "Crisis Reaches Breaking Point for Parnell," *The Irish Times*, December 2, 2009.

30　Valente, *Myth of Manliness*, 54.

31　Stoker, *Personal Reminiscences*, vol. 2, 29.

32　See George Edward Wright, *The Parnellite Split: Or, the Disruption of the Irish Parliamentary Party* (London: Routledge, 1891). Parnell also was considered a risk for a potential turn to the physical enforcement of Home Rule. After the divorce crisis and split of 1890, he made a political misstep in appealing to Fenian sentiment by taking on the violent language of Fenianism and Republicanism. Stoker was decidedly unsympathetic to this aspect of Parnell's version of Home Rule.

33 Sally Ledger, for instance, explicates the graphic scene of Lucy's second death in terms of sexual assault. She describes the "final, horrific mutilation of Lucy Westenra [as] partly a projection onto Lucy's body of the masculine fury provoked by the fact that she finally eludes all of her suitors [...]. It is also, of course, a violent revenge on the sexualized body of the New Woman" (Sally Ledger, *The New Woman: Fiction and Feminism at the Fin de Siècle* (Manchester: Manchester University Press, 1997), 104).

34 Forrest, "Scripting the Female Voice," 86. Forrest points out that the concept of the disembodied female voice "tested the boundaries of the male listener's comfort zone, challenging the social consensus regarding gender and voice when women were connected to communication technologies; [...] women facilitated the exchange of information, but were themselves considered unfit as emitters."

35 Forrest, "Scripting the Female Voice," 80.

36 Stoker, *Dracula*, 67.

37 Stoker, *Dracula*, 189–90.

38 Even years later she was vilified as "That bitch, that English whore [who] put the first nail in [Parnell's] coffin" by a character in James Joyce's *Ulysses*, a novel that takes place in 1904 and was written in 1922 (*Ulysses*, ed. Declan Kiberd (London: Penguin, 2000), 755). Joyce's depiction points to the longevity and intensity of this vitriolic viewpoint in Ireland.

39 Picker, *Victorian Soundscapes*, 135.

40 Stoker, *Dracula*, 153.

41 Stoker, *Dracula*, 62.

42 Stoker, *Dracula*, 99.

43 Stoker, *Dracula*, 79.

44 Picker, *Victorian Soundscapes*, 134.

45 Stoker, *Dracula*, 250.

46 F. D. Klingender, *The Condition of Clerical Labour in Britain* (London: Martin Lawrence, 1935), 108.

47 Jennifer Fleissner points out that it has become "commonplace enough to view Lucy's body as the primary site for the novel's conflicts over female desire. More recent criticism has thus turned to the typist Mina, arguing that her body emblematizes a different battleground, upon which the stakes concern women's relation to work and writing" (Jennifer L. Fleissner, "Dictation Anxiety: The Stenographer's Stake in *Dracula*," *Nineteenth-Century Contexts* 22, no. 3 (2000): 418, https://doi.org/10.1080/08905490008583519). Though Fleissner suggests that the typewriter was the primary object/technology for a discussion of gender

roles in *Dracula*, the phonograph holds an equally significant gender association, especially for stenographers.

48　Stoker, *Dracula*, 238–39, emphasis added.

49　Mina's use of the typewriter in this instance is a continuation of the female-as-typewriter motif implied in the "Phonographysteria" article and a phenomenon that Fleissner and Wicke pay particular attention to.

50　See Luke Gibbons, "'Some Hysterical Hatred': History, Hysteria and the Literary Revival," *Irish University Review* 27, no. 1 (1997): 7–23.

51　Stoker, *Dracula*, 10, 158, 197.

52　Stoker, *Dracula*, 185, 186, 245, 264, 361.

53　Stoker, *Personal Reminiscences*, vol. I, 344.

54　Stoker, *Personal Reminiscences*, vol. I, 344.

55　Valente, *Dracula's Crypt*, 40.

56　Valente, *Dracula's Crypt*, 41.

57　Stoker, *Dracula*, 402.

58　Stoker, *Dracula*, 236.

59　Stoker, *Dracula*, 236.

60　Stoker, *Dracula*, 237.

61　Picker, *Victorian Soundscapes*, 135.

62　Picker, *Victorian Soundscapes*, 135, emphasis original.

63　Stoker, *Dracula*, 238.

64　Stoker, *Dracula*, 236.

65　Stoker, *Dracula*, 237.

66　Carol A. Senf, "Dracula: Stoker's Responses to the New Woman," in *Gothic: Critical Concepts in Literary and Cultural Studies*, ed. Fred Botting and Dale Townshend (London: Routledge, 2004): 331–46.

67　Stoker, *Dracula*, 402.

68　George Bernard Shaw, "Preface for Politicians," in *Modern and Contemporary Irish Drama: Backgrounds and Criticism*, ed. John P. Harrington, 2nd ed. (New York: W. W. Norton, 2009), 473.

69　"Unionist Demonstration in Enniskillen: Speech by Right Hon. J.H. Campbell," *The Irish Times*, January 5, 1906.

70　"Home Rule: Debate in the Commons," *The Irish Times*, February 16, 1911.

71　"Gramophone Campaign," 7.

72　"Home Rule: Resolution at Derby," 7.

73　Joyce, *Ulysses*, 625.

74　Edith Œnone Somerville and Martin Ross, *Mount Music* (London: Longmans, Green, 1919), 250. Somerville wrote and published the book on her own, but credited Ross as her co-author since they had, years before Ross's death, conceptualized the novel together. Somerville and Ross also include gramophones in other works, though those references are more incidental than provocative. In *Some Experiences of an Irish R.M.*

(1899), a horse's breathing is described as "a cross between a grampus and a gramaphone [*sic*]" during a fox hunt (Edith Œnone Somerville and Martin Ross, *Some Experiences of an Irish R.M.* (London: Longmans, Green, 1906), 222). In a later work, *In Mr. Knox's County* (1915), someone's singing in another room is characterized as "a sound as of a gramophone in the next world" (Edith Œnone Somerville and Martin Ross, *In Mr. Knox's Country* [London: Longmans, Green, 1915], 156).

75 Bernard Shaw, *Pygmalion*, in *George Bernard Shaw's Plays*, ed. Sandie Byrne, 2nd ed. (New York: W. W. Norton, 2002), 289.

76 Shaw, *Pygmalion*, 289.

77 "Teaching by Phonograph," *Weekly Irish Times*, December 5, 1896.

78 George Bernard Shaw, *A Treatise on Parents and Children*, Project Gutenberg, https://www.gutenberg.org/files/908/908-h/908-h.htm.

79 Shaw, *Pygmalion*, 300.

80 Shaw, *Pygmalion*, 307, 308.

81 There are constant awkward moments with regards to the sexual implications of Eliza's interactions with the men at Wimpole Street: "dressing Eliza"—first with Doolittle, then with Mrs. Higgins—as well as the euphemistic "turn on" in the second and fifth acts. There is also the insinuation, when Eliza goes missing and Pickering tries to contact the police, that Pickering and Higgins are involved in "some improper purpose" with regards to the young woman (*Pygmalion*, 336). Though we know that nothing overtly sexual is occurring between Eliza and her mentors, Shaw perpetually underscores just how sexual this entire scenario appears through this use of dramatic irony. *Pygmalion* challenges preconceived notions about "kept women" by keeping the innuendos but negating any sexual frisson between Higgins and Eliza throughout the play.

82 Shaw, *Pygmalion*, 312.

83 Shaw, *Pygmalion*, 313.

84 Shaw, *Pygmalion*, 313.

85 Shaw, *Pygmalion*, 313.

86 On Higgins's part at least there is a certain tongue-in-cheek to paying Doolittle. He delights in the dustman's candor, rough logic, and absolute dissipation as a self-proclaimed member of the "undeserving poor." He views Doolittle in almost the exact same light as he does Eliza, proposing to make Doolittle a Member of Parliament with a little tutoring. Shaw clearly intends for Higgins's attitude toward everyone and everything to be that of a curious but indifferent scientist, but this does not entirely absolve his culpability in capitulating to Doolittle's demands for money in exchange for Eliza.

87 "Display Ad 22—No Title," *The Irish Times*, September 18, 1912.

88 J. Ellen Gainor argues that the 1938 film makes this sexualization and violence even more overt when Eliza is stripped of her clothing and bodily

attacked in the bathing scene. She argues that the scene's symbolic rape occurs under the direction of Higgins, though Mrs. Pearse is the one who carries out the bathing while he and Pickering bemusedly listen at the bottom of the stairs. When the nearly unrecognizable Eliza reenters the scene, she has been "robbed of all vestiges of her old identity, including a symbolic virginity" (J. Ellen Gainor, "The Daughter in Her Place," in *George Bernard Shaw's Plays*, ed. Sandie Byrne, 2nd ed. (New York: W. W. Norton, 2002), 526). This creates a strong parallel between Eliza's and Lucy Westenra's symbolic rapes as well as the #MeToo movement.

89 George Bernard Shaw, *Collected Letters*, vol. 2, ed. Dan H. Laurence (New York: Viking, 1985), 787.

90 Philip Klass and E. E. Kellett, "'The Lady Automaton' by E.E. Kellett: A *Pygmalion* Source?", *Shaw* 2 (1982): 75–100. John Picker explicates this potential *Pygmalion* source further by examining Kellett's more expanded text, "The New Frankenstein" (John M. Picker, "My Fair Lady Automaton," *Zeitschrift für Anglistik und Amerikanistik* 63, no. 1 (2015): 89–100, https://doi.org/DOI 10.1515/zaa-2015-0006).

91 E. E. Kellett, "The Lady Automaton," *Pearson's Magazine* 11 (1901): 663–57.

92 Kellett, "Lady Automaton," 665.

93 Kellett, "Lady Automaton," 666.

94 George Bernard Shaw, "George Bernard Shaw Discusses the Perils of Gramophones (1927)," *Great Audio Moments*, vol. 39 (Global Journey, 2013).

95 Shaw, "Perils of Gramophones."

96 Shaw, *A Treatise on Parents and Children*.

97 Shaw, *Pygmalion*, 323.

98 Shaw, *Pygmalion*, 324.

99 Shaw, *Pygmalion*, 326.

100 Shaw, *Pygmalion*, 327–28. I have altered the format, but not the content, of these speeches for the sake of clarity.

101 Shaw, *Pygmalion*, 328.

102 Shaw, *Pygmalion*, 328.

103 Stoker, *Dracula*, 357.

104 Stoker, *Dracula*, 356.

105 Homi Bhabha, "Of Mimicry and Man: The Ambivalence of Colonial Discourse," *October* 28 (1984): 127, https://doi.org/10.2307/778467, emphasis added.

106 Klass and Kellett, "Lady Automaton," 81.

107 Shaw, *Pygmalion*, 346.

108 Shaw, *Pygmalion*, 346.

109 Shaw, *Pygmalion*, 346.

110 Forrest, "Scripting the Female Voice," 75.

111 Theodor W. Adorno, "The Curves of the Needle," trans. Thomas Y. Levin, *October* 55 (1990): 54, https://doi.org/10.2307/778935.

112 Shaw, *Pygmalion*, 349.

113 Shaw, *Pygmalion*, 333.

114 Shaw, *Letters*, vol. 3, 160.

115 Shaw, *Pygmalion*, 303.

116 Shaw, *Pygmalion*, 331.

117 Picker points out that in the film version of *My Fair Lady*, Eliza becomes a hybrid of Audrey Hepburn as the physical manifestation and Marni Nixon as the voice for the musical performances. Hepburn pre-recorded the songs, but Nixon's voice was considered more viable for the part. This is in stark contrast to the fact that Rex Harrison, who had a negligible singing voice but rather spoke on pitch, refused to pre-record, and sound production accommodated his performance demands and innovated the wearable microphone (Picker, "My Fair Lady Automaton"). The subordinated priority of the recorded female voice to the male voice has fascinating layers of complexity in this work and its afterlives.

118 Cited in Ann L. Ferguson, *The Instinct of an Artist: Shaw and the Theatre* (New York: Cornell University Press, 1997), 34.

119 Shaw, "Preface for Politicians," 475.

120 Shaw, *Pygmalion*, 328.

121 Shaw, *Pygmalion*, 327.

122 Shaw, *Pygmalion*, 349.

123 Shaw, *Pygmalion*, 349.

124 Shaw, *Pygmalion*, 349.

125 Awam Amkpa, "Drama and the Languages of Postcolonial Desire: Bernard Shaw's 'Pygmalion,'" *Irish University Review* 29, no. 2 (1999): 296.

Chapter Three: Gramophonic Violence: The Gramophones of the Irish Revolution

1   John MacDonagh, Bureau of Military History Witness Statement (BMH WS-219), 1916.

2   Fearghal McGarry, *The Rising: Ireland, Easter 1916* (Oxford: Oxford University Press, 2010), 156.

3   MacDonagh, BMH WS-219, 2.

4   Seosamh de Brún, *The 1916 Diaries of an Irish Rebel and a British Soldier*, ed. Mick O'Farrell (Cork: Mercier Press, 2014), April 28, Kindle edition.

5   Gerard Shannon, "Today in Irish History, 9 July 1917: The Death of Muriel MacDonagh," *The Irish Story*, http://www.theirishstory.com/2016/07/09/today-in-irish-history-9-july-1917-the-death-of-muriel-macdonagh/#_

edn10. Information from a newspaper cutting of Muriel's account of last seeing Thomas (National Library of Ireland Manuscript 20,646/2).

6 Sean O'Casey, *Autobiographies II: Drums Under the Windows and Inishfallen, Fare Thee Well* (London: Faber and Faber, 2011), https://books.google.com/books?id=0TjDmbgP8DcC&source=gbs_navlinks_s.

7 O'Casey, *Autobiographies II.*

8 These gramophones replaced the large ornate horn with an inverted horn embedded in the lid of the box. Sound was carried from the needle on the record through a small, adjustable horn apparatus directed at the concave lid of the machine, which then amplified and refracted the sound outward.

9 Imperial War Museums. "The Decca Gramophone." Accessed April 22, 2021. https://www.iwm.org.uk/collections/item/object/31665.

10 Mary Evans, "Well or Wounded, They Love to Listen to Decca," *Illustrated London News*, n.d.

11 "Classified Ad 89," *The Irish Times*, October 13, 1915.

12 "Classified Ad 89," 4.

13 "Display Ad 16," *The Irish Times*, October 18, 1916.

14 A Part Worn Colonel, "Gramophones in Hospitals," *The Times*, February 12, 1916.

15 C.O., "Gramophones in Hospitals," *The Times*, February 15, 1916.

16 David Evans, Richard Clark, and Thaddeus O'Sullivan, "Episode 1," *The Crimson Field* (BBC 1, April 6, 2014).

17 Music therapy, which is clearly at work in my discussion of the gramophone's use in treatment, was still largely undefined and experimental before World War I. The gramophone had a great impact on the therapy's development, making such treatment widely accessible and viable during the war and afterward.

18 Brendan Kelly, *Hearing Voices: The History of Psychiatry in Ireland* (Kildare: Irish Academic Press, 2019), 143.

19 Jay Needham and Eric Leonardson, "Instruments of Tension: Gramophones, Springs and Performance of Place," *Leonardo Music Journal* 23 (2013): 37.

20 Theodor W. Adorno, "The Curves of the Needle," trans. Thomas Y. Levin, *October* 55 (1990): 55, https://doi.org/10.2307/778935.

21 Cited in Kelly, *Hearing Voices*, 139.

22 A. Collins, "The Richmond District Asylum and the 1916 Easter Rising," *Irish Journal of Psychological Medicine* 30, no. 4 (2013): 280, emphasis added.

23 Collins, "Richmond District Asylum," 280.

24 Collins, "Richmond District Asylum," 281.

25 Kelly, *Hearing Voices*, 139.

26 Kelly, *Hearing Voices*, 140.

27 Elizabeth Bowen, *The Last September* (New York: Anchor Books, 2000), 230, emphasis original.

28   Bowen, *The Last September*, 230.

29   Neil Corcoran, "Discovery of a Lack: History and Ellipsis in Elizabeth Bowen's *The Last September*," *Irish University Review* 31 (2001): 331, https://doi.org/10.2307/25504880.

30   Bill Brown, "Thing Theory," *Critical Inquiry* 28, no. 2 (2001), 4.

31   Elizabeth Bowen, *The Mulberry Tree: Writings of Elizabeth Bowen*, ed. Hermione Lee (London: Random House, 1999). Many other prominent works on Bowen equally emphasize her use of anthropomorphizing and highlighting objects over individuals. See Maud Ellmann, *Elizabeth Bowen: The Shadow Across the Page* (Edinburgh: Edinburgh University Press, 2004); Eluned Summers-Bremner, "Dead Letters and Living Things," in *Elizabeth Bowen: New Critical Perspectives*, ed. Susan Osborn (2009): 61–84; Patrick Moran, "Elizabeth Bowen's Toys and the Imperatives of Play," *Éire-Ireland* 46, no. 1 (2011): 152–76; and Simon During, "Accelerate: Why Elizabeth Bowen Likes Cars," in *Science, Technology, and Irish Modernism*, ed. Kathryn Conrad, Cóilín Parsons, and Julie McCormick Weng (2019): 113–27.

32   Matthew Brown, "Strange Associations: Elizabeth Bowen and the Language of Exclusion," *Irish Studies Review* 20, no. 1 (2012): 12, https://doi.org/10.1080/09670882.2011.624325.

33   Ellmann, *Elizabeth Bowen*, 97; Keri Walsh, "Elizabeth Bowen, Surrealist," *Éire-Ireland* 42, no. 3 (2007): 127.

34   Bowen, *The Last September*, 224.

35   Bowen, *The Last September*, 212.

36   Bowen, *The Last September*, 220.

37   The name by which it is called can have its own polarizing political and national connotations. While War of Independence is the most accepted and accurate, I often describe it in this chapter as the Anglo-Irish War to highlight the connection to the Anglo-Irish characters of Bowen's novel.

38   Bowen, *The Last September*, 209, emphasis original.

39   Bowen, *The Last September*, 49, emphasis original.

40   Bowen, *The Last September*, 49.

41   Bowen, *The Last September*, 224.

42   Bowen, *The Last September*, 212.

43   Bowen, *The Last September*, 295.

44   Bowen, *The Last September*, 219.

45   *The Last September* is filled with similar hauntings. Gerald, for example, is often ghostlike, which foreshadows his death: he is constantly considering shadows, the title of the last section of the novel ambiguously foretells the "Departure of Gerald," and throughout the work, Lois and Gerald take particular notice of the back of his head (*The Last September*, 70, 132, 224, 231), hinting at the shocking news to come,

that Gerald has been shot "through the head" by Irish rebels (*The Last September*, 293). One early scene between Gerald and Lois at the tennis party incorporates each of these allusions: "Gerald lay like a dark fine shadow [...]. His head was pleasant with bumps, that made planes of light and shadow over his polished hair. [... Lois] saw him as though he were dead, as though she had lost him, with the pang of an evocation" (*The Last September*, 70). Gerald's death is only one of the many examples of atemporal haunting that fill the pages of *The Last September*. The gramophone is another.

46 Bowen, *The Last September*, 210.

47 Bowen, *The Last September*, 218, 219.

48 Bowen, *The Last September*, 211.

49 Theodor W. Adorno, "The Form of the Phonograph Record," trans. Thomas Y. Levin, *October* 55 (1990): 56, https://doi.org/10.2307/778936.

50 Cited in Bowen, *Mulberry Tree*, 124. The preface to the American edition of *The Last September* was originally published in 1952 but is not generally included in current print editions of the novel.

51 Bowen, *The Last September*, 3.

52 Jessica Gildersleeve, *Elizabeth Bowen and the Writing of Trauma: The Ethics of Survival* (Amsterdam: Rodopi, 2014), 36.

53 Gildersleeve, *Elizabeth Bowen and the Writing of Trauma*, 46.

54 Virginia Woolf, *Mrs. Dalloway* (San Diego: Harcourt, 1925), 142.

55 Woolf, *Mrs. Dalloway*, 140.

56 Siegfried Sassoon, "Dead Musicians," in *Counter-Attack and Other Poems* (London: Heinemann, 1918), 58–59, lines 17–27.

57 Bowen, *The Last September*, 230; Sassoon, "Dead Musicians," line 27.

58 Bowen, *The Last September*, 230.

59 Bowen, *The Last September*, 154.

60 Bowen, *The Last September*, 155.

61 Bowen, *The Last September*, 155.

62 It is worth noting that the film adaptation of *The Last September* (1999) essentially opens with this scene. The gramophone—an ornate machine with the full exterior horn, rather than the more portable "trench gramophone"—is initially situated on the ground by itself as the shot pans up to Gerald and Lois's dancing feet. Then, after a sequence of shots of Danielstown, the two are shown dancing energetically down the avenue with Daventry holding the gramophone. He is depicted as conducting his own kind of twirling dance with the gramophone as his ostensible partner. And while I unreservedly applaud the choice to make Daventry the man who is connected to the gramophone in this early scene (it is more likely that another soldier named Armstrong was the one responsible for the bet), the decision to have him dancing with the machine is an utter impossibility in terms of consistent playback. The needle would

have skittered across the record so violently in this scenario that not only would replay have been immediately interrupted, but the record would have been damaged (*The Last September*, dir. Deborah Warner, Trimark, 1999).

63   Bowen, *The Last September*, 40.

64   Bowen, *The Last September*, 40.

65   Bowen, *The Last September*, 41.

66   Bowen, *The Last September*, 42. The "trench-coat" is yet another example of Bowen's objectification of people in favor of anthropomorphizing objects. It is also a reference to World War I and its trench warfare, making this encounter particularly fraught with violent imagery. For more about this particular object, its role in *The Last September*, and its connection to the larger scope of twentieth-century culture, see Celia Marshik, *At the Mercy of Their Clothes: Modernism, the Middlebrow, and British Garment Culture* (New York: Columbia University Press, 2017).

67   Bowen, *The Last September*, 42–43.

68   Bowen, *The Last September*, 43.

69   Part of Lois's anxiety about her ability to reproduce her gramophonic trauma stems from a distrust of her female perspective (as described in relation to the gendered object in Chapter 2 above). Lois's gramophonic experiences of the Anglo-Irish War therefore translate into a trauma narrative fraught with the protagonist's self-doubt and marginalized gender and social perspective, while the armed conflict seeps in from the peripheries of the novel's main action.

70   Bowen, *The Last September*, 64. Though the burning of Danielstown and the other Big Houses of the novel are constantly foreshadowed in *The Last September*, they are not the only burnings and reprisals, as the RIC barracks incident demonstrates.

71   Bowen, *The Last September*, 66.

72   Bowen, *Mulberry Tree*, 126.

73   Bowen, *Mulberry Tree*, 126.

74   Bowen, *The Last September*, 82.

75   Bowen, *The Last September*, 83, emphasis original.

76   Corcoran, "Discovery of Lack," 326.

77   Later in the novel, Bowen overtly draws out the tension in Lois's relationships with the English and Irish when Gerald informs the Danielstown residents that he has helped capture the Connors' son. The immediate Danielstown reaction is "I'm sorry to hear that. [...] His mother is dying. [...] We must remember to send up now and inquire after Mrs. Michael Connor" (*The Last September*, 131). Some time later, Sir Richard speculates that Gerald's death might have been retribution for his role in Connor's capture: "Peter Connor's friends: they knew everything, they were persistent: it did not do to imagine..." (*The Last September*, 298).

78   Bowen, *The Last September*, 180. Lois also makes comparisons between the crack in the wall and the House of Usher. Corcoran suggests that this crack is a widening of the one in Lois's basin, serving as "the fissure opening between a politically and historically exhausted past and a potentially non-existent future" ("Discovery of Lack," 318). Corcoran also suggests that Bowen's allusion to Poe's *The Fall of the House of Usher*, the way the cracks in that novel lead to the fall of the house after its secret is revealed, has a parallel in this mill, where "the terrible secret of Anglo-Irish history remain[s] architecturally articulate on the land" ("Discovery of Lack," 326). Gildersleeve comes to a similar conclusion when she writes, "Just as the silences in a text point to the impossibility of representing trauma, the unspeakable limit-event, so too the cracks and crevasses of the ruin figure the unrepresentable" (*Elizabeth Bowen and the Writing of Trauma*, 44).

79   Bowen, *The Last September*, 183.

80   Bowen, *The Last September*, 183. This description also draws parallels with Woolf's concept of sound as depicted in *Mrs. Dalloway*, when she describes the "leaden circles dissolv[ing] in the air" after Big Ben rings, the "ring after ring of sound" when another clock chimes, and the "faint sounds [rising] in spirals" throughout her home (*Mrs. Dalloway*, 186, 50, 38).

81   Bowen, *The Last September*, 182.

82   Bowen, *The Last September*, 230.

83   Bowen, *The Last September*, 231. This third mention of cracks seems to have gone unnoticed by previous scholars, Corcoran in particular, since he makes much of the previous two instances.

84   Bowen, *The Last September*, 230–31, emphasis original.

85   Bowen, *The Last September*, 300.

86   Cited in Bowen, *Mulberry Tree*, 126, emphasis original.

87   Bowen, *Mulberry Tree*, 126.

88   Molly Keane, *Mad Puppetstown* (London: Little Brown, 2013), 109.

89   Keane, *Mad Puppetstown*, 269.

90   John Banville, "Introduction," in J. G. Farrell, *Troubles* (New York: New York Review of Books, 2002), x.

91   Farrell, *Troubles*, 194.

92   "Sir Bryan Mahon's House Burned," *The Irish Times*, February 17, 1923.

93   "Sir Bryan Mahon's House Burned."

94   There are clear indicators of new money in the set pieces of the second act and in the scene descriptions by O'Casey, but the Boyles point out none particularly, except the purchase and arrival of the gramophone.

95   Sean O'Casey, *Juno and the Paycock*, in *Modern and Contemporary Irish Drama*, ed. John P. Harrington, 2nd ed. (New York: W. W. Norton, 2009), 218.

96 O'Casey, *Juno and the Paycock*, 219.
97 O'Casey, *Juno and the Paycock*, 219. Mary and her father discuss the quality of music played on a gramophone in a debate that touches on some of Walter Benjamin's principles presented in his influential essay, "The Work of Art in the Age of Its Technological Reproducibility." Benjamin directly considers the gramophone when he claims that authenticity in technical reproduction is impossible. In that same vein, Mary's choice of words when describing the gramophone's playback as "destructive of real music" suggests that she sides with Benjamin's contention that "the original underlies the concept of its authenticity" in any mechanical reproduction of art (Walter Benjamin, "The Work of Art in the Age of Its Technological Reproducibility," in *The Norton Anthology of Theory and Criticism*, ed. Vincent B. Leitch, 2nd ed. (New York: W. W. Norton, 2010), 978). Mary's description is not exclusively a commentary on mechanical reproduction, since O'Casey seems to hint at a satirical reading of the same statement. Mary undercuts her own intellectual concerns about the gramophone when she performs a type of gramophony on her own part (much like Eliza and Mina in the previous chapter). Mary is actually reciting Charlie Bentham's ideas in his absence. Boyle counters her argument, perhaps picking up on the irony of Mary's statement, when he does not respond to the statement as an argument, but rather bases his incredulity on (the absent) Bentham's character: "Desthructive of music—that fella ud give you a pain in your face" (*Juno and the Paycock*, 219).

Mary compounds her initial gramophony by citing her other suitor to add weight to her argument: "But, father, Jerry says the same" (*Juno and the Paycock*, 219). To which Boyle provides the same critique. Mary's echo of her male suitors is problematic and yet she continues to recite from them well into the last act of the play. Mary displays a rather remarkable ability for gramophonic replication when she recites back to Jerry Devine three complete stanzas of his own verse in the third act; these verses, she explains, were only ever read at a single Labour meeting, but they have stayed with her enough for her to point out their relevance in the face of her own current troubles. Perhaps it is the violence of the imagery in Devine's poem that helps Mary recall them so long after the initial recitation. The "eagle's tearin' claw," the "craters [and] their deadness," and the "agonizing horror / of a violin out of tune" use gramophonic imagery that replicates Mary's state of mind during a heart-rending expression of her own pain (*Juno and the Paycock*, 242).

98 O'Casey, *Juno and the Paycock*, 246.
99 O'Casey, *Juno and the Paycock*, 198.
100 Gabriel Fallon, *Sean O'Casey, the Man I Knew* (London: Little Brown, 1965), 17, emphasis added.

101 O'Casey, *Juno and the Paycock*, 200.

102 O'Casey, *Juno and the Paycock*, 200.

103 O'Casey, *Juno and the Paycock*, 200.

104 O'Casey, *Juno and the Paycock*, 213.

105 O'Casey, *Juno and the Paycock*, 214.

106 O'Casey, *Juno and the Paycock*, 200.

107 O'Casey, *Juno and the Paycock*, 219.

108 O'Casey, *Juno and the Paycock*, 219.

109 O'Casey, *Juno and the Paycock*, 219.

110 O'Casey, *Juno and the Paycock*, 230. Similar recitals occur on pp. 240 and 243.

111 Cited in Kelly, *Hearing Voices*, 27–28.

112 O'Casey, *Juno and the Paycock*, 200.

113 O'Casey, *Juno and the Paycock*, 221.

114 O'Casey, *Juno and the Paycock*, 221.

115 Adorno, "Phonograph," 56.

116 O'Casey, *Juno and the Paycock*, 222.

117 Susan Harris, "Sensationalizing Sacrifice," in *Modern and Contemporary Irish Drama*, ed. John P. Harrington, 2nd ed. (New York: W. W. Norton, 2009), 514.

118 Harris, "Sensationalizing Sacrifice," 514.

119 O'Casey, *Juno and the Paycock*, 199.

120 O'Casey, *Juno and the Paycock*, 227.

121 Joseph Holloway, *Joseph Holloway's Abbey Theatre: A Selection from His Unpublished Journal Impressions of a Dublin Playgoer* (Carbondale, IL: Southern Illinois University Press, 2009), 496.

122 Christopher Murray, "Juno and the Paycock," in *Modern and Contemporary Irish Drama*, ed. John P. Harrington, 2nd ed. (New York: W. W. Norton, 2009), 506.

123 O'Casey, *Juno and the Paycock*, 198, 227.

124 O'Casey, *Juno and the Paycock*, 227.

125 O'Casey, *Juno and the Paycock*, 227.

126 O'Casey, *Juno and the Paycock*, 229.

127 O'Casey, *Juno and the Paycock*, 229.

128 O'Casey, *Juno and the Paycock*, 229.

129 O'Casey, *Juno and the Paycock*, 230.

130 O'Casey, *Juno and the Paycock*, 230.

131 O'Casey, *Juno and the Paycock*, 230.

132 O'Casey, *Juno and the Paycock*, 230.

133 O'Casey, *Juno and the Paycock*, 243.

134 O'Casey, *Autobiographies II*, 144.

135 O'Casey, *Juno and the Paycock*, 243.

136 O'Casey, *Juno and the Paycock*, 243.

137 O'Casey, *Juno and the Paycock*, 244.
138 O'Casey, *Juno and the Paycock*, 245.
139 O'Casey, *Juno and the Paycock*, 245.
140 O'Casey, *Juno and the Paycock*, 246.

Chapter Four: Gramophonic Strain: Residual Tension in Post-War Literature

1   "Gramophones: How to Keep Them in Good Condition," *The Irish Times*, July 24, 1923.
2   "Gramophones."
3   Indemnity Act, 1923, §15, http://www.irishstatutebook.ie/eli/1923/ act/31/enacted/en/html.
4   "Irish Questions in Parliament," *The Irish Times*, July 24, 1923.
5   Les P. Pook, "An Introduction to Coiled Springs (Mainsprings) as a Power Source," *International Journal of Fatigue* 33, no. 8 (2011): 1018, https:// doi.org/10.1016/j.ijfatigue.2010.11.014.
6   See warnings against the Haller "time bomb" anniversary clock, for instance (Mervin Passmore, "The Haller Time Bomb Clock," 2009, https://silo.tips/download/copyright-mervyn-passmore-2009). The clock is called the "German time bomb" because the mainspring is known to occasionally fracture or slip from the ratchet that controls its unraveling, with consequences that range from a harmless but noisy unwinding to an explosive and destructive uncoiling. This type of failure in a clock might have been the inspiration for the failed assassination-by-clock-bomb plot point in Oscar Wilde's short story "Lord Arthur Savile's Crime," in *The Short Stories of Oscar Wilde: An Annotated Selection*, ed. Nicholas Frankel (Cambridge, MA: Harvard University Press, 2020): 39–92. And while there is no gramophone model that displays a parallel perpetual mainspring error, the "time bomb" clock is a particularly apt example of the consequences of fatigue failure in a mainspring.
7   Andrew E. Malone, "From the Stalls," *Dublin Magazine* (May 1925), 633.
8   "New Play at the Abbey Theatre: 'Portrait' by Mr. Lennox Robinson," *The Irish Times*, April 1, 1925.
9   Robert Goode Hogan and Richard Burnham, *The Years of Sean O'Casey, 1921–1926*, vol. 6, *The Modern Irish Drama: A Documentary History* (Dublin: Dolmen Press, 1975), 270. General audiences apparently agreed with the theater critics, since *Portrait* only had in total sixteen performances at the Abbey Theatre in 1925.
10   Malone, "From the Stalls," 633.
11   Malone, "From the Stalls," 633.
12   Malone, "From the Stalls," 634.

13 H.N.K., "A New Play by Mr. Lennox Robinson," *Manchester Guardian*, April 10, 1925.

14 Susan L. Mitchell, "'Portrait' at the Abbey Theatre," *Irish Statesman*, April 4, 1925.

15 Mitchell, "'Portrait,'" 114.

16 Mitchell, "'Portrait,'" 115, emphasis added.

17 Lennox Robinson, *The White Bird. Portrait* (Dublin: Talbot, 1928), 112.

18 Robinson, *Portrait*, 127.

19 "Gramophone Recital at Abbey Theatre," *The Irish Times*, December 9, 1924.

20 The plays include *The Round Table* (1922), *Portrait* (1925), *Ever the Twain* (1929), *Church Street* (1934), and *Bird's Nest* (1937).

21 Bill Brown, "Thing Theory," *Critical Inquiry* 28, no. 2 (2001), 4.

22 Robinson, *Portrait*, 108.

23 Robinson, *Portrait*, 107–8.

24 The references to iron and stone ages link to the Scottish Enlightenment's concept of stadialism, the theory of human cultural development that cast the Irish as at the dawn of their development, not yet civilized but on their way.

25 Bill Kissane, "'A Nation Once Again'?: Electoral Competition and the Reconstruction of National Identity After the Irish Civil War, 1922–1923," in *After Civil War: Division, Reconstruction, and Reconciliation in Contemporary Europe*, ed. Bill Kissane (Philadelphia, PA: University of Pennsylvania Press, 2015): 43–69.

26 Robinson, *Portrait*, 107.

27 Norreys O'Conor, "A Dramatist of Changing Ireland," *Sewanee Review* 30, no. 3 (1922): 277.

28 Kurt Eisen, "Lennox Robinson," in *Irish Playwrights, 1880–1995* (London: Greenwood Press, 1997): 308–21.

29 Hogan and Burnam, *The Years of Sean O'Casey*, 270.

30 Robinson, *Portrait*, 119, 116.

31 Robinson, *Portrait*, 96.

32 Robinson, *Portrait*, 96.

33 Robinson, *Portrait*, 121.

34 Robinson, *Portrait*, 121.

35 Robinson, *Portrait*, 106.

36 Robinson, *Portrait*, 106.

37 Robinson, *Portrait*, 106.

38 Robinson, *Portrait*, 106, 108.

39 Sean O'Casey, *Three Dublin Plays*, ed. Christopher Murray (London: Faber and Faber, 1998).

40 Robinson, *Portrait*, 107.

41 Robinson, *Portrait*, 101.

42   Robinson, *Portrait*, 102.

43   Robinson, *Portrait*, 102.

44   Robinson, *Portrait*, 102.

45   Robinson, *Portrait*, 103.

46   Robinson, *Portrait*, 111.

47   Robinson, *Portrait*, 113.

48   Frank O'Connor, *Leinster, Munster and Connaught* (London: Robert Hale, 1950).

49   "Come, Landlord, Fill a Flowing Bowl. H. De Marsan, Publisher, 54 Chatham Street, N. Y.," image, Library of Congress, Washington, D.C. 20540 USA, https://www.loc.gov/resource/amss.sb10068a/?st=text.

50   Robinson, *Portrait*, 122.

51   Robinson, *Portrait*, 124, 123.

52   Robinson, *Portrait*, 124.

53   Robinson, *Portrait*, 125.

54   Robinson, *Portrait*, 125.

55   Robinson, *Portrait*, 125.

56   Robinson, *Portrait*, 126.

57   Lennox Robinson, "Heritage of the Meek [Afterwards Called 'Portrait']," Manuscript, Lennox Robinson Papers, Special Collections Research Center, Morris Library, Southern Illinois University Carbondale, 1925, Box 3. While rehearsing the play, Robinson realized that Tom was the right character choice for such action. In the staging draft of the play, Robinson crossed out the lines and actions that were attributed to Charlie in obfuscating Peter's death and replaced Charlie with Tom. To suit word to action, Tom is also the one who turns the gramophone on and off for the death dance. (See Abbey Theatre, "Portrait" (n.d.), Abbey Theatre Digital Archive at National University of Ireland, Galway, 11036_S_0001, 31 Mar 1925. 1–26. [script].)

58   Lennox Robinson, *The Round Table: A Comic Tragedy in Three Acts* (London: Putnam, 1924), 46–47.

59   Robinson, *Portrait*, 127.

60   James Plunkett, *Farewell Companions* (London: Gainsborough Press, 1996), 21.

61   Louis MacNeice, "An Eclogue for Christmas," in *The Collected Poems of Louis MacNeice* (Oxford: Oxford University Press, 1967), 33.

62   MacNeice, "An Eclogue for Christmas," 33.

63   Barry Ward, "Interview with Barry Ward," in Paul Laverty, *Jimmy's Hall* (London: Route, 2014), Kindle edition.

64   Paul Laverty, "Introduction," in Laverty, *Jimmy's Hall*.

65   Laverty, *Jimmy's Hall*.

66   Laverty, *Jimmy's Hall*.

67   Brian Friel, *Dancing at Lughnasa* (London: Faber and Faber, 1990), 31.

68   Friel, *Dancing at Lughnasa*, 50.
69   Friel, *Dancing at Lughnasa*, 51, emphasis original.
70   Neil Jordan, *Nightlines* (New York: Random House, 1995), 60.
71   Jordan, *Nightlines*, 39.
72   Jordan, *Nightlines*, 127.
73   Francis Stuart, *Black List, Section H* (London: Penguin, 1996), 377. This account sounds eerily like *The Irish Times* article of February 17, 1923, which describes the burning of a Big House: "While the furniture was being piled to be burned, the raiders took a gramophone from the house, placed it on the doorstep, and set it going to a lively tune."
74   O'Brien's publishing house, Longmans, which housed the majority of the first run of the novel, was bombed during the London Blitz. O'Brien was quick to point out the "grim irony that is not without charm": that his book ultimately survived the war, whereas Hitler did not (William Gass "Introduction," in Flann O'Brien, *At Swim-Two-Birds* (Normal, IL: Dalkey Archive Press, 1998), v).
75   Gass writes, "[*At Swim-Two-Birds*] appeared in the same year (1939) as *Finnegans Wake* [...] but the beginning of the text (there are several 'openings') is pure Samuel Beckett" (Gass, "Introduction," v).
76   O'Brien, *At Swim-Two-Birds*, 59.
77   O'Brien, *At Swim-Two-Birds*, 60–61.
78   O'Brien, *At Swim-Two-Birds*, 96.
79   O'Brien, *At Swim-Two-Birds*, 98.
80   O'Brien, *At Swim-Two-Birds*, 98–99.
81   O'Brien, *At Swim-Two-Birds*, 99.
82   O'Brien, *At Swim-Two-Birds*, 100.
83   O'Brien, *At Swim-Two-Birds*, 98.
84   O'Brien, *At Swim-Two-Birds*, 98, 99.
85   O'Brien, *At Swim-Two-Birds*, 99.
86   O'Brien, *At Swim-Two-Birds*, 27, 40, 122.
87   O'Brien, *At Swim-Two-Birds*, 99.
88   O'Brien, *At Swim-Two-Birds*, 99. It is unclear whether this misspelling of anadiplosis is intentional or not, though its duplication as "anadipolsis" in at least two editions of the novel would indicate that it *is* intentional. This potentially serves as a critique of the student, who is none-too-dutiful as a scholar—his uncle asks him "Do you ever open a book at all?" (*At Swim-Two-Birds*, 4)—though his attention to detail and figures of speech throughout the novel would belie the assumption of sloppiness in his assessments. It does, however, contribute to the perception that the student, while assuming a posture of condescension toward and disdain of his uncle, is not as infallible as he would like to believe.
89   O'Brien, *At Swim-Two-Birds*, 98.
90   O'Brien, *At Swim-Two-Birds*, 99.

91 Jacques Chailley, *40,000 Years of Music: Man in Search of Music* (New York: Farrar, Straus and Giroux, 1964), 114. Chailley identifies the first electronic recording of classical music as taking place on March 21, 1925.

92 O'Brien, *At Swim-Two-Birds*, 99.

93 O'Brien, *At Swim-Two-Birds*, 144.

94 Declan Kiberd, *Irish Classics* (Cambridge, MA: Harvard University Press, 2001), 515.

95 Bonnie Kime Scott, "The Subversive Mechanics of Woolf's Gramophone in *Between the Acts,*" in *Virginia Woolf in the Age of Mechanical Reproduction,* ed. Pamela L. Caughie (New York: Garland, 2000), 105.

96 O'Brien, *At Swim-Two-Birds*, 99.

97 O'Brien, *At Swim-Two-Birds*, 99.

98 Kiberd, *Irish Classics*, 514.

99 O'Brien, *At Swim-Two-Birds*, 95.

100 O'Brien, *At Swim-Two-Birds*, 61–95.

101 James George O'Keeffe, *Buile Suibhne: Being the Adventures of Suibhne Geilt, A Middle-Irish Romance* (London: Irish Texts Society, 1913).

102 Seamus Heaney, *Sweeney Astray: A Version from the Irish* (New York: Farrar, Straus and Giroux, 1983).

103 T. S. Eliot, notably, incorporated aspects of the Sweeney legend into several of his poems: "Sweeney Among the Nightingales" (1918), "Mr. Eliot's Sunday Morning Service" (1918), "Sweeney Erect" (1919) and *The Waste Land* (1922); the latter work also famously alludes to a gramophone—both Sweeney and the gramophone appear in "The Fire Sermon." In 1932 additional fragments about Sweeney were published as *Sweeney Agonistes*. Eliot's depictions, however, are obviously not translations of *Buile Suibhne* specifically.

104 O'Brien, *At Swim-Two-Birds*, 65.

105 *Report of the War Office Committee of Enquiry into "Shell-Shock": Presented to Parliament by Command of His Majesty* (London: Imperial War Museum, repr. 2014), 139.

106 O'Brien, *At Swim-Two-Birds*, 65.

107 O'Brien, *At Swim-Two-Birds*, 67.

108 Denell Downum, "Citation and Spectrality in Flann O'Brien's 'At Swim-Two-Birds,'" *Irish University Review* 36, no. 2 (2006): 312.

109 Downum, "Citation and Spectrality," 312.

110 O'Brien, *At Swim-Two-Birds*, 65.

111 O'Brien, *At Swim-Two-Birds*, 65.

112 O'Brien, *At Swim-Two-Birds*, 65. O'Brien's translation of the text pays particular attention to the importance of alliteration—"madly mad-gone" and "fury and fits and frenzy and fright-fraught fear"—as a feature of pre-1600 Irish writing. His translations are a deeply scholarly

engagement with the traditions of Irish literature and myth, which the comic tone in the rest of his fiction often overshadows. Sweeny of *At Swim-Two-Birds* is one of the most violent and stylistic translations of the story, and it is thanks in part to O'Brien's translation that the story of Sweeny has been perpetuated in the twentieth and twenty-first centuries.

113 O'Brien, *At Swim-Two-Birds*, 123.
114 O'Brien, *At Swim-Two-Birds*, 134.
115 O'Brien, *At Swim-Two-Birds*, 135.
116 O'Brien, *At Swim-Two-Birds*, 236.
117 O'Brien, *At Swim-Two-Birds*, 228.
118 O'Brien, *At Swim-Two-Birds*, 237.
119 O'Brien, *At Swim-Two-Birds*, 238.
120 O'Brien, *At Swim-Two-Birds*, 238.

Coda: Gramophonic Echoes

1   Brian Friel, *Dancing at Lughnasa* (London: Faber and Faber, 1990), 28–29.
2   Friel, *Dancing at Lughnasa*, 30.
3   Elizabeth Bowen, "Songs My Father Sang Me," in *The Collected Stories of Elizabeth Bowen* (New York: Knopf, 1981), 650.
4   Bowen, "Songs My Father Sang Me," 654.
5   Bowen, "Songs My Father Sang Me," 651.
6   Elizabeth Bowen, *The Heat of the Day* (New York: Anchor Books, 2002), 71.
7   Bowen, *Heat of the Day*, 73.
8   Flann O'Brien, *The Poor Mouth: A Bad Story about the Hard Life*, trans. Patrick C. Power (Normal, IL: Dalkey Archive Press, 1996), 42–43. This echoes Mina Harker's assessment of the machine when she first encounters it in *Dracula*, describing it as "a wonderful machine" but "cruelly true" (*Dracula*, 237).
9   Magnetic wire recorders were available to the Commission's field workers, but the temperamental equipment and fragile wires were less rugged than the wax cylinders and analog process of the Ediphones. Hence the dated technology was still very much in use and visible in *Gaeltacht* communities in the 1940s.
10 O'Brien, *Poor Mouth*, 44.
11 O'Brien, *Poor Mouth*, 44–45.
12 O'Brien, *Poor Mouth*, 45.
13 O'Brien, *Poor Mouth*, 45.
14 Maebh Long, *Assembling Flann O'Brien* (London: Bloomsbury, 2014), 184.

15   Sean O'Faolain, "The Faithless Wife," in *The Oxford Book of Irish Short Stories*, ed. William Trevor (Oxford: Oxford University Press, 2010), 317.
16   O'Faolain, "Faithless Wife," 320, 329.
17   James Joyce, *Ulysses*, ed. Declan Kiberd (London: Penguin, 2000), 933. In the same year that Joyce published *Ulysses*, T. S. Eliot published *The Waste Land*, which famously also evokes a gramophone in conjunction with a stilted sexual encounter. The woman has "one half-formed thought": "Well now that's done: and I'm glad it's over." With her "automatic hand, [she] puts a record on the gramophone" (T. S. Eliot, *The Waste Land*, ed. Michael North (New York: W. W. Norton, 2001)). The gramophone's capacity to represent the rote and mechanical repetition of sex and relationships is a far-reaching one, as Mlle Morphy, Molly Bloom, and Eliot's unnamed young woman effectively demonstrate.
18   James Plunkett, "The Eagles and the Trumpets," in *Collected Short Stories* (Dublin: Poolbeg, 1977), 231.
19   Plunkett, "Eagles and Trumpets," 232.
20   Plunkett, "Eagles and Trumpets," 232–33.
21   Plunkett, "Eagles and Trumpets," 233.
22   Plunkett, "Eagles and Trumpets," 233.
23   Interestingly, BBC Radio 3 paired these two plays, *Embers* and *Krapp's Last Tape*, in a 2006 broadcast.
24   Sarah Keller, "'Once Wasn't Enough for You': Beckett, Technology, and Preservation," *Literature-Film Quarterly* 38 (2010): 233.
25   Samuel Beckett, *Embers*, in *The Complete Dramatic Works* (London: Faber and Faber, 2006), 255.
26   Beckett, *Embers*, 261.
27   Beckett, *Embers*, 261.
28   Edna O'Brien, *The Country Girls: Three Novels and an Epilogue* (New York: Farrar, Straus and Giroux, 2017), 34.
29   O'Brien, *Country Girls*, 98.
30   O'Brien, *Country Girls*, 224.
31   O'Brien, *Country Girls*, 308.
32   Edna O'Brien, "Irish Revel," in *The Oxford Book of Irish Short Stories*, ed. William Trevor (Oxford: Oxford University Press, 2010), 505, 509.
33   Patrick McCabe, *The Butcher Boy* (New York: Delta, 1994), 194.
34   Joyce, *Ulysses*, 598.
35   McCabe, *Butcher Boy*, 222–23, 19–21.
36   Frank McGuinness, "Surviving the 1960s: Three Plays by Brian Friel 1968–1971," in *The Cambridge Companion to Brian Friel*, ed. Anthony Roche (Cambridge: Cambridge University Press, 2007), 27.
37   Fintan O'Toole, *Critical Moments: Fintan O'Toole on Modern Irish Theatre* (Dublin: Carysfort Press, 2003), 211.
38   Brian Friel, *The Gentle Island* (London: Davis-Poynter, 1973), 19.

39 McGuinness, "Surviving the 1960s," 26.

40 José Lanters, "Violence and Sacrifice in Brian Friel's 'The Gentle Island' and 'Wonderful Tennessee,'" *Irish University Review* 26, no. 1 (1996): 164.

41 Chu He, "Nationalism and the West in Brian Friel's 'The Gentle Island' and Martin McDonagh's 'The Beauty Queen of Leenane,'" *Nordic Irish Studies* 13, no. 2 (2014): 5.

42 Seamus Deane, "Introduction," in Brian Friel, *Selected Plays* (London: Faber and Faber, 1984), 15.

43 Friel, *Gentle Island*, 34.

44 The gramophone on the remote and isolated Inishkeen also has connections to the cover image for this book: a gramophone brought to the very isolated island of Inishbiggle, Co. Mayo, as a novelty for the residents in 1900.

45 Friel, *Gentle Island*, 25.

46 Friel, *Gentle Island*, 31.

47 Friel, *Gentle Island*, 26.

48 Friel, *Gentle Island*, 37.

49 Friel, *Gentle Island*, 37.

50 Friel, *Gentle Island*, 35.

51 The Blasket Islands were evacuated in 1953. Denis Johnston's 1934 play *Storm Song* also plays on allusions to the Blasket biographies and satire of J. M. Synge's *Riders to the Sea*, set on the Aran Islands. Johnston's play, which was largely a flop, depicts a film director who comes to an island off the west coast, bringing with him a gramophone and film equipment; in his pursuit of an "authentic" experience, he drowns while trying to film the islanders during a storm. Flann O'Brien's *Poor Mouth* is also a satire of the Blasket biographies, creating a vivid network of allusion in Friel's play.

52 Muiris Ó Súileabháin, *Twenty Years A-Growing* (Nashville, TN: J. S. Sanders, 1998), 131.

53 Seán Mac an tSíthigh, "Deck Chair Recovered from *Lusitania* is Restored," *RTÉ*, August 29, 2018, https://www.rte.ie/news/munster/2018/0829/988306-lusitania/. In *Twenty Years A-Growing*, Ó Súilleabháin describes the islanders recovering the body of Henry Atkinson, an officer on the *Lusitania*.

54 Ó Súilebháin, *Twenty Years A-Growing*, 131.

55 Friel, *Gentle Island*, 35.

56 Friel, *Gentle Island*, 39.

57 Friel, *Gentle Island*, 43.

58 Friel, *Gentle Island*, 41.

59 Friel, *Gentle Island*, 41.

60 Friel, *Gentle Island*, 45.

61 Helen Lojek, "Brian Friel's Gentle Island of Lamentation," *Irish University Review* 29, no. 1 (1999): 48.

62 Lojek, "Brian Friel's Gentle Island," 48.
63 Denis Ireland, "The Backward-Looking Reason Why the I.R.A. Exists," *The Irish Times*, February 20, 1971, emphasis added.
64 Only three years later, another *Irish Times* journalist would further identify the politics surrounding Northern Ireland's conflicts as gramophonic. While debating aspects of the Sunningdale Agreement—an attempted tripartite power-sharing agreement between Britain, Northern Ireland, and the Republic of Ireland known collectively as the Council of Ireland, which was signed in 1973 and collapsed in 1974—Mr. Blaney, an MP, wanted to reaffirm a resolution passed in 1949 about the Republic's right to a whole and united Ireland. Senator Conor Cruise O'Brien countered Blaney's motion, pointing out that "to do this would be to declare that they had not been able to learn anything from the progress of events, and that they were incapable, not merely of new thinking, but of testing, qualifying, or modifying earlier thinking"; the article goes on to point out that Blaney's position "was like a needle stuck in the cracked groove of a gramophone record" ("Fianna Fail Votes in Support of Resolution: Nothing Done to Allay Fears on Sunningdale Pact," *The Irish Times*, February 28, 1974).
65 "What's on in the Arts," *The Irish Times*, November 29, 1971.
66 Michael Parker, "Telling Tales: Narratives of Politics and Sexuality in Brian Friel's *The Gentle Island*," *Hungarian Journal of English and American Studies (HJEAS)* 2, no. 2 (1996): 61.
67 Friel, *Gentle Island*, 44.
68 Friel, *Gentle Island*, 9.
69 Friel, *Gentle Island*, 48.
70 Friel, *Gentle Island*, 39.
71 Parker, "Telling Tales," 69.
72 Lojek points out that "homoeroticism itself" is not really the culprit of the violence in *The Gentle Island*, especially since the Sweeneys initially have no problem with Peter and Shane's relationship. She goes on to explain that

> Homoeroticism [...] does not appear to be either unusual (it is native to both coasts of Ireland) or a problem. Rather, problems arise when any erotic desire is repressed or misused. Manus's betrayal of the young girl he impregnates leads to his maiming and poisons his eventual marriage. Peter's twisting of gratitude to compel affection corrodes his relationship with Shane. Joe's inarticulateness prevents his marriage with Anna. Sarah's confinement to an island and to a marriage that frustrates her sexuality yields repressions that break out in violence. ("Brian Friel's Gentle Island," 58)

When Shane allegedly threatens the continuation of the island's future inhabitants through a non-procreative relationship with Philly, Sarah shoots Shane and we are left uncertain if he will live. This result suggests that a violent stance against anything other than traditional views of sexuality, nationality, or culture will ultimately result in a sterile relationship and a bleak future: the island's inhabitants are down to three (Philly, Sarah, and Manus), the island is a veritable ghost town, and Philly and Sarah's marriage will likely never result in offspring. The island is literally and figuratively barren and serves as a potential metonym for Ireland at large, and as a critique of the violence of the Troubles.

73 Friel, *Gentle Island*, 48.
74 Ann Kaplan, *Trauma Culture: The Politics of Terror and Loss in Media and Literature* (New Brunswick, NJ: Rutgers University Press, 2005), 70.

Index

#MeToo 80, 198n88

Abbey Theatre 75, 136, 146
abreaction 98–99, 102, 105, 107–9, 118,
    121
    see also repetition; therapies
Act of Union 58, 90, 195n24
Adorno, Theodor 6, 85–86, 91, 106
Alexander, Jeffrey 9–10
Amkpa, Awam 200n125
anachronism/anachrony 35, 37–38,
    179
    see also memory; trauma
Anglo-Irish 16, 62–63, 76, 94, 100–102,
    109, 113, 115–16, 118, 128, 156,
    202n37, 205n78
Anglo-Irish War 103, 113, 115, 202n37,
    204n69
    see also War of Independence
Armistice 103
    see also World War I (also The Great
    War)
Asquith, H. H. 76, 86
At Swim-Two-Birds 3, 16–17, 134–36,
    150–51, 158–59, 163–64, 181, 188,
    211n74–75, 211n88, 212n112
    Mr. Corcoran (character) 152–53,
    156, 158, 163

Sweeny, Mad King (character)
    151–52, 159–63, 169, 181,
    212n112
    see also O'Brien, Flann
automaton 79–82, 84–90, 110, 148
    see also "Lady Automaton"
autonomy 4, 8–9, 14, 58–59, 64, 72,
    75–76, 78, 86, 90–91, 181
    political 4, 9, 14, 58–59, 64, 72, 75–76
    sexual 14, 58–59, 64, 72, 75, 78, 90,
    181
Auxiliaries (Black and Tans) 102–3
    see also War of Independence

Ballybeg (*Baile Beag*) 172–73
    see also *Dancing at Lughnasa*; Friel,
    Brian; *Gentle Island*; *Philadelphia
    Here I Come*; *Translations*
Banville, John 203n62, 205n90
Barnett, Kyle S. 57
Barraud, Francis 190n41
    see also Nipper the terrier
Beal Bocht, An see Poor Mouth, The
    see also O'Brien, Flann
Beckett, Samuel 135, 150–51, 170,
    211n75
    Dream of Fair to Middling Women
    135

Embers 170
Krapp's Last Tape 170
"More Pricks than Kicks" 135
Benjamin, Walter 5, 206n97
Berliner, Emile 7, 32, 190n39
Between the Acts 2
    see also Woolf, Virginia
Beyond the Pleasure Principle 191n48
    see also Freud, Sigmund
Bhabha, Homi 84
Big House 77, 102, 109, 115–17, 150,
    174, 204n70, 211n73
    Bowen's Court 115, 117
        see also Bowen, Elizabeth
    burning 115–17, 150, 174, 204n70
        211n73
    Danielstown 102, 104, 109, 111–12,
        115, 203n62, 205n70, 205n77
    Mad Puppetstown 116n205
    Sir Bryan Mahon's estate 117,
        211n73
Bird's Nest 135
    see also Robinson, Lennox
Black List, Section H 135, 150, 211n73
    see also Stuart, Francis
Blasket biographies 168, 176, 215n51
    in *Gentle Island* 176
    in *Poor Mouth* 167–69, 215n51
    in *Storm Song* 215n51
    Twenty Years A-Growing 176
Blasket Islands 168, 176, 215n51
Bloom, Leopold (character) 1–3, 77
    see also Ulysses
Bloom, Molly (character) 169, 214n17
    see also Ulysses
Boddice, Rob 189n19
Bowen, Elizabeth 2, 16, 94, 100–103,
    106–8, 111–17, 135, 167, 180,
    202n31, 202n37, 204n66, 204n77,
    205n78
    Bowen's Court 115, 117
    correspondence with Woolf 101–2
        see also Woolf, Virginia
    Death of the Heart 135
    fascination with objects 101–2

Friends and Relations 135
Heat of the Day 167
Last September, The 3, 16, 94,
    100–102, 105–6, 108–9, 115–17,
    128, 167, 180, 202n45, 203n62,
    204n66, 204n77, 205n78
Mulberry Tree 202–5
"Songs My Father Sang Me" 167
To the North 135
"Boy Who Swapped a Bog for a Gramo-
    phone, The" 135
    see also Cannon, Moya
Boyle, Captain (character) 16, 117–18,
    121, 124
    see also Juno and the Paycock
Boyle, Johnny (character) 16, 117–28,
    142, 174, 180–81
    see also Juno and the Paycock
Boyle, Juno (character) 117–21, 123–24,
    126–28
    see also Juno and the Paycock
Boyle, Mary (character) 117–19, 123,
    126–28, 206n97
    see also Juno and the Paycock
Bracefield, Hillary 187n20
Bradshaw, Brendan 12
brain 13, 22–26, 28–29, 33, 38, 69–70,
    97, 108, 121, 149, 189n15, 189n19
    fever 25–26, 29
    gender in brain debate 26, 189n19
    vs mind 189n15
    see also mind
Brandon, Peter (character) 17, 136–37,
    139–47, 152, 174, 181, 210n57
    see also Portrait
breakage 17, 134, 139, 151, 154–56,
    160–64
    see also At Swim-Two-Birds;
        mainspring
Breuer, Josef 33
    see also Studies in Hysteria
Briody, Mícheál 48
Brown, Bill 6, 101
Brown, Matthew 202n32
Buile Suibne 160–62

see also O'Keefe, J. G.; Sweeney
    (general mythic figure)
Burnham, Richard 136, 140
Butcher Boy, The 171–72
    see also McCabe, Patrick

Cahill, Donnacha 11, 187n20
Campbell, J. H. 76
Campbell, Mrs. Patrick 89
Cannon, Moya 135
    see also "Boy Who Swapped a Bog for
    a Gramophone, The"
Caruth, Cathy 34
Chamberlain, Austen 58, 77
Charcot, Jean-Martin 26
"Charge of the Light Brigade, The" 41
    see also Tennyson, Alfred, Lord
cholera 21, 43–44
Church Street 135, 209n20
    see also Robinson, Lennox
Civil War 12, 15–16, 94, 117–18, 120,
    125, 132, 134–35, 140, 143, 149–50,
    152, 154–56, 181
    Anti-Treaty 16, 118, 120, 155
    Pro-Treaty 150, 155
Clarke, Tom 94
Collins, A. 99
Connolly, James 94
Conversation Piece 135
    see also Keane, Molly
Corcoran, Neil 101, 113
Cosgrave, W. T. 150
Country Girls, The 171
    see also O'Brien, Edna
Crimson Field, The 98
cultural trauma 9–11, 13–14, 18, 20,
    43–45, 52, 100, 128, 163, 179–80,
    182–83
    assimilation of 5, 20, 34–35, 182
Curtin, Adrian 185n7
Curtis, L. Perry 194n7
cylinder (for phonograph) 6–7, 20,
    23–25, 37–38, 41, 51–52, 67, 73–74,
    78–79, 89, 91, 174, 180, 188n12,
    190n39, 213n9

Dáil Éireann 103, 115, 178
dance/dancing 103–8, 110–14, 116, 138,
    145, 148–49, 158, 165, 171, 177, 181,
    n203n62, 210n57
    in *At Swim-Two-Bird* 158
    in *Dancing at Lughnasa* 165
    in *Gentle Island* 177–81
    in "Irish Revel" 171
    in *Jimmy's Hall* 148–49
    in *Last September* 101, 103–8,
    110–12, 203n62
    in *Portrait* 138, 144–45, 181, 210n57
    in *Troubles* 116
Dancing at Lughnasa 135, 149, 165, 167,
    172–73
    Evans, Gerry (character) 149, 165–67
    Mundy, Chris (character) 165
    see also Friel, Brian
Daventry (character) 16, 100–109, 114,
    118, 124, 128, 203n62
    see also Last September
Davoren, Donal (character) 120, 142
    see also Shadow of a Gunman, The
de Brún, Seosamh 93
de Valera, Éamon 149, 155, 162
"Dead Musicians" 107–8
    see also Sassoon, Siegfried
"dead silence" 16, 116, 118, 121, 124–25,
    128–29, 170
dead/death 1, 4–5, 16, 32, 41, 43–44,
    48, 61, 65, 68–69, 80, 89, 101, 105–9,
    114–17, 119, 121–29, 135, 138, 145,
    147, 155, 158, 162, 167, 170, 178–81,
    185, 194n19, 196n33, 197n74, 20n45,
    204n77, 208n97, 210n57
    see also ghosts; undead
Deane, Seamus 174
Death of Cúchulainn 162
    see also Sheppard, Oliver
Death of the Heart 135
    see also Bowen, Elizabeth
Decca (gramophone) 3, 95–97
    advertisement for 95–96
    trench gramophone 15, 95, 97
    see also gramophone

Derrida, Jacques 5, 8
Devoted Ladies 135
   see also Keane, Molly
dictation 6, 46, 48, 57, 60, 69, 89
   see also Ediphone; oral culture;
      phonograph; secretaries; tran-
      scribe/transcription; typist
Dignam, Paddy (character) 1, 3–4, 17
   see also *Ulysses*
disk (gramophone record) 2, 7, 22–23,
      30, 83, 88–90, 153, 190n38–39
   see also cylinder, record (noun,
      object)
Donelon, John O'Conor 99
Doolittle, Eliza (character) 15, 59, 78–92,
      174, 181, 198n81, 198n88, 200n117,
      206n97
   see also *Pygmalion*
Dougherty, Jane Elizabeth 124
Downum, Denell 160
Dracula 2, 14–15, 19–23, 25–30, 32–40,
      42–46, 50–53, 59–63, 65–66, 68–70,
      72, 75, 80, 84, 180–81, 188n3, 188n5,
      188n12, 190n38, 192n74, 192n84,
      196n47, 213n8
   Dracula (character) 20, 26, 28–30,
      32, 34–35, 37, 39, 66, 68, 74, 118,
      188n3, 189n19, 189n24
   Harker, Jonathan (character) 22,
      25–26, 28–29, 33–37, 50, 68–71,
      188n5, 192n74
   Harker, Mina (née Murray) (char-
      acter) 15, 21–22, 24, 26, 29, 33–37,
      41–42, 47–48, 50–51, 59–62, 66,
      68–75, 84, 92, 181, 188n5, 189n19,
      191n56, 194n19, 196n47, 197n49,
      206n97, 213n8
   Renfield (character) 20, 22, 26, 29–33,
      48–49, 71
   Seward, John (character) 14–15,
      19–26, 29–38, 42, 46–53, 61,
      66–71, 174, 180, 188n3, 188n12,
      189n15, 190n38, 193n90, 194n19
   Seward's mental asylum 14, 19–21,
      32, 37

Westenra, Lucy (character) 15, 20–21,
      26, 34, 36–37, 48, 59–63, 65–70,
      72, 74, 81, 92, 189n24, 194n19,
      196n33, 196n47, 198n88
   see also Stoker, Bram
Dream of Fair to Middling Women 135
   see also Beckett, Samuel
du Maurier, George 60
Dublin Castle 63, 76, 86, 178–79
During, Simon 202n31

"Eagles and the Trumpets, The" 169
   see also Plunkett, James
Eagleton, Terry 192n73
Easter Rising, 1916 3, 10–11, 14–16, 59,
      87, 91–95, 99–100, 116–17, 119–21,
      128, 132, 135, 158, 162, 177–78, 180
   accounts of 93–94
   commemoration of 10–11
   shock in relation to 15–16, 99–100
   see also General Post Office (GPO);
      Jacob's biscuit factory
"Eclogue for Christmas, An" 135, 148
   see also MacNeice, Louis
Ediphone 46–48, 50–51, 168, 213n9
   see also Irish Folklore Commission;
      oral culture
Edison, Thomas 6, 19, 24–25, 32–33,
      38–40, 48, 57, 60, 110, 114, 189n14
Eisen, Kurt 140
Eliot, T. S. 2, 212n103, 214n214
   see also *Waste Land, The*
Ellmann, Maud 102
Embers 170
   see also Beckett, Samuel
End of the Beginning 135
   see also O'Casey, Sean
Engh, Barbara 57
Evans, Gerry (character) 149, 165–67
   see also *Dancing at Lughnasa*
Ever the Twain 135
   see also Robinson, Lennox

"Faithless Wife, The" 169
   see also O'Faolain, Sean

Fallon, Gabriel 119, 123, 127
Famine, the (The Great Famine) 14, 20,
    42–46, 52–53, 180
Farewell Companions 135, 148
    see also Plunkett, James
Farquar, Lois (character) 16, 100–102,
    104–6, 109–15, 118, 124–25, 128, 174,
    202n45, 203n62, 204n69, 204n77,
    205n78
    see also *Last September, The*
Farrell, J. G. 116
    see also *Troubles* (novel)
Feaster, Patrick 190n42
Feis Ceoil 47, 49
    see also oral culture
female voice 60, 66, 85–86, 91, 194n13,
    196n34
    see also gender; record/recording
    (verb); women
Fenianism 72, 196n32
Ferguson, Ann L. 200n118
Fianna Fáil 155
Finnamore, Joseph 189n13
"Five Entries from a Fictional Diary"
    135
    see also Power, Angela
Fleissner, Jennifer 74, 196n47, 197n49
folklore 14, 20–21, 38–39, 42–53, 168,
    191n66, 192n74
    see also Irish Folklore Commission
Forrest, Jennifer 66, 85, 194n13, 196n34
Frattarola, Angela 185n7
Freedgood, Elaine 7
Freud, Sigmund 26, 33–34, 38, 102,
    137
    Beyond the Pleasure Principle 191n55
    *Observations of the Psychical
        Mechanism of Hysterical
        Phenomenon* 26
    Studies in Hysteria 33
    see also Breuer, Josef
Friel, Brian 17, 135, 165, 172–74, 177–82
    Ballybeg (Baile Beag) 172–73
    Dancing at Lughnasa 135, 149, 165,
        167, 172–73

Gentle Island, The 17, 172–74,
    176–82, 215n40, 216n72
    Philadelphia Here I Come 172
    Translations 172
Friends and Relations 135
    see also Bowen, Elizabeth

Gaelic see Irish language (Gaelic)
Gaelic League 46, 49
    see also Oireachtas
Gaeltacht 167, 213n9
Gainor, J. Ellen 198n88
Galatea 78, 82, 88–89
    see also *Pygmalion*
Garratt, Robert F. 12
Gass, William 211n74, 21n75
gender 58–60, 64, 66, 68–69, 73, 75,
    77, 181–82, 189n19, 191n64,
    193n5, 194n7, 196n34, 196n47,
    204n69
    gender in brain debate 26, 189n19
    gendered politics 3–4, 58–60,
        62–63, 69, 76, 80, 91–93
    hysteria (gendered) 26, 33, 41, 57,
        70–71, 181
    see also sexuality; women
General Post Office (GPO) 93–94, 106,
    162
    see also Easter Rising 1916
Gentle Island, The 17, 172–74, 176–82,
    216n72
    "Oh! Susanna" 177, 180
    Quinn, Peter (character) 173,
        175–77, 180, 216n72
    Shane (character) 173–77, 179–82,
        216n72
    Sweeney, Joe (character) 173, 175–77,
        181, 216n72
    Sweeney, Manus (character) 173,
        175–76, 180–82, 216n72
    Sweeney, Philly (character) 173,
        176–77, 180–81, 216n72
    Sweeney, Sarah (character) 173–74,
        176–77, 181–82, 216n72
    see also Friel, Brian

ghosts 94, 107–8, 121–22, 128–29, 170, 182
  see also dead/death; haunting
Gibbons, Luke 197n50
Gildersleeve, Jessica 106, 205n78
Gladstone, William Ewart 62, 64–65
"God Save the King" 93, 143
  see also music
Gore, Donal (character) 150
  see also Nightlines
Gouraud, George Edward 40
Government of Ireland Act 1914 87
Gralton, Jimmy 148–49
  see also Jimmy's Hall
gramophone 1–18, 20, 22, 24, 26, 28, 30–32, 34, 36, 38, 40, 42, 44, 46, 48, 50–52, 56–60, 62, 64, 66, 68, 70, 72, 74, 76–102, 104–18, 120–22, 124–29, 131–40, 142–83, 185n7, 186n10, 187n20, 190n38–39, 190n41, 197n74, 197n74
  advertisements for 10, 39–40, 48, 95–97
  as media object 5, 10, 183
  as therapy 33, 97–99, 201n17
  atemporality 105, 107, 202n45
  Decca 3, 95–97, 201n8
  differences from phonograph 6–7, 58, 76, 89–91
  gramophony (mimicry) 84, 118, 126–27, 206n97
  His Master's Voice (HMV) 3–4, 32, 156–57, 171
  needle 1, 3, 7–8, 13, 20, 22–25, 28, 30, 62, 66, 91, 93, 98, 105, 110, 116, 128, 131, 153, 185n7, 201n8, 203n62, 216n64
  salesman 149, 165
    see also Evans, Gerry (character)
  trench models 15, 95, 97, 203n62
    see also Decca
  wants "dead silence" 16, 116, 118, 121, 124–25, 128–29, 170
    see also Juno and the Paycock
  see also Berliner, Emile; mainspring; music; record (object)

Griffith, D. W. 137
Groth, Helen 5
guns 102, 104, 111, 127, 136, 141–46, 154, 174, 178
  parallels to gramophones 143, 145, 174
  see also Shadow of a Gunman, The
Guyau, Jean-Marie 22–24

Halliday, Sam 5
Hamlet 140–41
Harker, Jonathan (character) 22, 25–26, 28–29, 33–37, 50, 68–71, 188n5, 192n74
  see also Dracula
Harker, Mina (née Murray) (character) 15, 21–22, 24, 26, 29, 33–37, 41–42, 47–48, 50–51, 59–62, 66, 68–75, 84, 92, 181, 188n5, 189n19, 191n56, 194n19, 196n47, 197n49, 206n97, 213n83
  see also Dracula
Harris, Susan 122–23
Harrison, Rex 200n117
haunting 13, 42, 105–6, 118, 122, 128, 170, 202n45
  see also ghosts
He, Chu 174
Healy, Tim 64
Heaney, Seamus 159
  see also Sweeney Astray
Heat of the Day 167
  see also Bowen, Elizabeth
Hepburn, Audrey 200n117
"Her Table Spread" 135
  see also Bowen, Elizabeth
Hibernia 2–3, 58, 70
Higgins, Henry, Professor (character) 15, 59, 78–80, 82–91, 189n81, 198n86, 198n88
  see also Pygmalion
Hindle, Maurice 188n2
His Master's Voice (HMV) 3–4, 32, 156–57, 171
  see also gramophone; Nipper the terrier

Hogan, Roger 136, 140
Holloway, Joseph 123
Home Rule 15, 58–59, 62–65, 68, 70–72,
    75–78, 86–87, 89, 91–92, 174, 179,
    195n28, 195n32
    First Home Rule Bill 179
    Second Home Rule Bill 15, 63–65,
        196n32
    Third Home Rule Bill 15, 59, 76–77,
        86–87
Hone, Penelope 5
Hsieh, Chih-Hsien 185n7
Hughes, Tom (character) 93–94, 136,
    139–47, 152, 154, 210n57
    see also Portrait
Hutcheson, Michael 43
hysteria 26, 33, 41, 57, 70–71, 181
    see also phonographysteria

"If you're Irish, Come into the Parlor"
    124–25
    see also music
immortal 19, 38
    see also undead
In Mr. Knox's Country 197n74
    see also Somerville and Ross
Inishbiggle 187m20, 215n44
Inishfallen, Fare Thee Well 126
    see also O'Casey, Sean
"Invisible Giant, The" 20, 43–44
    see also Stoker, Bram
Ireland, Denis 178
Irish Citizen Army 94
Irish Folklore Commission 45, 47,
    49–50, 168, 192n83
    see also Ediphone; folklore; Irish
        language (Gaelic)
Irish Free State 115, 132, 136, 140, 147, 154
Irish language (Gaelic) 14, 45–46, 49, 52,
    76, 167–69, 176, 180
    see also folklore; Irish Folklore
        Commission; oral culture
"Irish Question" 58, 63, 132
Irish Republican Army (IRA) 16, 94,
    103–4, 116–17, 119–20, 122–27, 142

"Irish Revel" 171
    see also O'Brien, Edna
Irish Times 19, 25, 40, 55, 57, 70, 76, 79,
    87, 97, 117, 131–32, 136, 144, 147,
    154, 164, 178–79
Irving, Henry 40–41, 63, 71–72
    see also Stoker, Bram

Jacob's biscuit factory 93–95, 99
    see also Easter Rising, 1916
Jimmy's Hall 135, 148–49
    see also Gralton, Jimmy
John Bull 58
John Bull's Other Island 75–76
    see also Shaw, George Bernard
Johnston, Denis 135, 215n51
    see also Storm Song
Jordan, Neil 135, 150
    see also Nightlines
Joyce, James 1–5, 8, 77, 151, 196n38,
    214n17
    see also Ulysses
Joyce, Joe 195n29
Juno and the Paycock 2, 16, 94, 116–17,
    123, 128, 142, 146, 170, 180,
    206n97
    Boyle, Captain (character) 16,
        117–18, 121, 124
    Boyle, Johnny (character) 16, 117–28,
        142, 174, 180–81
    Boyle, Juno (character) 117–21,
        123–24, 126–28
    Boyle, Mary (character) 117–19, 123,
        126–28, 206n97
    Tancred, Robbie (character) 16,
        122–28, 142, 146
    see also O'Casey, Sean

Kaplan, Ann 183
Keane, Damien 186n7
Keane, Molly 116, 135
    Conversation Piece 135
    Devoted Ladies 135
    Knight of Cheerful Countenance 135
    Mad Puppetstown 116

Rising Tide 135
Taking Chances 135
Keller, Sarah 170
Kellet, E. E. 80–82, 84, 87, 199n90
    see also "Lady Automaton"
Kelly, Brendan 100
Khader, Jamil 35
Kiberd, Declan 158
Killycreggs in Twilight 135
    see also Robinson, Lennox
Kissane, Bill 140
Kittler, Friedrich 5, 8, 33, 186n10,
    192n84
Klass, Phillip 80, 84
Klingender, F. D. 196n46
Knight of Cheerful Countenance 135
    see also Keane, Molly
Knowles, Sebastian 185n2
Krapp's Last Tape 170, 214n23
    see also Beckett, Samuel

"Lady Automaton" 80–82, 85, 88–89
    see also Kellet, E. E.
Lanters, José 174
Last September, The 3, 16, 94, 100–102,
    105–6, 108–9, 115–17, 128, 167, 180,
    202n45, 203n62, 204n66, 204n77,
    205n78
    dancing in 101, 103–8, 110–12,
       203n62
    Daventry (character) 16, 100–109,
       114, 118, 124, 128, 203n62
    Farquar, Lois (character) 16, 100–102,
       104–6, 109–15, 118, 124–25, 128,
       174, 202n45, 203n62, 204n69,
       204n77, 205n78
    film adaptation 203n62
    Lesworth, Gerald (character) 103–4,
       106, 110, 112–15, 202n45, 204n77
    see also Bowen, Elizabeth
Laverty, Paul 135, 148
Ledger, Sally 196n33
Leinster, Munster and Connaught 135
    "God Save the King" 143
    gramophones as guns 143, 145, 174

"Soldier's Song, A" 143
    see also O'Connor, Frank
Leonardson, Eric 201n19
Lesworth, Gerald (character) 103–4,
    106, 110, 112–15, n202–4
    see also Last September, The
Lojek, Helen 177–78, 216n72
Lonely Girl, The 171
    see also O'Brien, Edna
Long, Maebh 213n14
"Lord Arthur Saville's Crime" 208n6
    see also Wilde, Oscar
Lord Lieutenant of Ireland 87, 90
Lusitania 176, 215n53
Lyons, F. S. 12

Mac on tSíthigh, Seán 215n53
MacBride, John 93
MacDonagh, John 93
MacDonagh, Muriel 93
MacDonagh, Thomas 93
MacNeice, Louis 135, 148
    see also "Eclogue for Christmas, An"
Mad Puppetstown 116
    see also Keane, Molly
madness 26, 103, 107, 109, 152, 159–60,
    163
    see also Daventry (character);
       Renfield (character); Sweeney
       (general mythic figure); Sweeny,
       Mad King (character)
Magic Mountain 2
    see also Mann, Thomas
mainspring (gramophone motor)
    131–34, 139, 144–45, 147, 164,
    208n6
    "breakage" in the 17, 134, 139, 151,
       154–56, 160–64
    strain in the 16–18, 37, 70, 98, 105,
       120, 131–33, 135–41, 143, 145,
       147, 149, 151, 153–57, 159, 161,
       163–64, 166, 183, 208n6
    tensile strength of the 131, 134, 136,
       139, 147, 164
    torque of the 134, 136, 164

see also gramophone

Malcolm, Ian 77

Malone, Andrew E. 136–38

Mann, Thomas 2

  see also Magic Mountain

Marshik, Celia 8, 204n66

material culture 8

  see also thing theory

McCabe, Patrick 17, 171

  see also Butcher Boy, The

McCormack, W. J. 195n20

McGarry, Fearghal 200n2

McGuiness, Frank 173–74

McLuhan, Marshall 187n19

media object 5, 10, 183

  see also media studies

media studies 2, 4–6, 9, 18, 183

  see also media object

memory 1, 5, 9, 12–14, 18, 20, 22–25,
    27, 29, 33–39, 45–46, 94, 98, 102,
    107–9, 111, 116, 127, 154, 158,
    166–67, 170, 172, 182–83, 187n20
  atemporal 105, 107
  linear 34–35, 37, 115, 179
  phonograph as analogous to 22–24
  see also trauma

mental health facility (asylum) 14,
    19–20, 99, 121
  Richmond District Asylum 99–100
  Richmond War Hospital 15, 98–100,
    118
  Seward's asylum in *Dracula* 14,
    19–21, 32, 37
  see also abreaction; music therapy;
    therapy

Miller, Julie Ann 193n6

mimicry 83–84, 90, 114
  see also gramophony

mind 9, 12–13, 25, 28–30, 33–34, 68,
    83, 99, 102, 104–5, 114–15, 126,
    139, 142, 147, 161, 163, 185n7,
    189n15, 206n97
  brain vs mind 189n15
  see also brain

Mitchell, Susan 137–38, 147

Modern Painting 58

  see also Moore, George

modernism 2, 4–5, 8, 13, 151, 182

Moore, George 58

  see also Modern Painting

Moran, Patrick 202n31

Morash, Christopher n191

"More Pricks than Kicks" 135

  see also Beckett, Samuel

Moss, Stephanie 26–27, 189n24

Mount Music 77, 197n74

  see also Somerville and Ross

Mrs. Dalloway 107, 205n80
  Smith, Septimus Warren (character)
    107
  see also Woolf, Virginia

Mulberry Tree 202n31

  see also Bowen, Elizabeth

Mundy, Chris (character) 165

  see also Dancing at Lughnasa

Murphet, Julian 5

Murray, Christopher 123

music 8, 22, 47, 49–50, 77, 83, 90, 93, 95,
    98–99, 105, 108–10, 112, 118, 139,
    145, 148, 150, 153, 156, 158, 167,
    177, 181, 187n20, 189n14, 200n117,
    201n15, 206n97, 212n91
  "Butcher Boy, The" 172
  "Come, Landlord, Fill the Flowing
    Bowl" 143
  "God Save the King" 93, 143
  "If you're Irish, Come into the Parlor"
    124–25
  Madama Butterfly 98
  music therapy 99, 201n17
  "Oh! Susanna" 177, 180
  Patience 153, 156
  "Silent Night" 171
  "Soldier's Song, A" 143
  "When I first put this uniform on"
    156

music therapy 99, 201n17
  see also mental health facility
    (asylum)

My Fair Lady (film) 89, 200n117

My Fair Lady (musical) 89
Myers, W. H. 26–27

Needham, Jay 201n19
needle (gramophone and phonograph)
    1, 3, 7–8, 13, 20, 22–25, 28, 30, 62,
    66, 91, 93, 98, 105, 110, 116, 128, 131,
    153, 185n7, 201n8, 203n62, 216n64
New Woman 14–15, 58–60, 68–69,
    196n33
    see also gender; women
Nightlines 135, 150
    see also Jordan, Neil
Nipper the terrier 4, 32, 171, 185n7,
    190n42
    see also Barraud, Francis; His Master's
    Voice (HMV)
Nixon, Marni 200n117
Nordau, Max 26
Northern Ireland 58, 132, 172, 178–79,
    181, 216n64
    see also Sunningdale Agreement;
    Troubles, the

Ó Dálaigh, Seosamh 51
Ó Murchadha, Tadhg 51
Ó Súilebháin, Muiris 175
    see also Twenty Years A-Growing
O'Brien, Edna 17, 171
    Country Girls, The 171
    "Irish Revel" 171
    Lonely Girl, The 171
O'Brien, Flann 3, 16–17, 134–35,
    150–51, 153, 155–56, 158–62, 167,
    169, 181, 192n83, 211n74, 212n112,
    215n51
    At Swim-Two-Birds 3, 16–17, 134–36,
    150–51, 158–59, 163–64, 181,
    211n74, 211n88, 212n112
    Poor Mouth, The (*An Beal Bocht*)
    167–68, 192n83, 213n8, 215n51
*Observations of the Psychical Mechanism
    of Hysterical Phenomenon* 26
    see also Freud, Sigmund
O'Callaghan-Westropp, F. Colonel 77

O'Casey, Sean 2, 16, 94, 117–20,
    123–27, 135, 141–43, 146, 205n94,
    206n97
    End of the Beginning 135
    Inishfallen, Fare Thee Well 126
    Juno and the Paycock 2, 16, 94,
    116–17, 123, 128, 142, 146, 170,
    180, 206n97
    memories of Civil War 126–27
    memories of Easter Rising 94
    Shadow of a Gunman, The 120,
    141–42
O'Connor, Frank 135, 143, 148
    *see also Leinster, Munster and
    Connaught*
O'Conor, Norreys 140
O'Faolain, Sean 169
    see also "Faithless Wife"
"Oh! Susanna" 177, 180
    see also music
Oireachtas 47, 49
    see also Gaelic League
O'Keefe, J. G. 159
    see also Buile Suibne
Oppenheim, Nathan 27–29, 33
oral culture 14, 21, 39, 45, 52
    orality 14, 19, 21, 32, 38–40, 42,
    45–46, 48–53
    see also dictation; Ediphone; *Feis
    Ceoil*; folklore; Irish language
    (Gaelic)
O'Shea, Katharine 63–65, 67–68, 112
O'Sullivan, Sean 193
O'Toole, Fintan 173, 179

Page, Leanne 49, 193n90
Pall Mall Budget 61, 194n15
Parker, Michael 216n66
Parnell, Charles Stewart 62–65, 68, 120,
    195n28, 195n32, 196n38
Passmore, Mervin 208n6
Pateman, Carole 195n26
Patience 153, 156
    see also music
Pearse, Patrick 94, 199n88

Personal Reminiscences of Henry Irving
63
see also Stoker, Bram
Philadelphia Here I Come 172
see also Friel, Brian
phonograph 6–7, 14–15, 19–25, 28,
32–33, 36–43, 46–53, 55–63, 66–76,
78–85, 89–92, 110, 174, 180–81,
186n10, 189n14, 190n38–39,
190n41–42, 191n56, 192n83, 193n90,
193n5, 194n15, 194n19, 196n47,
197n49
analogous to memory 22–24
cylinder 6–7, 20, 23–25, 37–38, 41,
51–52, 67, 73–74, 78–79, 89, 91,
174, 180, 188n12, 190n39, 213n9
differences from gramophone 6–7,
58, 76, 89–91
phonographysteria 14, 55, 57, 69–71,
91, 191n64, 197n49
needle 1, 3, 7–8, 13, 20, 22–25, 28,
30, 62, 66, 91, 93, 98, 105, 110,
116, 128, 131, 153, 185n7, 201n8,
203n62, 216n64
see also dictation; *Dracula*; Guyau,
Jean-Marie; *Pygmalion*
phonographysteria 14, 55, 57, 69–71, 91,
191n64, 197n49
see also hysteria (gendered)
Picker, John 60, 67, 69, 73, 189n14,
194n15, 198n81, 199n90, 200n117
Plunkett, James 17, 135, 148, 169
"Eagles and the Trumpets, The" 169
Farewell Companions 135, 148
Póirtéir, Cathal 45–46
Pook, Les 133
Poor Mouth, The (An Beal Bocht)
167–68, 192n83, 213n8, 215n51
see also O'Brien, Flann
Portrait 16–17, 134–40, 142–43, 146–48,
152, 154–55, 164, 181, 208n9,
210n57
Brandon, Peter (character) 17,
136–37, 139–47, 152, 174, 181,
210n57

dancing 138, 144–45, 181, 210n57
Hughes, Tom (character) 93–94, 136,
139–47, 152, 154, 210n57
see also Robinson, Lennox
post-traumatic stress disorder (PTSD)
94
see also trauma; shell-shock
Power, Angela 135
see also "Five Entries from a Fictional
Diary"
"Preface for Politicians" 75, 119
see also Shaw, George Bernard
prostitute/prostitution 2–3, 66, 77–78
see also kept woman; sexuality
Punch (periodical) 60
Pygmalion 2, 15, 59, 76, 78–80, 84–87,
89, 91–92, 181, 198n81, 199n90
Doolittle, Eliza (character) 15, 59,
78–92, 174, 181, 198n81, 198n86,
198n88, 200n117, 206n97
film 88
Galatea 78, 82, 88–89
Higgins, Henry, Professor (character)
15, 59, 78–80, 82–91, 198n81n,
198n86, 198n88
phonograph and gramophone in 76,
89–91
see also Shaw, George Bernard

Quinn, Peter (character) 173, 175–77,
180, 216n72
see also *Gentle Island*

record/recording (verb) 6–7, 9, 13,
20–21, 24, 40, 46–48, 57, 60, 66–67,
77, 85–86, 89–91, 111, 122, 156, 168,
170, 185n7, 190n38, 194n13, 194n19,
200n117, 212n91
imagery 23, 28, 91, 110–11, 113–14
female voice 60, 66, 85–86, 90,
194n13, 196n34
recording event 13, 20, 23, 37–38, 42,
98–99, 111, 113–14, 118
record/recording (noun, object) 2–8,
13–14, 18, 20–23, 25, 28, 32, 37–38,

40–42, 47–51, 53, 56, 60–61, 66–67,
69–71, 74, 77–79, 81–82, 85–86,
90–94, 97–99, 105, 107, 110–111,
113–114, 118, 120, 122, 125, 128, 131,
138, 143, 145, 148–50, 153, 156, 158,
168–69, 171–73, 176–80, 183, 185n7,
194n15, 201n8, 204n62, 214n17,
216n64
  broken 114
  scratched 13
  see also cylinder, disk
record (noun, account) 12, 19, 30, 39, 42,
45–46, 50, 53, 65, 113, 120, 194n19
"Remorse for Intemperate Speech" 12
  see also Yeats, William Butler
Renfield (character) 20, 22, 26, 29–33,
48–49, 71
  see also Dracula
repetition 27–28, 35, 41, 84, 88, 98,
105–6, 118, 120, 125–28, 155, 161,
169, 179, 214n17
  see also abreaction
Report of the War Office Committee of
Enquiry into "Shell-Shock" 160
Republic of Ireland 172, 216n64
Richards, Leah 194n19
Richmond District Asylum 99–100
  see also mental health facility
    (asylum)
Richmond War Hospital 15, 98–100,
118
  see also mental health facility
    (asylum); shell shock; World War I
Riders to the Sea 215n51
  see also Synge, John Millington
Rising Tide 117, 135
  see also Keane, Molly
Robert, Goode Hogan 208n9
Robinson, Lennox 16, 39–40, 134–43,
145–47, 152, 154, 181, 210n57
  Bird's Nest 135, 209n20
  Church Street 135, 209n20
  Ever the Twain 135, 209n20
  Killycreggs in Twilight 135
  Round Table, The 145–46

  see also Abbey Theatre
Ross, Martin 197n74
  see also Somerville and Ross
Round Table, The 145–46
  see also Robinson, Lennox
Royal Irish Constabulary (RIC) 103, 112,
204n70

Saint-Amour, Paul 4–5, 8
Sassoon, Siegfried 107–8
  see also "Dead Musicians"
scars 20, 25, 94, 99, 105, 110–11, 113–14,
120, 128–29, 180
Schloss, Carol 193n6
Scott, Bonnie Kime 212n95
Scriabin, Alexander 145
secretary 55, 57
  see also dictation; stenography/
    stenographers; transcribe/tran-
    scription; typist; women
Senf, Carol 74
Seward, John (character) 14–15, 19–26,
29–38, 42, 46–53, 61, 66–74, 174,
180, 188n3, 188n12, 189n15, 190n38,
193n90, 194n19
  Seward's mental asylum 14, 19–21,
    32, 37
  see also Dracula
sexuality 2, 15, 60–69, 71–75, 79–80,
92, 169, 174, 181, 194n13, 198n81,
198n88, 214n17, 216n72
  sexual autonomy 14, 58–59, 64, 72,
    75, 78, 90, 181
  sexual violence 37, 65–66, 80, 151,
    171, 196n33, 198n87
  sexualized 58–63, 69, 73, 77, 80, 87,
    90, 181
  see also gender; women
Shadow of a Gunman, The 120, ·
141–42
  see also O'Casey, Sean
Shane (character) 173–77, 179–82,
216n72
  see also Gentle Island
Shannon, Gerard 200n5

Shaw, George Bernard 2, 15, 59, 75–76, 78–82, 84–86, 88–89, 91–92, 198n81, 198n86
  John Bull's Other Island 75–76
  "Preface for Politicians" 75–76
  Pygmalion 2, 15, 59, 76, 78–80, 84–87, 89, 91–92, 181, 198n81, 199n90
  Treatise on Parents and Children, A 79
  see also Abbey Theatre
shell shock 15, 94–95, 97–98, 100–102, 121, 128, 139, 160, 163
  gramophone as therapy for 33, 97–99, 201n17
  see also post-traumatic stress disorder (PTSD); *Report of the War Office Committee of Enquiry into "Shell-Shock"*; Richmond War Hospital; trauma; World War I (also The Great War)
Sheppard, Oliver 162
  see also Death of Cúchulainn
shock (distinct from shell shock) 16, 26, 29, 41, 95, 97, 99–100, 105, 109, 121, 128, 172
  see also trauma
"Silent Night" 171
  see also music
Smart, Robert A. 43
Smith, Septimus Warren (character) 107
  see also Mrs. Dalloway
Snake's Pass, The 20
  see also Stoker, Bram
"Soldier's Song, A" 143
  see also music
soldier 15–16, 93–95, 97–103, 106, 111, 113, 116–21, 124–25, 127–28, 143, 149, 159, 167, 203n62
  Boyle, Johnny (character) 16, 117–28, 142, 174, 180–81
    see also Juno and the Paycock
  Daventry (character) 16, 100–109, 114, 118, 124, 128, 203n62
    see also Last September, The

Gore, Donal (character) 150
  see also Nightlines
Hughes, Tom (character) 93–94, 136, 139–47, 152, 154, 210n57
  see also Portrait
Lesworth, Gerald (character) 103–4, 106, 110, 112–15, 202n45, 203n62, 204n77
  see also Last September, The
Sassoon, Siegfried 107–8
  see also "Dead Musicians"
Tancred, Robbie (character) 16, 122–28, 142, 146
  see also Juno and the Paycock
Some Experiences of an Irish R.M. 197–98
  see also Somerville and Ross
Somerville and Ross 77, n197–98
  In Mr. Knox's Country 198
  Mount Music 77, n197
  Some Experiences of an Irish R.M. 197n74
  see also Ross, Martin; Somerville, Edith Œnone
Somerville, Edith Œnone 77, 135, 197n74
  States through Irish Eyes, The 135
  see also Somerville and Ross
"Songs My Father Sang Me" 167
  see also Bowen, Elizabeth
Spanish Civil War 149–50
States through Irish Eyes, The 135
  see also Somerville, Edith Œnone
stenography/stenographers 48, 55–56, 69, 196n47
  see also secretaries; transcribe/transcription
Stoker, Bram 2, 14, 19–22, 24–27, 29, 34, 36, 39–46, 50, 52–53, 59, 62–66, 68–72, 75, 80, 84, 190n38, 191n66, 195m24, 195n32
  Dracula 2, 14–15, 19–23, 25–30, 32–40, 42–46, 50–53, 59–63, 65–66, 68–70, 72, 75, 80, 84, 180–81, 188n3, 188n5, 188n12,

190n38, 192n74, 192n84, 196n47, 213n8

"Invisible Giant, The" 20, 43–44

Personal Reminiscences of Henry Irving 63

Snake's Pass, The 20

Stoker, Charlotte (mother) 20–21, 43–44

worked for Henry Irving 40–41, 71–72

Stoker, Charlotte 20–21, 43–44

Storm Song 135, 215n51

  see also Johnston, Denis

Straight, Alyssa 188n5

strain (force or tension) 16–17, 65, 70, 98, 105, 120, 131–32, 136, 138, 140, 142, 147, 154–56, 163–64, 166

  see also gramophone; mainspring; mind; tension

  strain (line or lineage) 18, 37, 183

Stuart, Francis 135, 150, 211n73

  see also *Black List, Section H*

Studies in Hysteria 33

  see also Breuer, Josef; Freud, Sigmund

suffrage 15

  see also New Woman; women

Summers-Bremner, Eluned 202n31

Sunningdale Agreement 216n64

  see also Northern Ireland; Troubles, the

Sweeney (general mythic figure) 169–71, 181, 212n103

  see also *At Swim-Two-Birds*; *Buile Suibne*; "Eagles and the Trumpets"; Eliot, T. S.; madness; *Sweeney Astray*

Sweeney Astray: A Version from the Irish 159, 212n102

  see also Heaney, Seamus; Sweeney (general mythic figure)

Sweeney, Joe (character) 173, 175–77, 181, 216n72

  see also *Gentle Island*

Sweeney, Manus (character) 173, 175–76, 180–82, 216n72

  see also *Gentle Island*

Sweeney, Philly (character) 173, 176–77, 180–81, 216n72

  see also *Gentle Island*

Sweeney, Sarah (character) 173–74, 176–77, 181–82, 216n72

  see also *Gentle Island*

Synge, John Millington 215n51

  see also *Riders to the Sea*

Taking Chances 135

  see also Keane, Molly

Tancred, Robbie (character) 16, 122–28, 142, 146

  see also *Juno and the Paycock*

Tennyson, Alfred 41

  see also "Charge of the Light Brigade"

tension 4, 16–18, 59, 79, 93, 98–99, 102, 113, 116, 131–34, 136, 140, 143–48, 150–52, 163–64, 166, 172, 178–79, 181–83, 204n77

  see also strain

Terry, Ellen 80

therapy 33, 70, 98–99, 109, 201n17

  abreaction 98–99, 102, 105, 107–9, 118, 121

    see also repetition

  music as 99, 201n17

  talking cure 33

  see also mental health facility (asylum)

thing theory 6, 8, 18, 183

  see also Brown, Bill; material culture

To the North 135

  see also Bowen, Elizabeth

torque 134, 136, 164 *see* mainspring

transcribe/transcription 42, 48–52, 55, 60, 69, 71–72

  see also dictation; secretaries; stenography/stenographers; typist

translation 49, 159–61, 174, 212n103, 212n112

  see also Irish language (Gaelic)

Translations 172

  see also Friel, Brian

trauma 9–21, 23–25, 27–29, 31, 33–39,
    41–47, 49–53, 57, 92, 99–102,
    105–11, 113–15, 118–21, 125,
    127–29, 132, 138–39, 141, 155,
    159–60, 163, 166–67, 179–80,
    182–83, 204n69, 205n78
  assimilation of 5, 20, 34–35, 182
  narratives 10, 14, 34–35, 37, 42–43,
    50, 115, 179, 204n69
  post-traumatic stress disorder 94
  shock (mental) 16, 26, 29, 41, 95, 97,
    99–100, 105, 109, 121, 128, 172
  therapy 33, 70, 98–99, 109, 201n17
    see also abreaction; mental health
      facility (asylum)
  see also atemporality; scars; shell shock
Treatise on Parents and Children, A 79
  see also Shaw, George Bernard
Tree, Herbert Beerbohm 88
trench gramophone 15, 95, 97, 203n62
  see also Decca
Trotter, David 5
Troubles (novel) 116
  see also Farrell, J. G.
Troubles, the 17, 172, 178–79, 182,
    216n62
  see also Northern Ireland; Sunning-
    dale Agreement
Twenty Years A-Growing 176, 215n53
  see also Ó Súilebháin, Muiris
typewriter 5, 19, 55, 57, 68–70, 73–74,
    191n56, 196n47, 197n49
  see also dictation; secretaries;
    transcribe/transcription
typist 55–56, 69, 196n47
  see also dictation; secretaries;
    transcribe/transcription

Ulysses 1–2, 4–5, 8, 77, 169, 172, 185n7,
    196n38, 214n17
  Bloom, Leopold (character) 1–3, 77
  Bloom, Molly (character) 169,
    214n17
  Dignam, Paddy (character) 1, 3–4, 171
  see also Joyce, James

undead 14, 19–21, 38–40, 42, 48, 50,
    52–53, 65–66, 189n24
  see also dead/death; Dracula;
    immortal; vampire
Unionism/Unionist 58, 87, 178–79

Valente, Joseph 43, 63–64, 72, 195n24,
    194n28
vampire 14, 20–22, 25–26, 29, 32–42, 46,
    48–50, 52–53, 62, 65–67, 69–70, 84,
    180, 188n3, 189n14, 191n56, 192n74,
    192n84
  see also Dracula; undead
violence 3–4, 9–10, 12–13, 15–18, 25,
    30–31, 35, 59, 72, 90–107, 109–29,
    131–36, 138–39, 141, 143–45, 147,
    151–62, 166, 169, 172–82, 195n32,
    196n22, 198n88, 204n62, 204n66,
    206n97, 213n112, 216n72
  causing trauma 9–10, 12–13, 16, 35,
    92, 94, 99, 101, 106, 121, 128, 139,
    161, 172
  political 9–10, 16–17, 59, 91–92, 128,
    144, 159, 162, 172, 177–79, 181
  prolonged 104, 110, 112, 121, 129,
    132, 134, 138, 141, 154, 158–61,
    168
  related to the gramophone 3–4,
    13, 15, 25, 91–92, 122, 124, 126,
    139, 145, 147, 158, 169, 172–75,
    181–82, 206n97
  sexual 37, 65–66, 80, 151, 196n33,
    198n87

Walsh, Keri 102
War of Independence 10, 12, 15, 94, 101,
    103, 113, 116–17, 120, 141, 148, 150,
    154–56, 179, 202n37
  see also Anglo-Irish War; Auxiliaries
    (Black and Tans)
Ward, Barry 210n63
Waste Land, The 2, 212n103, 214n17
  see also Eliot, T. S.
Westenra, Lucy (character) 15, 20–21,
    26, 34, 36–37, 48, 59–63, 65–70, 72,

74, 81, 92, 189n24, 194n19, 196n33,
    196n47, 198n88
  see also Dracula
Western Front 16, 94, 100, 109, 128
  see also World War I
Wicke, Jennifer 191n56, 197n49
Wilde, Lady Jane "Speranza" 191n66
Wilde, Oscar 191n66, 208n6
  see also "Lord Arthur Saville's Crime"
women 14–15, 55–62, 65–70, 73–75,
    77–80, 82–88, 90–92, 99–100, 104,
    111–13, 116–17, 135, 151, 181,
    189n19, 193n5, 196n33034, 196n46,
    198n81, 214n17
  female voice 60, 66, 85–86, 91,
    194n13, 196n34, 200n117
    see also recording
  kept woman 79, 198n81
  New Woman 14–15, 58–60, 68–69,
    196n33, 198n81
  prostitute/prostitution 2–3, 66, 77–78
  secretaries 55, 57
  sexual autonomy 14, 58–59, 64, 72,
    75, 78, 90, 181

stenographers 48, 55–56, 69, 196n47
suffrage 15
typist 55–56, 69, 196n47
Woolf, Virginia 2, 101, 107, 205n80
  Between the Acts 2
  correspondence between Bowen and
    Woolf 101–2
  Mrs. Dalloway 107, 205n80
World War I (also The Great War)
    15–16, 58, 91, 94–95, 99–101, 104,
    106–7, 118, 128, 154–55, 159–60,
    167, 176, 201n17, 204n66
  see also Richmond War Hospital;
    shell shock; soldiers; Western
    Front
World War II (also "The Emergency")
    150, 167
Wright, George Edward 195n32

Yeats, William Butler 12, 75
  see also "Remorse for Intemperate
    Speech"

Printed and bound by CPI Group (UK) Ltd, Croydon, CR0 4YY

23/01/2023

03183014-0001